'A fabulous read – finding out about these cinemas was almost like reading detective fiction – unveiling, as the book does, the enigmatic nature of small nations' cinemas and giving the reader insights and knowledges heretofore squirreled away.'

Professor Susan Hayward, University of Exeter

'It's astonishing that we have had to wait until now to get our hands on this timely, informative, and lively volume. *The Cinema of Small Nations* offers us a rich overview of what this very important but underappreciated phenomenon might mean. How do films get produced and, under the sign of various national cultures, attached to states that are on the small side, geographically, demographically, and politically? How do these works then circulate on local turf and across the globe? These questions are addressed via rich and theoretically informed case studies from leading scholars in each area. After reading this book, it is impossible to speak of world cinema, national cultures, or globalization in easy platitudes.'

Professor Faye Ginsburg, New York University

THE CINEMA OF SMALL NATIONS

Edited by
Mette Hjort and Duncan Petrie

EDINBURGH UNIVERSITY PRESS

For Anicë, Siri and Erik

© in this edition Edinburgh University Press, 2007
© in the individual contributions is retained by the authors

Edinburgh University Press Ltd
22 George Square, Edinburgh

Typeset in 10/12.5 Adobe Sabon
by Servis Filmsetting Ltd, Manchester, and
printed and bound in Great Britain by
Cromwell Press, Trowbridge, Wilts

A CIP record for this book is available from the British Library

ISBN 978 0 7486 2536 9 (hardback)
ISBN 978 0 7486 2537 6 (paperback)

The right of the contributors
to be identified as authors of this work
has been asserted in accordance with
the Copyright, Designs and Patents Act 1988.

CONTENTS

INTRODUCTION

Mette Hjort and Duncan Petrie

The Cinema of Small Nations

In a recent article entitled 'An Atlas of World Cinema', Dudley Andrew concludes his discussion in the following way:

> Let me not be coy. We still parse the world by nations. Film festivals identify entries by country, college courses are labelled 'Japanese Cinema', 'French Film', and textbooks are coming off the presses with titles such as *Screening Ireland*, *Screening China*, *Italian National Cinema*, and so on. But a wider conception of national image culture is around the corner, prophesied by phrases like 'rooted cosmopolitanism' and 'critical regionalism'. (Andrew 2006: 26)

Andrew's concluding remarks reference the recent emergence in film studies of a new critical vocabulary – 'world cinema', 'transnational cinema', 'regional cinema' – while his discussion of world cinema more generally responds to, and thus reflects, the need for fully developed conceptual models that will lend analytic precision to the terms in question. Particularly relevant in the present context is the way in which Andrew's reference to nations and to their inevitable persistence in film culture also acknowledges, at least implicitly, that innovative ways of understanding national elements must be part of the critical shift that is currently occurring in film studies.

There can be little doubt that film studies today requires models that go well beyond conceptions of the nation as a monadic entity involved at most, perhaps, in an unfortunate relationship with a single dominant other, Hollywood (Morris et al. 2005; Nagib 2006). A guiding premise motivating *The Cinema of Small Nations* is that careful analysis of a range of small national cinemas, with a focus for the most part on the last few decades, will suggest a number of conceptual models for understanding the persistence of nation in various transnational constellations. Small nations or states, it is widely recognised in the specialised literature, are necessarily a relational phenomenon: 'A state is only small in relation to a greater one. Belgium may be a small state in relation to France, and France a small state in relation to the USA . . . . *small state should be therefore considered shorthand for a state in its relationship with greater states*' (emphasis added, Erling Bjöl, cited in Chan Yul Yoo 1990: 12). Some small nations or states are marked by a history of colonial rule and thus by an important relational complexity that emphases on American cultural and economic imperialism tend to obscure. And many small filmmaking nations have sought alliances in recent times with nations that are similarly perceived to be grappling with the inequities that size, under some definition of that term, generates. As an analytic tool in the context of film studies, the concept of small nation promises to shed light on at least some of the ways in which subnational, national, international, transnational, regional and global forces dovetail and compete in the sphere of the cinema.

Conceived as a collaborative and collectivist project, *The Cinema of Small Nations* encompasses twelve case studies by authoritative scholars with specialised knowledge of a particular small nation and its cinema. Contributors were asked, where relevant, to provide information about the institutional parameters governing cinematic production in their context, to identify some of the persistent challenges faced by filmmakers in that context, and to discuss and assess the impact of any solutions that might have been explored over the years. In addition, the hope was that the various essays would help to draw attention to some of the key cinematic texts or tendencies associated with the cinemas in question, as well as to any features that these films might share by virtue of their production by film practitioners operating within the constraints and opportunities that a given small nation affords. The overall result of this collectivist project is, we believe, a set of reliable data that can be, and indeed should be, mobilised for comparative purposes. An influential view in the field of small states studies has it that 'small states are not simply scaled-down versions of larger states but instead have an ecology of their own' (Bray and Packer 1993: xix). At the same time, '[i]t is not always easy to discern which features of individual small states are reflections of small size and thus can be generalised, and which features merely reflect the specific cultural, economic or other features of the particular states in question' (xxiii). The comparative picture that *The Cinema of Small Nations* presents allows film scholars to begin to determine which features of particular small filmmaking nations are generalisable and why.

What soon becomes apparent, if the comparativist invitation that lies at the heart of this project is taken up, is that the possibility of full generalisability across all cases is rare. However, small filmmaking nations clearly do tend to confront certain types of problem and to have recourse to certain types of solution, depending on the particular form of small nationhood in question.

DEFINING SMALL NATION

Small Nation, Global Cinema (Hjort 2005) attempts a definition of 'small nation' relevant to the study of film, but for the most part the concept of small nation has not been central to the concerns of film scholars, who have yet to engage with the rich literature on the topic produced by other disciplines. Small nationhood figures mostly as a general intuition, rather than a clearly defined analytic tool, in the work of film scholars. For example, in a chapter devoted to films from the silent era in *Film History: An Introduction*, David Bordwell and Kristin Thompson include a section entitled 'Smaller Producing Countries', where traits held to be common to films produced 'in the smaller producing nations' (2003: 78) are identified: 'First, many were shot on location . . . Second, filmmakers frequently sought to differentiate their low-budget films from the more polished imported works by using national literature and history as sources for their stories' (78). These traits, Bordwell and Thompson further claim, reflect enduring strategies relevant not only to the silent era but also to contemporary cinema: 'The strategies of using national subject matter and exploiting picturesque local landscapes have remained common in countries with limited production to the present day' (79). Countries referred to in this short section on 'Smaller Producing Countries' include Mexico, India, Colombia, New Zealand, Australia, Ireland and Canada. While the section heading evokes a concept of small nationhood, the discussion itself gives priority to the question of levels of production, thereby blurring the distinction between the idea of a small country that produces films and the idea of a country that produces a small number of films. While the two categories may overlap, and often do, they do not necessarily coincide. What is more, the inclusion of India is coherent if the focus is indeed on levels of production during the silent era, and questionable if the aim is to say something about the early involvement of small countries with film. The point, quite simply, is that intuitions about small nationhood do inform writing on film, but in ways that highlight the contributions that conceptual elaboration and clarification might make.

In disciplines such as sociology, education, political science and international relations, research on small nations, countries and states was very much prompted by their proliferation, particularly after 1945 (Bray and Packer 1993: xxiii). In *Education in Small States: Concepts, Challenges and Strategies*, Mark Bray and Steve Packer work with a definition of small states that adopts population as the 'main indicator of size', with the upper-level 'cut-off' being set, quite arbitrarily, they admit, at 1.5 million (xx). This particular definition of a small state allows them to note that 18 out of 71 states qualified as small in 1939, as compared with 42 out of 156 in 1976, and 47 out of 168 in 1986 (xxiii). Even a significantly higher cut-off figure, they remark, supports the claim that 'the world is a world of small states. Over half the sovereign states have populations below five million, and 54 have populations below 1.5 million' (xix). The proliferation of small states is the result primarily of the process of decolonisation (Olafsson 1998: 1) and, in more recent times, of the collapse of the former Soviet Union (Bray and Packer 1993: xxiii–xxiv). Bray and Packer's 'cut-off' at 1.5 million reflects a second phase in the literature on small states, the first having been concerned with significantly larger entities. Indeed, in his influential study entitled *The Inequality of States: A Study of the Small Power in International Relations*, David Vital identified the upper level as a population of between 10 and 15 million 'in the case of economically advanced countries', and as a population of between 20 and 30 million 'in the case of underdeveloped countries' (1967: 8). Vital's definition includes '[n]o lower limit', the assumption being 'that the disabilities that are a consequence of size where the population is ten million will clearly be intensified where it is five or ten times smaller' (8).

For many researchers on small states the 'most important measure of size is population', although most agree that a definitive definition of small state cannot be provided. Emphasis on population helps to draw attention to this measure's implications for 'social structure and processes', a key point being the extent to which population size determines 'the size of the internal market before the foreign trade factor comes into operation' (Olafsson 1998: 9). This particular market correlation has clear relevance for film as a high-cost industry, and as a result the vast majority of the seventy-nine small states identified by Bray and Packer (including such places as Liechtenstein, Andorra, Aruba, Kiribati and Oman) have no pertinence in the context of the present study. A noteworthy exception, however, is Iceland, with a population of just over 300,000 and a film industry that has produced sixty feature films since 1978. As a film-producing microstate, Iceland is included here as a case allowing for an exploration of the extra-small factor. It is clear, however, that in the context of film studies a definition that lies somewhere between Vital's and Bray and Packer's is needed if a comparative project focusing on small nationhood and film as an institutional practice is to get off the ground. Yet, in developing the framework for *The Cinema of Small Nations*, we did make a point of ensuring that our cases span the full spectrum, ranging from Bray and Packer's microstates to what Vital would call a developing small nation, with a clear concentration in the population range of 4–10 million. Focusing on a series of independent states, a city state, a special administrative region and a sub-national entity with a significant degree of self-determination, the small nations/states that provide a basis for the case studies have populations as follows: Taiwan: 23,036,087; Burkina Faso: 13,902,972; Cuba: 11,382,820; Tunisia: 10,175,014; Bulgaria: 7,385,367; Hong Kong: 6,940,432; Denmark: 5,450,661; Scotland: 5,062,011; Singapore: 4,492,150; New Zealand: 4,076,140; Ireland: 4,062,235; Iceland: 309,699.

The literature on small states and nations identifies 'geographical scale or area' as a 'second measure of size' (Olafsson 1998: 9). Discussion of this measure includes considerations having to do with whether total area or only habitable land should be counted (Lloyd and Sundrum 1982: 20–1), as well as the possibility of establishing 200-mile Exclusive Economic Zones in the case of islands and archipelagos that are 'remote and isolated from large markets' (Olafsson 1998: 7). Some approaches to small nationhood pay scant attention to geographical scale, however, as Ernest Gellner points out in his commentary on Miroslav Hroch's work:

> State-endowment would seem to be more important than size in a literal sense, in so far as the Danes appear to be consigned to the 'large nation,' which can hardly be correct in some simple numerical sense. This makes the Danes a large nation, and the Ukrainians a small one. (Gellner 1996: 135)

We have opted to follow the lead of Gellner and many other scholars in taking geographical scale seriously as an indicator of small nationhood. Our largest small filmmaking country, Burkina Faso, is thus half the size of France and eleven times smaller than India. The small filmmaking nation with no independent state, the Hong Kong Special Administrative Region, is approximately six times the size of Washington DC. The Hong Kong case is particularly interesting inasmuch as it provides an opportunity to look closely at the cinematic activities of a small nation that is destined in the course of fifty years to be absorbed into the largest nation-state on earth. The following figures establish the scope of analysis in *The Cinema of Small Nations*, with regard to this second measure of size: Burkina Faso: 273,800 sq km; New Zealand: 268,021 sq km; Tunisia: 163,610 sq km; Cuba: 110,860 sq km; Bulgaria: 110,550 sq km; Iceland: 103,000 sq km; Scotland: 78,772 sq km; Ireland: 70,280 sq km; Denmark: 42,394 sq km; Taiwan: 32,260 sq km; Hong Kong: 1,042 sq km; Singapore: 682.7 sq km.

A third size variable figuring centrally in analyses of small states and nations is gross national product (GNP) (Chan Yul Yoo 1990: 11). This particular variable is held to be an 'indicator of the size of the internal market' as well as 'an indicator of military potential' relevant to 'the study of political power' (Olafsson 1998: 10). Our cases range from affluent European and Asian countries that fail the test of small nationhood with regard to the GNP indicator while meeting it in other respects, to one of the poorest countries of the world, Burkina Faso. On the assumption that smaller figures are easier to compare than larger ones, the break-down provided here refers to GNP on a per capita basis and in US dollars: Ireland: 41,000; Iceland: 35,700; Denmark: 34,800; Hong Kong: 34,000; Singapore: 28,600; Taiwan: 27,500; New Zealand: 25,300; Scotland: 23,622; Bulgaria: 9,600; Tunisia: 8,200; Cuba: 3,500; Burkina Faso: 1,200.

Miroslav Hroch introduces yet another conceptual element to the discussion. In his classic work, *The Social Preconditions of National Revival in Europe: A Comparative Analysis of the Social Composition of Patriotic Groups among the Smaller European Nations*, Hroch foregrounds domination as a core component of small nationhood:

> We only designate as small nations those which were in subjection to a ruling nation for such a long period that the relation of subjection took on a structural character for both parties. (Hroch 1985: 9)

With its history of colonial rule in the North, Denmark must be classified as a large rather than a small nation if rule by non-co-nationals is adopted as a sole indicator of small-nation status. In all of the other eleven cases, however, questions having to do with domination, the struggle for autonomy, spheres of influence, and a balance of power are crucial for any genuine understanding of the more general social and political frameworks for small-nation filmmaking. Nine became fully independent nation-states in the twentieth century, in the case of Tunisia, Burkina Faso and Singapore between 1956 and 1963. Bulgaria has experienced independence twice: first in 1908 from the Ottoman Empire and then again in 1989 from Soviet-controlled Eastern Europe. Cuba, which became independent of Spain in 1902, was subsequently transformed by the Marxist revolution of 1959. Of the two remaining case studies, Hong Kong, once a British colony, became one of several special administrative regions of China in 1997, a change of status that was widely perceived at the time as a form of re-colonisation; and in 1999 Scotland became a devolved nation within the United Kingdom. The histories of power relevant to the small-nation status of such a range of specific places are complicated and do not lend themselves to easy generalisations or quick comparisons. The various contributions to *The Cinema of Small Nations* do, however, support the idea that the structural character assumed by rule by non-co-nationals over time is a constitutive element of small nationhood.

The Cinema of Small Nations presents a multifaceted working definition of small nationhood encompassing four indicators of size. The twelve cinemas were selected not only with these indicators in mind, but also with a view to bringing other potentially relevant issues into focus, particularly with regard to the thematic aboutness of a given nation's films, or the role that film might play as a form of public criticism or critical intervention. Some of the states or nations are ethnically and culturally homogeneous while others are highly diverse. Some of the contexts are officially bilingual, others officially monolingual, and others unofficially multilingual. These differences may ultimately have no implications for the general concept of small nationhood, but they do have a clear bearing on the particular way in which small nationhood manifests itself in any given case.

It is important to underscore that the term 'small nation', which contrasts with 'large nation', is not proposed here as a definitive categoriser reflecting essential and unchangeable properties, nor as an implicit affirmation of putatively great nations. The point of an analytic of small nationhood in connection with the institutional bases and outputs of a range of cinemas marked by partially overlapping problems is not to engage in a process of demeaning labelling, but to identify inequities and injustices that call for change. In this sense, small nationhood, at least with regard to some of its facets, refers to a situation requiring change. This is particularly true of low GNP and domination as features of the small nation phenomenon. A second motivation for the development of a comparative analytic of small nationhood has to do with the possibility of identifying strength in apparent weakness, and solutions that might be transferable.

An important feature of the literature on small nations, and particularly of those writings produced by members of small nations, is to call attention not only to the challenges of small nationhood, but also, potentially, to the opportunities. Working primarily with population as a measure of size, Olafsson, for example, argues that 'the citizen of a small state has a better possibility to influence decision making than a citizen in a large state' (1998: 14), and this is a point that harmonises with at least some of our cinematic cases. And in *Realism and Interdependence in Singapore's Foreign Policy*, N. Ganesan evokes a 'siege mentality' associated with concerns about 'political survival and national viability' in the face of 'limited land area, small population base and the relative absence of natural resources' in order subsequently to show that such adverse factors have led to policies that effectively augment the 'state's limited endowments' (2005: 1–2). Small nationhood need not be a liability nor a clear sign of sub-optimality, and the task in any analytic of small nationhood associated with film is thus a dual one: to identify those factors that are genuinely debilitating and caught up with questionable power dynamics; to pinpoint strategies that ensure access, visibility and participation; and to transform these strategies, through analysis, into cultural resources that can be appropriated in, and adapted to, other circumstances.

THE VEXED QUESTION OF THE NATION IN FILM STUDIES

The absence of fully developed concepts of small nationhood in film studies has required an engagement with the findings of other fields. It is time now, however, to return to film studies, and to situate *The Cinema of Small Nations* in relation to the current debates concerning national and transnational cinema. To return to Dudley Andrew's observation at the beginning of this introduction, the concept of 'national cinema' continues to feature strongly in Anglophone film studies and global film culture more generally. Moreover, the increasing interest on the part of Western film scholars in the idea of 'world cinema' has extended the range of studies of individual national cinemas beyond the long-established focus on North American and European cinemas to embrace the post-colonial and emergent national cinemas of Asia, Africa and Latin America.

Yet all of this is happening at the same time that the status of the nation state – as the primary unit of economic, political and cultural differentiation in the world system – is being brought into question by the impact of globalisation. Key factors here include the aggressively transnational imperative of finance capital, the deregulation of markets, the increasing geographical mobility of labour, and the global penetration of communications networks facilitating business, information, entertainment and other forms of cultural exchange. These developments have rendered the boundaries of the nation-state porous and have also weakened the regulatory control of governments, thereby eroding the sense, and indeed the reality, of national autonomy. While advocates of globalisation argue that such change has brought greater freedom, opportunity, choice and diversity (Cowen 2002), it is also clear that globalisation has served the economic, political and cultural interests of certain parties more than others, raising concerns about a new era of American or Western imperialism and attendant cultural homogenisation or standardisation (Jameson 2000). Certain manifestations of resistance to the negative effects of globalisation may have taken a defensive nationalist form, but neo-liberal globalisation has also led to the emergence of alternative oppositional networks including various non-governmental organisations (or NGOs) that can be seen as constituting alternative forms of globalisation, or 'globalisation from below' (Appadurai 1997, 2001).

With regard to the cinema, one of the most visible consequences of globalisation has been the consolidation of the American motion picture industry as the dominant international player. While aggressively engaged in the cultivation of overseas markets from as early as the 1910s, Hollywood has been able to intensify its grip on global distribution and exhibition as a result of the impact of neo-liberalism on trade practices and terms. The US government has actively assisted Hollywood's efforts along these lines, and Hollywood's apparently unassailable position within the domain of screen entertainment is one that corresponds closely to America's political, economic and military status as the world's only super-power in the post-Cold War era. As Toby Miller et al. note in their detailed analysis of 'global Hollywood', over the past fifteen years American films have doubled their share of the international market, accounting for between 40 and 90 per cent of national box office revenues around the world (Miller et al. 2005). This process of consolidation has been reinforced by a vigorous campaign by the American motion picture industry through the General Agreement on Tariffs and Trade (GATT), and since 1995 the World Trade Organization (WTO). As is well known, the relevant global trade negotiations have often been a matter of the United States exerting pressure on competitors to reduce or eliminate any barriers to free and open access to markets. A poignant recent example of this can be found in South Korea, where a thriving film industry with regional significance and considerable local support, both at the level of audiences and in terms of cultural policy, found itself reeling from US demands concerning screen quotas.

The transformative effect of globalisation on the international motion picture industry has had other significant implications for the nature of national film industries and film policy. As Miller et al. argue, the traditional binary model that pitted an essentially commercial, free-market and internationally oriented industrial model (Hollywood) against a culturally-informed and state-subsidised model (European national cinemas) has been superseded by a 'new international division of cultural labour' (Miller et al. 2005: 50–110). Once again building on established practice, this new order is founded on an intensification of Hollywood's direct participation in the production sectors of other national film industries – most notably Canada, the UK and Eastern Europe – through an increase in runaway and co-production initiatives. While fluctuating currency exchange rates have dictated the relative cost benefits of producing films in various countries, American producers have also been enticed by a number of inducements offered by national governments including tax breaks, subsidies and related forms of assistance. What is significant here is the indication that national film policy has become less concerned with protecting local production or culture perceived as being under threat from Americanisation, and instead is embracing the putative benefits of the new international division of cultural labour, most notably the substantial levels of inward investment that major Hollywood-funded productions bring in terms of local employment and the purchase of goods and services. This shift from a cultural to an economic imperative may chime with the neo-liberal turn in world trade but it has also generated a great deal of anxiety about the erosion of cultural difference and non-commercial filmmaking practices that might be entailed by acquiescence to a Hollywood/American agenda.

At the same time, the operation of the new international division of cultural labour in the motion picture industry can also have the effect of boosting the international status and visibility of small or minor players. For example, the annual New Zealand Screen Production Survey for 1999–2000 noted a 62 per cent increase in total production financing from the previous year, a rise due to the production of *The Lord of the Rings* and another Hollywood-funded project, *Vertical Limit* (*Survey of Screen Production in New Zealand* 2001). *The Lord of the Rings* trilogy also provides an apposite example of just how transnational motion picture production has become. This adaptation of a well-known novel written by an Oxford don is directed by a pre-eminent New Zealand filmmaker, financed by an American studio and a German investment bank with considerable assistance from the New Zealand government through tax breaks, shot and post-produced in New Zealand by a predominantly local crew, and featuring an international cast led by American, British and Australian actors. This example interestingly suggests that cinematic transnationalism need not be synonymous with an affirmation of American imperialism. While the idiom of Jackson's trilogy may be clearly in line with the mode of popular Hollywood genre cinema, the films are clearly identified in New Zealand as local product. Much of the trilogy's profits inevitably flowed back to Los Angeles, yet the substantial inward investment generated by this US$600 million production has led to a significant upgrading of the basic infrastructure in the New Zealand film industry, and in ways that continue to benefit local as well as offshore productions.

Miller et al.'s analysis focuses primarily on industrial process issues, and the shift in film studies away from a concern with national cinema in a narrow sense towards greater interest in a transnational frame of reference also embraces questions of culture. One notable example of this kind of shift is provided by the work of the British film historian Andrew Higson. The author of a very influential essay on 'the concept of national cinema' (Higson 1989), whose wider work on British cinema has mobilised such concepts as national consensus and national heritage, Higson has more recently begun to question some of the assumptions that underpinned his earlier position. Influenced by certain strains of post-colonial thinking, Higson now advocates a post-national approach that recognises the extent to which national cultures are characterised by plurality, heterogeneity and diversity. As he puts it, 'all nations are in some sense diasporic . . . forged in the tension between unity and disunity, between home and homelessness' (Higson 2000a: 64–5). Within a specifically British context, Higson acknowledges the implications of the multi-ethnic transformation of British culture in recent decades, especially in connection with the emergence of a 'post-national' British cinema marked by cultural difference and diversity. But Higson also brings this understanding of hybridity to bear on earlier periods in British cinema, including those identified in his earlier work as forging a strong sense of national cultural consensus along ethnic lines. The suggestion at this point is that film scholars must take seriously a previously neglected yet long-standing tradition of cosmopolitanism in British cinema, at the level of both creative personnel and textual meaning. A similar argument is developed by Tim Bergfelder in relation to European cinema, which, he contends, needs to be studied in terms of its transnational and cross-cultural dimensions and not merely as a loose federation of differentiated and bounded national cinemas. Bergfelder also invokes the significance of migration for the discursive construction of national cinemas in Europe, pointing to, among other things, the historical legacy of the dynamic inter-relations amongst the cultural centres and margins of Europe. Particularly relevant in this connection are the cosmopolitan and hybrid production studios that emerged at various historical moments in Berlin, Paris, London and Rome. Bergfelder's rejection of the more traditional conception of European cinema as a defensive response to the economic and cultural encroachment of Hollywood effectively disputes the idea of American cinema as the primary determining cultural and industrial force in the creation of European cinema on both a national and a regional level, highlighting instead the workings of a quite different kind of internal geo-cultural dynamic.

The search for alternative perspectives on transnational relations in cinema where Hollywood does not play the predominant role and is not the major beneficiary is taken up in a non-European context by Meaghan Morris in relation to Hong Kong action cinema. Morris writes:

> In an inter-Asian context, [Hong Kong action cinema] . . . allows us to reflect historically on transnational industrial as well as aesthetic imaginings, which do not solely derive from the West and which 'flow', as it were, towards and through Western cinemas as well as around the region itself. (Morris 2004: 182)

Morris goes even further, suggesting that the model of national cinema itself has to be superseded if film scholars are to avoid falling back on a situation where the norms for discussing cinema are defined by Hollywood. Hong Kong action cinema repays study, then, inasmuch as it is linked to a specific geographical production location that has brought together filmmakers from a variety of places (including East and South East Asia, Australia and the United States) and thus has helped to foster transnational interaction with a local film industry and the creation of a genuinely transnational film genre.

The above references to Miller et al., Higson, Bergfelder and Morris point to the centrality of transnational relations and interactions in the context of contemporary film studies. At the same time, questions having to do with various forms of nationhood persist. Indeed, as the discussion thus far has demonstrated, national categories continue to be invoked with reference to sites of production, exhibition, acquiescence, resistance or some form of transformation.

The unequal character of globalisation also raises the problem of structural domination and subordination within a system that may be global and international, but in which nation-states continue to function as key actors within prevailing patterns of power relations. Within film studies, the problem of such relations is probed in a provocative way by Paul Willemen, who identifies some of the problems associated with the increasing international focus in Western cinema studies. (This essay was initially published in 1994 before the recent vogue for trans- or even post-national discourse but the caution remains pertinent, particularly given the kind of progressive claims frequently made for extra-national perspectives.) The problems Willemen identifies include the neo-colonial imposition of Euro-American paradigms on non-Western films; the assumed universality of film language, which has the effect in some contexts of undermining local knowledge; and the forced (as well as elective) internationalism imposed on national film industries, frequently on economic grounds, which can serve to marginalise non-mainstream and oppositional practices in the name of marketability. Willemen is also at pains to differentiate discourses of nationalism and national identity from those centred on the specificity of a given national or cultural formation. While the former have tended to reinforce the kind of homogenising perspectives on national cinema that have inspired some critics to turn to more transnational frameworks, the engagement with national or cultural specificity remains, in Willemen's view, both legitimate and necessary. In their introduction to a recent volume of essays theorising national cinema, Willemen and his colleague Valentina Vitali describe the complex relationship between cinema and the national as follows:

> It is precisely as discursive terrains for struggle between dominant and non-dominant forces over the power to fix the meaning of the given narrative stock that films can be seen not to 'reflect', but to 'stage' the historical conditions that constitute 'the national' and, in the process, to 'mediate' the socio-economic dynamics that shape cinematic production along with the other production sectors governed by national industrial regulation and legislation. (Vitali and Willemen 2006: 8)

Following this line of argument, the most important dimension of a national cinema is its mode of address. For Willemen this cultural *raison d'être* is a much more fundamental consideration than the nationality of the filmmaker or the origin of the production finance (Willemen 2006: 34).

In a similar vein, Chris Berry reaffirms the significance of a national frame of reference in film studies by calling for a paradigm shift in how the relationship between national and transnational concepts and questions is to be understood. Berry identifies three examples (pertaining to global relations, the international film industry, and the discourses of film studies) of the kinds of developments that require attention to both national and transnational issues. First, while the onward march of economic globalisation and free trade has eroded the idea of the nation-state as the primary actor within the world system, new nation-states and national disputes continue to proliferate around the world, frequently stimulated by the very same processes of globalisation. Second, in the context of cinema production the growth of international co-productions and transnational networks of distribution and exhibition has cast doubt on the idea of national film industries as a paradigm; yet, anxiety about local film production and film culture continues to inform policy, and national labels remain salient in the international marketing and understanding of particular films. Third, the emphasis on a more transnational perspective in cinema studies coexists with, and sometimes even articulates, an abiding interest in national phenomena that are sustained by the very forces that threaten them. Berry thus insists on the need to explore the full range of ways in which a concept of nation remains relevant to film studies. His most recent book, entitled *China on Screen* and co-authored with Mary Farquhar, takes up this task with great force and lucidity. Indeed, the case of Chinese cinema, which embraces the cinematic production of Hong Kong, Taiwan and the People's Republic, facilitates a productive analysis of transnational/national dynamics in which culture and ethnicity, rather than territorial boundaries, play a dominant role. For Berry and Farquhar, the challenge is precisely to transform the study of national cinemas into the study of cinema and its relation to national phenomena, the ultimate goal being to grasp the specificity of various contemporary and historical conjunctures rather than imposing a necessarily reductive or homogenising framework of national identity upon the complexity of a particular cultural, spatial and political conjuncture.

LOCATING SMALL NATIONAL CINEMAS

These debates in film studies are marked by a certain conceptual slippage between an array of different terms – international, transnational, postnational, global and even diasporic – deployed to describe and analyse relationships and systems operating above and beyond the level of the nation. Greater specificity is required here, particularly if we are to develop a more nuanced understanding of the complexity of the global system and how it impacts upon the individual and collective examples of small national cinemas considered in this volume. A useful start to such a conceptual differentiation is provided by the political scientist Peter Katzenstein, who two decades ago wrote a very illuminating book on the political and economic advantages enjoyed by small European nations during the initial stages of what we now understand as the emergence of a new global phase in late capitalism (Katzenstein 1985). In a new work entitled *A World of Regions: Asia and*

Europe in the American Imperium, Katzenstein focuses on the nature of contemporary global and international relations in a world defined in terms of 'porous regions interacting with an American imperium'. For our purposes here, two key elements in Katzenstein's account prove particularly useful. First, his conceptualisation of a global system in which a central player achieves a position of pre-eminence while being transformed by the very process in question helps to clarify the workings of a global film industry dominated by Hollywood and its new international division of cultural labour. The latter may have served to promote American national interests, but has also worked against these same local interests inasmuch as it has facilitated the involvement of non-American corporate interests (such as Sony's and Vivendi's) in Hollywood as well as an increase in offshore production, the result being high levels of unemployment in the California labour market. Second, Katzenstein makes a cogent case for viewing globalisation and internationalisation as distinct phenomena contributing in different if interlocking ways to the dynamics of a contemporary world of regions:

> I define *globalisation* as a process that transcends space and compresses time. It has novel transformative effects on world politics. I define *internationalisation* as a process that refers to territorially based exchanges across borders. It refers to basic continuities in the evolution of the international state system. Globalisation highlights the emergence of new actors and novel relations in the world system, internationalisation the continued relevance of existing actors and the intensification of existing relations. Territorially based international processes permit continued differences in national practices. Nonterritorial global processes push toward convergence of national differences and also toward a wide variety of local processes of specific adaptation to global changes. (2005: 13)

Globalisation, Katzenstein claims, serves to erode the cohesion of nations, whereas internationalisation reaffirms the nation-state as the primary actor in the world system. While the concepts of globalisation and internationalisation lie at the heart of divergent interpretations of the contemporary world system, what is important is the interaction between the two and how they serve to make regions essentially porous. The call for careful attention to both globalisation and internationalisation, and especially their reciprocal dynamics, is relevant to the study of film where it points to some possible solutions to the recurrent conundra associated with discussions of national, transnational and global issues. As analysed by Katzenstein, the complementary inter-relation between globalisation and internationalisation provides a framework for understanding the kinds of tension between national and global perspectives or commitments which Berry identifies. Globalisation may underpin the emergence of the new international division of labour, including the new emphasis on transnational production and distribution and a near-simultaneous global release, and lend credence to cosmopolitan or diasporic perspectives on cultural production, but internationalisation informs the national schemes of film funding that continue to exist in many countries. Internationalisation is also at work in the branding of films as particular national products aimed at a global market place, just as it informs the ways in which audiences make sense of films (including those from Hollywood) as expressions of particular nationally specific cultures.

Limited size has arguably rendered the impact of these processes of globalisation and internationalisation even more intense in the case of small nations than in large nations. Small nations by definition have very limited domestic markets for all locally produced goods and services – including culture – and so have been forced by the neo-liberal economic and political pressures of globalisation into a greater dependency on external markets. At the same time many small nations have emerged out of twentieth-century processes of decolonisation and liberation struggles and consequently have a strong vested interest in nation-building and the maintenance of a strong sense of national identity relevant both internally and externally to the nation. The specific ways in which these apparently contradictory forces are negotiated are a recurring theme in the various case studies here. Some of the small nations featured in this volume have been producing films since the silent era, but the idea of a specifically national cinema gained currency across the world in the 1970s and 1980s as part and parcel of the wider transformations that have refashioned global relations over the last thirty years. While the cultural and political value of the moving image in nation-building was quickly recognised in some nations, particularly following independence from former colonial rule and in connection with other revolutionary struggles, in other cases the opportunities for filmmakers to address the complex specificity of national formations, post-colonial or otherwise, took time to arise. In examples where the state has assumed a central role in determining the political or ideological content of films, internal tensions and even conflicts have also arisen around the production of independent or oppositional representations and as a result of various systems of censorship. The essays on Tunisia, Cuba, Burkina Faso and Singapore all identify such tensions, which are integral to the process of development towards democratic institutions and the recognition of an inclusive and heterogeneous civil society. Filmmakers can also experience forms of creative limitations if non-commercial funding is scarce or the local industry is over-reliant on overseas sources of production finance or markets. This has been an issue in nations with a tradition of single party domination such as Taiwan and Bulgaria, but also in more politically pluralistic small nations such as Ireland, New Zealand and Scotland.

Central to the creation and consolidation of a national cinema has been the establishment of national institutions – such as the Irish Film Board, the Danish

Film Institute, the New Zealand Film Commission, the Instituto Cubano de Arte e Industria Cinematográficos, and the Société Anonyme Tunisienne de Production et d'Expansion Cinématographique – and of funding initiatives designed to encourage, nurture and support film production and a wider national film culture. The impulse in question has found diverse expression in different parts of the world. In Western Europe, for example, a concept of culture has played a decisive role, with film being construed as deserving of public, state support *qua* culture. In Third World post-colonial or revolutionary states, such as Burkina Faso, Tunisia and Cuba, state support for the moving image has served a more properly political function linked to the project of building a new independent nation and forging a national identity. South East Asia brings to light yet another permutation, for here state involvement has traditionally been aligned with more regionally focused commercial imperatives that have created opportunities for production but often within tightly defined cultural and generic parameters. However, in Europe, the traditional sense of bounded and differentiated national cinemas has always been more difficult to maintain in the case of small nations and consequently, in addition to nationally specific initiatives, filmmakers have benefited from sources of pan-European support (MEDIA, Eurimages), regional initiatives (the Nordic Film and TV Fund) or co-production sources often located in the metropolitan centres (Channel Four, Canal +). Former colonial relationships – for example, the UK with Ireland, France with Burkina Faso, Spain with Cuba – have also ensured a source of external funding for filmmakers in some small nations, predicated in each case on a cultural or linguistic bond. But whether particular institutional arrangements favour a primarily centrifugal or centripetal momentum in terms of national engagement (i.e. either oriented outwards by creating nationally branded culture for a wider international arena/market or inwardly focused and addressing a specifically domestic audience), there is evidence of both cultural diversity and a simultaneous inward/outward impulse in all of the small national film industries/film cultures presented here.

Under globalisation state support has been influenced by a new international division of cultural labour, with economics competing with, and at times eclipsing, culture as the primary rationale for funding. In some small nations this has led to a certain tension between two conflicting visions, the one favouring subsidies for film as both culture and a vehicle for a politics of recognition, and the other a more market-oriented investment in cultural industries allied to other potential sources of foreign earnings, such as tourism. While the emergence of a cultural industries agenda in places like New Zealand and Scotland may have raised fears of the overt commodification of culture, in some of the more economically vulnerable nations globalisation has had serious consequences for the actual viability of local production. The essays on Burkina Faso, Cuba and Bulgaria drive this point home, and in ways that have clear relevance for other

African, Latin American and Eastern European cinemas. In different ways the smallness of small national cinemas has ensured that the effects of the external forces that structure and drive the global system are felt all the more keenly, a constant reminder of the predicament of small nations as actors in the global economy.

However, this does not give us the whole picture. The WTO's neo-liberal economic agenda has also had an impact on the film industries of richer countries such as Taiwan, Singapore and New Zealand, where it has allowed the dominant players in the global system to enhance their market positions, although not always with purely negative local effects. The analysis of contemporary small national cinemas also reveals the emergence of regional networks and alliances that are providing transnational alternatives to the neo-liberal model of globalisation driving contemporary Hollywood. In some instances these alternatives find a basis in supranational initiatives aimed at both large and small nations, examples including the aforementioned MEDIA and Eurimages programmes launched by the European Union. In other cases, transnational networks have been fuelled by a focal awareness of small nationhood, and by film practitioners' desire to build lasting relationships with people who are perceived to be grappling with similar problems or to be inspired by similar ideals. Relevant in this connection are the now quite substantial relations between Denmark and Scotland, and the 'affinitive transnationalism' (Hjort, forthcoming) to which sustained interaction between this small nation and sub-national entity gives rise. What this affinitive transnationalism also highlights is the important role that individual initiatives and artistic leadership can play as a complement or alternative to cultural policy in small-nation contexts. The most visible example of this form in the past decade has been the Danish Dogme 95 initiative which not only helped to rejuvenate the fortunes of one small national cinema, but also became an alternative form of global cinema based on a radically different set of aesthetic, economic and cultural priorities and practices from those underpinning Hollywood (Hjort 2005). The Dogme legacy can also be discerned in the new 'Advance Party' initiative involving Danish and Scottish filmmakers working closely together in ways that represent a new moment of devolution away from the idea of national specificity in the Scottish case (Murray, this volume).

The essays in this volume all engage with ways in which the form and content of films connect with both national and global determinants. In line with many of the most incisive accounts of cinema and nation, the analyses call attention to the complexity of national formations, and to the differences and conflicts that are key features of their histories. Sometimes the tensions that inform and animate, or occasionally hamper, national production relate directly to questions of political power and censorship, as well as to a process of self-critique aimed at creating the conditions for pluralistic and democratic modes of expression. In other cases the decisive tensions have to do with competing national and cosmopolitan or international frames of reference. Some small national cinemas are comprised of what Dina Iordanova calls 'parallel industries'. Whereas one of these industries is small and both locally focused and anchored, the other is externally owned and run, and in every way part of the global film industry. In other small national cinemas difference manifests itself in distinct types of product, aimed at specific audiences. This kind of differentiation draws on various models of cinematic practice such as the First/Second/Third Cinema framework and its possible extension to Fourth or indigenous cinema, as in the case of settler societies such as New Zealand. What is also significant is that, in the case of a small national cinema, all of these dimensions are oriented towards a global as well as a local audience, whether that of the ubiquitous multiplex, the cosmopolitan art house or the specialised festival.

While globalisation and internationalisation may have impacted negatively on some small national cinemas, they have created opportunities that others have grasped, with some enjoying unprecedented international visibility as a result. By virtue of an ecology that is specific to various measures of size, small national cinemas repay careful attention at a time when film scholars are looking for positive definitions of world cinema, for evidence of the diverse ways in which global forces affect local cinematic contexts, and for conceptual models that acknowledge that cinema is caught up in a web of international relations and not merely in an ongoing drama with Hollywood.

Works Cited

Andrew, Dudley. 2006. 'An Atlas of World Cinema'. In Stephanie Dennison and Song Hwee Lim (eds), *Remapping World Cinema: Identity, Culture and Politics in Film*. London: Wallflower. pp. 19–29.

Appadurai, Arjun. 1997. *Modernity at Large: Cultural Dimensions of Globalization*. Minneapolis, MN: University of Minnesota Press.

Appadurai, Arjun. 2001. 'Introduction'. *Globalization*. Durham, NC: Duke University Press. pp. 1–21.

Bergfelder, Tim. 2005. 'National, Transnational or Supranational Cinema? Rethinking European Film Studies' *Media. Culture & Society*, Vol. 27, No. 3. pp. 315–31.

Berry, Chris. 2006. 'From National Cinema to Cinema and the National: Chinese-Language Cinema and Hou Hsiao-hsien's "Taiwan Trilogy"'. 'In Valentina Vitali and Paul Willemen (eds), *Theorising National Cinema*. London: British Film Institute. pp. 148–57.

Berry, Chris, and Mary Farquhar. 2006. *China on Screen*. New York: Columbia University Press.

Bordwell, David, and Kristin Thompson. 2003. *Film History: An Introduction*. London: McGraw-Hill.

Bray, Mark, and Steve Packer. 1993. *Education in Small States: Concepts, Challenges and Strategies*. Oxford: Pergamon.

Chan Yul Yoo. 1990. *The International Relations of Korea as a Small State*. Baltimore, MD: Johns Hopkins University dissertation.

Cowen, Tyler. 2002. *Creative Destruction: How Globalisation is Changing the World's Cultures*. Princeton, NJ: Princeton University Press.

Ganesan, N. 2005. *Realism and Interdependence in Singapore's Foreign Policy*. London: Routledge.

Gellner, Ernest. 1996. 'The Coming of Nationalism and its Interpretation: The Myths of Nation and Class'. In Gopal Balakrishnan (ed.), *Mapping the Nation*. London: Verso. pp. 98–145.

Higson, Andrew. 1989. 'The Concept of National Cinema'. *Screen*, Vol. 30, No. 4. pp. 36–46.

Higson, Andrew. 2000a. 'The Limiting Imagination of National Cinema'. In Mett Hjort and Scott Mackenzie (eds), *Cinema and Nation*. London: Routledge. pp. 63–74.

Higson, Andrew. 2000b. 'The Instability of the National'. In Justine Ashby and Andrew Higson (eds), *British Cinema: Past and Present*. London: Routledge. pp. 35–48.

Hjort, Mette. 2005. *Small Nation, Global Cinema*. Minneapolis, MN: University of Minnesota Press.

Hjort, Mette. Forthcoming. 'Affinitive and Experimental Transnationalism: The "Advance Party" Initiative'. In Dina Iordanova, David Martin-Jones and Belén Vidal (eds), *Cinema at the Periphery*. Detroit, MI: Wayne State University Press.

Hroch, Miroslav. 1985. *The Social Preconditions of National Revival in Europe: A Comparative Analysis of the Social Composition of Patriotic Groups among the Smaller European Nations*. Cambridge: Cambridge University Press.

Jameson, Fredric. 2000. 'Globalization and Political Strategy'. *New Left Review* 4, July/August. pp. 49–68.

Katzenstein, Peter J. 1985. *Small States in World Markets: Industrial Policy in Europe*. Ithaca, NY: Cornell University Press.

Katzenstein, Peter J. 2005. *A World of Regions: Asia and Europe in the American Imperium*. Ithaca, NY: Cornell University Press.

Lloyd, P. J., and R. M. Sundrum. 1982. 'Characteristics of Small Countries'. In B. Jalan (ed.), *Problems and Policies in Small Economies*. London: Croom Helm. pp. 17–38.

Miller, Toby, and Nitin Govil, John McMurria, Richard Maxwell, Ting Wang. 2005. *Global Hollywood 2*. London: British Film Institute.

Morris, Meaghan. 2004. 'Transnational Imagination in Action Cinema: Hong Kong and the Making of a Global Popular Culture'. *Inter-Asia Cultural Studies*, Vol. 5, No. 2. pp. 181–99.

Morris, Meaghan, and Stephen Chan, Li Siu-leung (eds). 2005. *Hong Kong Connections: Transnational Imagination in Action Cinema*. Hong Kong: Hong Kong University Press.

Nagib, Lúcia. 2006. 'Towards a Positive Definition of World Cinema'. In Stephanie Dennison and Song Hwee Lim (eds), *Remapping World Cinema: Identity, Culture and Politics in Film*. London: Wallflower. pp. 30–7.

Olafsson, Björn G. 1998. *Small States in the Global System: Analysis and Illustrations from the Case of Iceland*. Aldershot: Ashgate.

Vital, David. 1967. *The Inequality of States: A Study of the Small Power in International Relations*. Oxford: Clarendon.

Vitali, Valentina, and Paul Willemen. 2006. 'Introduction'. In Vitali and Willemen (eds), *Theorising National Cinema*. London: British Film Institute. pp. 1–16.

Willemen, Paul. 2006. 'The National Revisited'. In Valentina Vitali and Paul Willemen (eds), *Theorising National Cinema*. London: British Film Institute. pp. 29–43.

PART ONE

EUROPE

1. DENMARK

Mette Hjort

Defending the inherent interest of contemporary Danish cinema to non-Danes almost two decades ago involved making much of the Academy of Motion Picture Arts and Sciences' decision to honour Gabriel Axel's *Babette's Feast* (*Babettes gæstebud*) and Bille August's *Pelle the Conqueror* (*Pelle Erobreren*) with Best Foreign Feature awards in 1987 and 1988 respectively. The indisputable talent of Lars von Trier, as manifested in an early work like *Element of Crime* (1984), was also important to anyone seeking to affirm the value of Danish film. Yet in the late 1980s von Trier was still very much an emerging figure, both at home and abroad, having directed only two feature films, the haunting film noir, *Element of Crime*, and the far less successful *Epidemic* (1987), both of which belong to the so-called 'Europe trilogy'. Valiant attempts could be made to introduce viewers, critics and scholars to those many deserving filmmakers (especially in the area of films for children and young people) who warranted far greater visibility outside Denmark. In focusing on difficult issues faced by young people, filmmakers such as Nils Malmros, Søren Kragh-Jacobsen and Morten Arnfred had for years provided important alternatives (worthy of careful consideration elsewhere) to Disney's ideologically suspect 'candyfloss' (Zeruneith 1995). And then there was always the argument by authority: Danish cinema was once truly great, and recognised as such worldwide; surely it would be reasonable to assume that some of the remarkable qualities associated with a company such as Nordisk, a star such as Asta Nielsen, and filmmakers such as Benjamin Christensen and Carl Th. Dreyer would continue somehow to shape Danish film. However, the fact is that it was extraordinarily difficult to establish the value of contemporary Danish cinema in the late 1980s. Any enthusiasm could easily be challenged by means of a simple observation: even Danes had little or no time for Danish cinema. If Danes themselves viewed Danish film as the well-meaning but boring result of state subsidies, then why should the rest of the world pay attention to this small national cinema? The answer, difficult to make convincing at the time, was: because signs of change suggested a far more interesting future.

The situation has indeed changed, and whereas the Danish film industry once served as a virtually paradigmatic example of the failings and challenges associated with small national cinemas, there is now considerable interest in the so-called New Danish Cinema and in the underlying 'Danish model' that is its apparent condition of possibility. In order to grasp the extent of the transformation of Danish cinema over the last two decades, it is necessary to paint a comparative picture. In 1989:

- Denmark produced ten feature-length films, a figure significantly below the minimal level of film production deemed necessary to keep a core group of professionals actively involved in their craft.
- Danish directors could hope to direct films once every three or four years (Danish Film Institute (DFI) 2006b: 10).
- Danish films accounted for 15 per cent of box office receipts.
- American films generated 63 per cent of box office sales. (www.dfi. dk/talogstatistik/biograftal/entre1980_2000/entre1980_2000.htm)

Almost two decades later, figures from the DFI's 'Facts and Figures 2006: Production and Exhibition Figures for 2005' (DFI 2006a) point to a quite different reality:

- Denmark released thirty feature films.
- Danish directors could as a result hope to direct a film once a year or once every two years.
- Danish films took 32 per cent of the national market share.
- The market share for American films was 56 per cent.

Other noteworthy facts include:

- The average number of viewers per Danish film was 128,000, as compared to 56,000 for American films.
- With a population of 5.4 million, Danes had access to 164 cinemas across the country.
- Danish TV producers were increasingly involved in co-producing Danish films, which were also shown on TV.

- Six Danish features figured in the list of 'Ten Most Popular Films'.
- Danish films received eighty-one prizes and awards at international festivals.

If lack of confidence is a typical marker of small nationhood, then Denmark would appear to have transcended its small-nation status in recent years, at least with regard to film. Writings about Danish film by policymakers, journalists, scholars and politicians alike bespeak high levels of confidence rooted in a lived experience of success. For example, in his 'Preface' to 'New Goals: Challenges and Perspectives for Danish Film 2007–2010', a document written in connection with government negotiations about film funding for the next four-year period, the Chief Executive Officer of the DFI, Henning Camre (replaced by Henrik Bo Nielsen in 2007), describes Danish film as follows:

> [f]ilm . . . takes Denmark out into the world where it makes us visible and present in a forceful way that is *completely out of proportion to Denmark's size* (emphasis added) . . . Through film and moving images we stage ourselves, we conquer a right to a place on the international stage, where our culture and identity becomes visible and is given a voice . . . far too many countries have no opportunity to see their own world and culture reflected in film and images. They only see films that reflect a foreign – and often American – culture . . . For them film becomes an expression of how 'the others' live. This is not the situation in Denmark. (DFI 2006b: 3)

As a heavily subsidised industry, Danish film has been caught up with what Charles Taylor (1992) calls a politics of recognition, the desire to see expressions of culturally inflected identities recognised as valuable both internally and externally. Camre's statements clearly suggest that the harmful lack of recognition so typical of the lot of small nations no longer obtains in the area of Danish film. If anything, recognition is now widely believed to exceed what a small nation can reasonably expect and hope for.

The sense of self-efficacy that success generates is evident in the leadership role that the DFI assumed as co-organiser (along with the Greater Copenhagen Authority, the Nordic Film and TV Fund, and the Nordic Film Foundation) of the recent 'Think Tank on European Film and Film Policy'. Hosted by the DFI, this invitation-only event took place in Copenhagen in the summer of 2006, with discussions to continue at subsequent meetings and through a dedicated internet site. The initial Think Tank meeting aimed to bring together 'directors of European, national and regional film funds and film professionals (filmmakers, festival directors, distributors, exhibitors, critics), as well as policymakers and educators' in order to create what was dramatically referred to as a ' "big bang" in European film and film policy' (DFI 2006b: 48). The intention, more prosaically, was 'to examine why and how we use public funds to support film, and how we could support film more effectively in terms both of advancing public policy objectives and improving film's artistic quality and its ability to prosper in the market place' (ibid.). The DFI's role, as initiator and host, was clearly linked to the self-validating success in recent times of the Danish model for filmmaking, and, interestingly, to Denmark's small-nation status:

> We have shown that Danish film can place itself on a level where few [European cinemas] can follow us, but at the same time we are not perceived as a threat on account of our small size. The larger countries with larger film industries have trouble making others believe that ambitious initiatives like this one aren't motivated by self-interest alone. (ibid.)

EXPLAINING THE SUCCESS OF CONTEMPORARY DANISH FILM

What constitutes 'success' in the context of small-nation filmmaking is to some extent an open question. The assumption here is that the term is appropriate when the films produced by a given small national cinema provide evidence of a diversity of cinematic expression, secure a more than respectable share of the domestic box office, win numerous prizes on the international festival circuit, achieve some measure of international distribution, attract funding from various public and private sector sources at the national, supranational and international levels, and provide a platform for actors, directors, cinematographers and other professionals to pursue filmmaking opportunities both within and outside the national film industry on the kind of regular basis that allows skills to be maintained and further developed. Together these indicators constitute success inasmuch as they each stand in marked contrast to the conditions that typically obtain in small filmmaking countries. Success may, of course, involve certain costs, some of them artistic, and I will return briefly to this issue towards the end of this chapter. The most immediate task at hand, however, is to identify the causal factors that have made Danish cinema both viable and visible. I will approach this task by focusing on two key issues: cultural policy and artistic leadership.

Cultural Policy

Cultural pride in the golden age of Danish cinema (1910–1914) no doubt helps to explain the long-standing existence in this country of cultural policies and institutions that are variously designed to encourage contributions to film as art and as cultural expression. The Film Act of 1964, for example, led to the creation of both a film fund and a national film school, and subsequent Acts introduced further measures in support of film. Yet, if we are to understand the dramatic transformation evoked above, continuity of support is only a small part of the story that needs to be told. The landscape of Danish cultural policy has changed considerably over the last two decades, and the favourable position currently enjoyed by Danish cinema is very much the result of these changes, although artistic leadership, as we shall see, has also been crucial. It is impossible, in the present context, to provide an exhaustive list of all relevant policy changes, and I shall thus limit myself to those that have had an indisputable impact.

A new definition of Danish film

Whereas the Film Act of 1972 specified that any film that was to qualify as Danish (and thereby for state support) would have to be in Danish, the Film Act of 1989 introduced a new, disjunctive definition that allowed a film to receive support if it either was a Danish-language film or made a clear artistic or technical contribution to film art and film culture in Denmark, whether or not the language spoken in the film was Danish. The revised definition was prompted by the scandal that erupted when Lars von Trier's *Element of Crime*, which won the Prix Technique at Cannes in 1984, was refused DFI funding on account of its use of English and German, rather than Danish. This gesture was decisive, for it ended up paving the way for the production of a series of ambitious English-language films by von Trier that confirmed his status as Denmark's undisputed auteur. *Europa* (1991), *Breaking the Waves* (1996), *Dancer in the Dark* (2000) and *Dogville* (2003) were all partially funded by the DFI, the virtually guaranteed support serving in each instance to leverage the kind of further funding that was required in order to produce these, by small-nation standards, highly expensive co-productions.

The DFI as open-minded facilitator rather than dogmatic tastemaker

The Film Act of 1989 introduced another crucial change having to do with the mechanism by which films are deemed deserving of state support administered by the DFI. Up until 1989 filmmakers intent on securing public funds for their films were required to submit their proposals to one of a number of film consultants who were appointed by the DFI on three-year contracts. While generally supported in principle, this process had none the less drawn fire from the film milieu over the years, with charges ranging from favouritism and a dogmatic commitment (on the part of individual consultants) to a single and highly prescriptive conception of Danish film, to rhythms of assessment entirely at odds with the rather faster-moving realities of film production. In response to such charges, and to the stunning absence of a national audience for Danish film, the Film Act of 1989 called for an alternative funding process that would complement rather than replace the consultant scheme. The 50/50 scheme that was introduced by the DFI effectively allowed filmmakers to circumvent, and thus neutralise, the very gatekeepers that this institution had appointed as expert evaluators. Essentially the idea was that a producer could apply to the DFI for matching funds for his or her initial investment, up to a ceiling of 3 million Crowns (approximately 405,000 Euros). In 1997 the balance of public and private monies became 60/40 respectively, with a new ceiling of 5 million for the former. While controversial at first as a result of some highly dubious productions and widespread skepticism about the wisdom of loosening the experts' control over the state's allocations for film, the 50/50 (60/40) policy proved to be an ingenious intervention. Filmmakers such as Ole Bornedal and Nicolas Winding Refn produced their first features – *Nattevagten* (*Nightwatch*, 1994) and *Pusher* (1996) – by means of the 50/50 policy, having first struggled unsuccessfully with the consultancy system. Working in clear conversation with filmmaking traditions elsewhere – at the level of genre formulae, production design and narrative conventions – Bornedal produced a film that enthralled Danish viewers by virtue of the novel combination of Danish settings, the Danish language and the thriller genre. Inspired by an encyclopaedic knowledge of film, Refn developed a harrowing and cinematically compelling portrait of criminality in urban Denmark. Providing a stark contrast to the edifying tradition of the heritage film and related literary adaptations, *Pusher* became something of a cult phenomenon amongst younger generations. Had the DFI not somehow understood the seemingly paradoxical logic of seeking new faces and new ideas by neutralising its very own gatekeepers, these films, which together count as one of several turning points in contemporary Danish cinema, might never have been made. *Nightwatch* and *Pusher* paved the way for a younger generation of filmmakers intent on working more intensely, and innovatively, with (especially international) genre formulae.

A *change of regime*

The Film Act of 1997 called for far-reaching restructuring and integration of key film-related public institutions with an eye to rationalisation. The DFI, Danish Film Museum and National Film Board of Denmark were all fused into a new Danish Film Institute located in a specially designed Film House in central Copenhagen. Ib Bondebjerg, Professor of Film Studies at the University of Copenhagen, was appointed Chairman of the Board of this new body by then Minister of Culture, Elsebeth Gerner Nielsen, and Bondebjerg and his Board were responsible in a subsequent moment for hiring Henning Camre as the DFI's new chief executive officer (CEO). Camre's effectiveness as a leader, not least as an individual capable of building a highly competent team with the kind of mix of experience that defines his own background, has been decisive for the development of the Danish film policies that figure centrally in the 'Danish model'. Camre's development plans have all been clear, detailed, innovative, ambitious, and carefully attuned to the need both to consolidate existing strengths and to anticipate new challenges. Moreover, his various skills, strikingly absent in some of the former DFI administrators, have made Camre a highly effective spokesperson for Danish film, especially in negotiations about funding with the earlier Social Democratic government.

More money

The favourable situation currently enjoyed by Danish film rests crucially on the dramatic increase in funding that Camre and Bondebjerg secured during talks with relevant politicians in the spring of 1998. Film had long been demonstrably under-funded in comparison with other state-funded art-forms, such as theatre. What is more, by 1998 Danish film was associated with the kind of kudos that can be parleyed into monetary support. Danish films had won Academy awards in 1988 and 1989; von Trier had definitively established himself as a major auteur with *Breaking the Waves* (1996); then emerging directors such as Bornedal and Winding Refn had demonstrated beyond a doubt that Danish viewers could be persuaded to watch Danish films; and a prestigious Jury's Special Prize at Cannes in May 1998 for Thomas Vinterberg's second feature film, the Dogme film *Festen* (*The Celebration*), suggested that Danish film might well be on the cusp of producing the very film movement that von Trier had announced with such bravado in 1995, at a centennial celebration for film in Paris (Hjort and MacKenzie 2003: 1). The DFI's negotiations with the government resulted in an additional 440 million Crowns (approximately 59 million Euros) for Danish film from 1999 to 2002, a net increase of 75 per cent (Hjort and Bondebjerg 2000: 12).

New funding initiatives

The DFI's significantly enhanced budget was by no means used to pursue business as usual. It was not, in other words, simply a matter of making more films with budgets comparable to earlier productions, although quantity was a key issue. In 1998 the DFI view was that twenty features per year constituted the minimal level of production for a viable Danish cinema, and measures were thus taken to create the relevant critical mass.[1] However, the Danish film milieu post-1998 also witnessed a concerted effort to professionalise and develop various phases of the filmmaking process, from pre-production to marketing and distribution. The DFI emphasised support for script development in an effort to encourage original stories rather than adaptations. It also insisted on a more systematic approach to film distribution, with marketing strategies and target groups figuring centrally in even the earliest thinking about new film projects. The DFI provided subsidies for test screenings and exit polls, as well as for the production of multiple prints allowing for a film's simultaneous release throughout the country and thereby for the stimulation of cinephilia in the non-urban areas. Considerable effort was put into preventing the demise of cinemas in small towns through subsidies for the renovation of existing cinemas and for the creation of new cinemas. In addition to its role as funding body, the DFI assumed an advisory role in connection with the revival and expansion of Denmark's screens. It also helped to facilitate collaboration between private investors and various local governments in the area of film exhibition. The overall result was a significantly expanded network of cinemas throughout the country.

The project of securing domestic viewers for Danish cinema motivated the introduction of various measures aimed at ensuring an appreciation of moving images amongst children and young people. Film-X, a studio in the DFI's Film House, provides school-age children with an opportunity to explore some of the practical and technical aspects of the film production process. The DFI also established a Centre for Children and Young People in the Film House, the goal being to produce a wide range of materials that support the teaching of film narrative, aesthetics and appreciation, as well as the analysis of particular films, in Danish schools.

The DFI's approach to the actual funding of films has been guided to a considerable extent by two key issues: sustainability and cultural or artistic renewal. One aim has been to ensure that aspiring and emerging film directors have reasonable access to funding. In order to achieve this goal, it is not enough simply to enhance state support for Danish filmmaking, for such monies are quickly spent by established filmmakers with ambitious film projects requiring large budgets. Access can only be guaranteed if competition is held in check and if the zero-sum features of competitive funding practices are attenuated. Several of the DFI's funding programmes have been designed to do precisely this. I will briefly mention just two of the most noteworthy: New Fiction Film Denmark and New Danish Screen.

Introduced in 1994, New Fiction Film Denmark provided a crucial stepping stone between the Film School and the world of full-time professional filmmaking for about a decade. By keeping allocations below a relatively low funding ceiling of 3 million Crowns (approximately 402,000 Euros), and by encouraging filmmakers to limit their films to sixty minutes, this particular programme helped to create what I have called a 'zone of limited risk' (Hjort 2005) where recent film school graduates could refine their skills before assuming the high-risk role of feature-length filmmaker. The most noteworthy film associated with the programme is Jonas Elmer's largely improvised breakthrough film, a comedy shot in black and white, entitled *Let's Get Lost* (1997).

New Danish Screen, a programme aimed at 'young directors, producers, [and] scriptwriters' who are between the 'initial manifestation of talent' and 'its mature expression' (DFI 2002: 18), is a collaborative initiative involving the DFI and two Danish TV stations, DR and TV2, and a budget of approximately

14 million Euros (100 million Crowns) for an initial three-year period. New Danish Screen is a response both to the constraints of small-nation filmmaking and to the dangers that success entails:

> 'Danish film has been enjoying a remarkable run over the last ten years. But too much success can be a problem,' [then programme director Vinca] Wiedemann says. 'It happens when you try to copy things that did well. Or when filmmakers assume that having a hit entitles them to a much bigger production next time, now that they are rich and famous! However, as a small nation, Denmark is completely limited by the available film subsidies . . . Every time someone makes a film they should be thinking low-budget,' she contends. (Skotte 2006)

Influenced no doubt by core elements of the Dogme 95 movement, New Danish Screen provides a low-budget space where already competent filmmakers can unlearn the habits that create a comfort zone – but also obstacles to innovation and creativity – in the high-risk business of expensive feature-length filmmaking. New Danish Screen limits risk through budgetary restrictions, thereby creating the conditions under which filmmakers can take meaningful risks: 'what matters [Wiedemann points out in conversation with Kim Skotte] is . . . whether [a film] shows personal expression . . . the project's central creative forces [must] have inner drive and something to risk' (Skotte 2006). What we have here is creativity under budgetary constraint, and constrained risk as a condition of possibility for thoughtful risk-taking.

In some ways New Danish Screen recalls the apparently paradoxical logic of the 50/50 (60/40) scheme, for it was initiated as what Wiedemann calls a 'strategic countermove' designed to thwart some of the perverse effects of government subsidies: inertia and the abrogation of (fiscal) responsibility (Skotte 2006). Reflecting some of the core commitments of the new DFI, New Danish Screen insists on teamwork amongst producers, writers and directors, the point being to enhance commitment through involvement. New Danish Screen experienced various start-up problems, but established a decisive institutional presence in 2006 with Pernille Fischer Christensen's *En Soap* (*A Soap*, 2006) and Christoffer Boe's *Offscreen* (2006). A film about the suicidal transvestite and would-be transsexual Veronica (David Dencik) and his interaction with his new neighbour, the somewhat cynical Charlotte (Trine Dyrholm), *A Soap* won the Silver Bear at the Berlin Film Festival and went on to further success on the international festival circuit. *Offscreen* casts actor Nicolas Bro as himself, tracing his interactions, through the camera with which he films an unravelling life, with actor Lene Maria Christensen, director Christoffer Boe, director Jakob Cedergren, actor Trine Dyrholm and dramaturge Katrine Wiedemann, all as 'themselves'. Featured at two major film festivals in 2006 (the Venice Film

Festival and the London Film Festival), *Offscreen* promises to cement Boe's reputation as an uncompromising art director.

New Fiction Film Denmark and New Danish Screen are but two of a plethora of DFI funding programmes. In the context of small-nation filmmaking they provide evidence of a much-needed commitment to youth, creativity and bridging opportunities, to the equitable distribution of resources, and to inventive countermoves that can neutralise the perverse effects of the very subsidy system on which many small national cinemas inevitably rely.

Artistic Leadership

Danish cinema is a thriving undertaking these days in part on account of its ability to attract talented young people with the kind of energy and commitment that stands in stark contrast to pervasive welfare state mentalities. In order to understand the role that Danish film now plays as a powerful magnet in the pool of small-nation talent, it is necessary to look to the question of artistic leadership. And this, quite simply, means understanding the various contributions that Denmark's most significant auteur, Lars von Trier, has made to the landscape of Danish film.

The extent of von Trier's influence on contemporary Danish film highlights the paradoxes of individual agency in small-nation contexts. While smallness can impede external visibility, it also makes possible a considerable internal impact. The efficacy of individual filmmakers is thus both limited and potentially enhanced by their small-nation status, and the trick is to understand the complex dynamics that govern relations between limitations and opportunities. In the case of von Trier, the internal impact (mediated through external success) of this individual's agency has been so strong that there is genuine reason to doubt whether talk of a Danish model (or miracle, as some journalists would have it[2]) would even be possible without his galvanising presence.

Von Trier's contributions to Danish film have been wide-ranging, and it is most helpful here to focus on a number of general attitudes or principles that are variously reflected in a series of particular initiatives. Von Trier has helped to reverse the fortunes of small-nation filmmaking in Denmark in four crucial ways. He has systematically rejected the logic of what Robert H. Frank and Philip J. Cook (1995) call a 'winner-take-all' market and society, thereby counteracting the paralysing and self-limiting pathos of small-nation insecurities. Rather than accepting the limitations of existing cultural policies, he has sought to complement such policies with initiatives that provide solutions to the problems of small-nation filmmaking. He has put considerable energy into the work of institution-building. And, finally, in a culture where various forms of petty-minded egoism are celebrated as expressions of egalitarian virtues and where generosity is delegated to various government agencies charged with dispensing 'gifts' on behalf of the state, von Trier has thwarted the zero-sum reasoning that typically accompanies objective scarcity in small-nation filmmaking milieus through a commitment to what looks like a highly productive concept of gift culture. Let us look at each of these crucial interventions in turn.

The rejection of winner-take-all markets

According to Frank and Cook (1995) we can speak of a 'winner-take-all' society when differences in performance or talent translate into incommensurable differences at the level of income or rewards, with rewards being concentrated in the hands of a few top performers. Small-nation filmmakers who manage to make it on to the international radar inevitably encounter the logic of a winner-take-all market in the form of dramatically enhanced opportunities that encourage such filmmakers literally to sever their connections to their national context and community in favour of especially Hollywood filmmaking and star-level rewards. International visibility for a small-nation filmmaker involves a positional reward, and this new and far more favourable position within the international arena of cultural production effectively cancels many of the limiting features of the original small-nation context, but only at an individual and highly exceptional level. Favourable positioning in relation to rewards and opportunities, what I want to call positionality, itself promises further material and immaterial rewards that are simply unthinkable in most small-nation contexts and certainly in those where commitments to horizontal social structures, and to the kind of redistribution of wealth that is necessary to maintain them, are strong.

The logic of winner-take-all reasoning serves to make what Albert Hirschman (2006) would call 'exit' the inevitable next step for many a successful small-nation filmmaker, and in the Danish context Bille August's long-term absence from Denmark following the Academy award for *Pelle the Conqueror* illustrates the point. What is striking about von Trier is his systematic rejection of exit as the logical corollary of international success. Rather than embracing the possibility of a radical separation from the Danish filmmaking milieu, von Trier has used success to leverage various collectivist projects that have served dramatically to enhance the reputation of his collaborators, all of whom have been able as a result to enjoy the new opportunities that positionality generates. Instead of opting for exit, von Trier has chosen to remain in Denmark, where he has shown, time and again, that various manifestations of small nationhood need not be limiting, and can even be enabling.

Cinematic experimentation as a complement to cultural policy

Von Trier's most important contribution to the area of cinematic experimentation as an alternative to official cultural policy is the well-known Dogme 95 initiative. Announced in Paris in 1995, this back-to-basics, manifesto-driven and rule-governed approach to filmmaking gained legitimacy when Dogme #1, Vinterberg's *The Celebration*, won the Jury's Special Prize at Cannes in 1998. Dogme 95 went on to become a global movement, and at this point the Dogme legacy includes a considerable number of films made according to the rules dictated by the so-called 'Vow of Chastity', as well as many films that reflect the influence of the Dogme brethren's stance without strictly abiding by the rules. What is relevant here is that many of the rules specified in the 'Vow of Chastity' provide a cogent solution to the problems of cost and competition that small national cinemas inevitably face. Essentially the rules had the effect of proscribing the dominant Hollywood practices that shape viewers' expectations of what counts as a worthwhile film while being entirely beyond the economic reach of small-nation filmmakers. The ingenuity of Dogme, however, lies not only in its programmatic rejection of cost-intensive practices, but in the way that the manifesto's framing devices effectively legitimated the low-budget counter-aesthetic that the proscriptions favoured in practice. Without these devices this counter-aesthetic might have had little or no impact, and might even have registered as an expression of sub-competent filmmaking.

Inasmuch as Dogme involves what Jon Elster (1992, 2000) calls 'creativity under constraint', the stimulation of creativity through the imposition of constraints, this cinematic intervention combined important creative values with a genuinely pragmatic understanding of inevitable economic constraints. As scholars, critics, filmmakers and even policymakers discussed the impact and achievements of Dogme in Denmark and elsewhere, this particular mix of creative and instrumental values, of substantive and means-end rationalities, became virtually a preferred national brand, and certainly a considerable source of inspiration for producers and directors in the film industry. Nordisk Film's 'Director's Cut' programme, which was introduced in 2002, is, for example, clearly influenced by Dogme. Defined as a low-budget initiative (Gundelach Brandstrup 2002), this programme has produced a number of features, some of them quite remarkable. Examples include Christoffer Boe's first feature, *Reconstruction* (2003), a narrative about love and personal identity which won the Caméra d'Or at Cannes and a Golden Plaque for Manuel Alberto Claro's wide-screen cinematography. With its gritty images resulting from manipulation of Super 16 images during post-production, this film established Boe as someone capable of contributing complexity and originality to the visual styles of the New Danish Cinema. Another noteworthy 'Director's Cut' film is Jacob Thuesen's *Anklaget* (*Accused*, 2005). Based on a script by one of Denmark's most productive young scriptwriters, Kim Fupz Aakeson, *Accused* tells a psychologically nuanced and compelling story about incest. The film features actors who are very much associated with the New Danish Cinema: Troels Lyby (*Dogme #2, Idioterne/The Idiots*) in the role of the father who is (rightly) accused of incestuous desire by his young daughter, and Sofie Gråbøl (*Nattevagten/Nightwatch*, 1994; *Dogme #3, Mifunes sidste sang/Mifune*, 1999) as the wife and mother who must confront an unthinkable truth.

The artistic leadership that is evident in Dogme 95 has also had clear implications for policymaking. For evidence supporting this claim we need look no further than Vinca Wiedemann and her remarks about New Danish Screen as a framework within which creativity and limited resources are integrally connected. The point is that Dogme effectively validated low-budget filmmaking as a means for promoting creativity amongst already established and experienced filmmakers. Dogme is an excellent example of how the success of proposals sometimes depends as much on the status and identity of the person who articulates them as it does on their actual contents. As Ole Bornedal remarked in an interview, 'If a producer had proposed the Dogme concept, he would have been collectively slaughtered by every director in the country, but the proposal just happened to come from an artist, so now suddenly it's brilliant. It's that simple' (Hjort and Bondebjerg 2000: 233). Dogme essentially provided a kind of blueprint for artistically probing and economically viable filmmaking with a collectivist dimension oriented towards solidarity and sharing rather than individualism and zero-sum rationality. Having noted the various successes associated with Dogme, policymakers have been able simply to spell out various versions of the blueprint in officially institutionalised spin-off initiatives such as New Danish Screen. It is worth noting in passing that one of von Trier's most recent projects, the transnational Scottish–Danish Dogme project known as *Advance Party*, is an ingenious attempt to make cinematic experimentation do the work of much-needed yet non-existent cultural policies (Hjort forthcoming).

Institution-building

Von Trier's most significant contribution to institution-building has been the creation, together with his producer partner Peter Aalbæk Jensen, of a Film Town in the former army barracks in Avedøre, on the outskirts of Copenhagen. Established in the late 1990s, *Filmbyen* is now home to twenty companies and Northern Europe's most intensive site of film production (www.filmbyen.com). The guiding idea throughout has been to create a productive environment where competitive zero-sum games are constrained by a set of alternative practices. *Filmbyen*, more specifically, was designed to foster synergies, through shared resources and space, amongst individuals who are competitors, sparring partners and collaborators as the need or occasion arises. *Filmbyen* has a unique culture, very much shaped by Aalbæk Jensen and evident to anyone who spends a few hours in the central building known as the Old People's Home (a designation that reflects the presence of some of the oldest employees and departments associated with von Trier and Aalbæk Jensen's company Zentropa).

A suggestive example of Aalbæk Jensen's influence is the assembly-style singing from the Danish Folk High School's song book that takes place in *Filmbyen* on Fridays (Niels Aalbæk Jensen in Jacobsen 2001: 79). An occasion, quite clearly, for social effervescence and an intense experience of the social bond, these song sessions mirror an ethos of solidarity and loyalty that is the ideal, if not always the reality, associated with *Filmbyen*.

While *Filmbyen* was conceived by von Trier and Aalbæk Jensen as a home for Zentropa, the point was by no means to exclude competitors. Birgitte Hald and Bo Ehrhardt's Nimbus Film is thus, for example, located in *Filmbyen*, where it plays the role of plucky newcomer in relation to the more and more established operation associated with von Trier and Aalbæk Jensen, itself once a rebellious undertaking in a landscape dominated by Nordisk Film. Nimbus Film has played a crucial role in the renewal of Danish film, having produced many of the films that define the New Danish Cinema. Nimbus Film produced two of the most successful Dogme films, Vinterberg's *The Celebration* (1998) and Kragh-Jacobsen's *Mifune* (1999). In 2004 Nimbus released Nicolaj Arcel's feature debut, the compelling political drama *Kongekabale* (*King's Game*, 2004) with a remarkable performance by Anders Berthelsen (*Mifune*) as the investigative journalist, Ulrik Torp. The second feature by the Danish-trained Icelandic filmmaker, Dagur Kári, is also a Nimbus Film production. *Voksne Mennesker* (*Dark Horse*, 2005) is a visually and aurally compelling comedy in high-contrast black and white about a graffiti artist (played by Jakob Cedergren, Danish Shooting Star 2005), his best friend, Morfar (Nicolas Bro), and their life-changing encounter with a young woman called Franc (Tilly Scott Pedersen). Fischer Christensen's *A Soap* (2006) brought further recognition for Nimbus Film in the form of a second Silver Bear, and their most recent feature film production at the time of writing, Ole Christian Madsen's *Prag* (*Prague*, 2006), also seems set to meet with critical acclaim. With a manuscript by Kim Fupz Aakeson and performances by Mads Mikkelsen and Stine Stengade (who also played lead roles in Madsen's Dogme film, *En kærlighedshistorie* [*Kira's Reason*, 2001]), *Prague* was described as 'challenging with superb performances' and as a 'truly rewarding experience' by *Variety* following its premiere at the Toronto Film Festival in 2006.

With regard to the process of institution-building it is finally important to note that *Filmbyen* has become the site of many collaborative ventures involving both the public and private sector. Station Next is a project that builds on the successes of the New Danish Cinema and aims to foster cinephilic attitudes amongst teenagers through hands-on experience with professional filmmaking equipment in *Filmbyen*. Station Next was initiated in 1999 by Zentropa, the DFI, Statens Pædagogiske Forsøgscenter (the National Innovative Centre for General Education) and Danmarks Radio (Denmark's national broadcasting corporation) and has been backed in more recent years by the Danish Ministry of Culture and the European Commission for Education and Culture. The very positive result of Station Next has been a considerable number of young people (with diverse cultural backgrounds reflecting the ethnic composition of the suburbs south of Copenhagen) engaged in productive dialogue with film professionals in *Filmbyen*. Aalbæk Jensen has expressed his views on Station Next on numerous occasions, and the following is a characteristic comment that highlights the community- or milieu-developing aspirations behind *Filmbyen*:

> In Sweden you had enormous progress with Ingmar Bergman, Jan Troell, and Bo Widerberg, but they completely forgot about the grassroots. They didn't initiate a bloody thing that could help to carry the torch forward, and this has cost them 20 to 25 years of depression, in terms of film. That's why I won't stand quietly by and watch us make the same mistake in Denmark, and that's why education is so incredibly important to me. It is very encouraging (*mycket bekräftande*) as they say over there (*hinsidan*) to see young 12 or 13 year old brats running around making films here at *Filmbyen* (Station Next). (Peter Aalbæk Jensen, in Jacobsen 2001: 87)

Gift culture

Many of von Trier's projects have a collaborative dimension that has had far-reaching consequences for the Danish filmmaking milieu. In some cases von Trier's endeavours have involved an almost wilful sharing of prestige, reputation and talent. A case in point is *De fem benspænd* (*The Five Obstructions*, 2003), in which von Trier's former teacher, the much older and far less well-known filmmaker, Jørgen Leth, is required to remake one of his early successes, *Det perfekte menneske* (*The Perfect Human*, 12 minutes, 1967) according to a series of obstructive rules imposed by von Trier. The externally imposed obstructions create the conditions under which Leth is able to resolve a creative crisis and thus to renew his individual style. At the same time, the prestigious identity of the person imposing the relevant rules, von Trier, helps to lift Leth into the very sphere that is typically reserved for the kind of top performers who define a winner-take-all society. *The Five Obstructions* is at once a clear manifestation of Trier's rejection of winner-take-all thinking and an ingenious solution to the problems having to do with relative invisibility and poor positioning within a global cultural arena, with which most small-nation filmmakers grapple.

It is difficult to chart the precise impact of von Trier's commitment to what I am calling gift culture. What is clear, however, is that the Danish film milieu stands in stark contrast to the dominant mentalities of the welfare state, where citizens learn from an early age to work the system of benefits, and to insist that any activity remotely describable as labour be duly and justly remunerated.

The Danish film milieu is an environment where the concept of engaging in practices for the sake of intrinsic values provides a powerful source of motivation. The related idea of intrinsic rewards is, as Andrew Ross (2000) has pointed out, one that has long been associated with both the arts and academe, having given rise in some contexts to the rather unfortunate phenomenon of 'discounted labour'. In a welfare state, however, the worry is not so much that labour will go unremunerated, but rather that citizens, on account of the potent presence of the state and especially its robust safety nets, will fail to develop a truly passionate relationship to the activities that they perform as work. The Danish film milieu has seen the proliferation of various undertakings that emphasise the concept of gift culture in connection with the idea of intrinsic rewards. A key example is Super 16, an alternative film school that was created in 1999 by a number of film enthusiasts who had failed to gain admission to the highly competitive National Film School of Denmark. Super 16, which offers training in the evenings over a three-year period, admits eight directors and eight producers per year. The school has established itself as a highly respected and effective training ground for serious film professionals and has produced a number of increasingly visible film practitioners, amongst them Carsten Myllerup, one of its founding members. Super 16 is made possible by good will and gifts alone. It receives none of the monies that the Danish Film Institute administers on behalf of the Danish state, and relies on private sponsorships, the savings of the participating students, and, most importantly in the present context, on gifts from the film milieu. Nordisk Film, for example, provides Super 16 with a properly professional site for its activities at no charge. The students who attend Super 16 are mostly already active in various ways in the film milieu, and classes are thus conducted in the evenings, when Nordisk Film's studios are empty and available for alternative use.

The culture of generosity that is at least one of the features of the Danish film milieu is significant because it helps to generate a highly motivating and deeply rewarding social imaginary that has intrinsic values at its core. At the same time, generosity is clearly being practised by von Trier and others as a conscious milieu-developing strategy that is particularly necessary, and perhaps also feasible, in small-nation contexts.

Von Trier has been a remarkable figure in the landscape of Danish film and a source of considerable inspiration for many. Yet this filmmaker has always courted controversy and his recent critical outbursts about Danish film more generally, and the work of Susanne Bier and especially Anders Thomas Jensen more specifically, did little to endear him to certain colleagues.[3]

Jensen, who was accused by Trier of creating a steady stream of films that systematically avoid the creative psychological costs of soul-searching, personal filmmaking, is the director of a number of award-winning features: *Blinkende lygter* (*Flickering Lights*, 2000), *De grønne slagtere* (*The Green Butchers*,

2003) and *Adams æbler* (*Adam's Apples*, 2005); a prolific scriptwriter, he has also provided scripts for a long list of films including Bier's *Efter brylluppet* (*After the Wedding*, 2006), Jannik Johansen's *Mørke* (*Murk*, 2005), Tomas Villum Jensen's *Solkongen* (*The Sun King*, 2005), Bier's *Brødre* (*Brothers*, 2004), Jannik Johansen's *Rembrandt* (*Stealing Rembrandt*, 2003), Bier's Dogme film, *Elsker dig for evigt* (*Open Hearts*, 2002), Lasse Spang Olsen's *Gamle mænd i nye biler* (*Old Men in New Cars*, 2002), Kristian Levring's Dogme film, *The King is Alive* (2000), Kragh-Jacobsen's Dogme film, *Mifune* (1999), and Spang Olsen's *I Kina spiser de hunde* (*In China They Eat Dogs*, 1999). Von Trier's explicit critique of Jensen, and thereby of many of the films that make up the canon of the New Danish Cinema, prompted a scathing cinematic rejoinder: Tomas Villum Jensen's *Sprængfarlig bombe* (*Clash of Egos*, 2006), with a script by Jensen, tells a story about a self-centred, choleric, Brecht-inspired, pseudo-intellectual filmmaker whose works are hailed as masterpieces although nobody wants to see them. That von Trier is the referent here is made clear on countless occasions, and time will tell whether this filmmaker, now in his early fifties and increasingly synonymous with the Establishment of Danish film, will continue to be viewed by emerging filmmakers as a cultural resource or something else entirely.

THE CURRENT CHALLENGES FOR DANISH CINEMA

While there is every reason to be optimistic about the state of contemporary Danish filmmaking, there are new challenges on the horizon. The most important concerns the question of continued state support at current levels. Anders Fogh Rasmussen's right-of-centre coalition government has been making noises for some time about the possibility of significantly cutting funding for Danish film, the reason cited being its undeniable success. Ellen Trane Nørby, one of the government's spokespersons, has been particularly vocal in this connection, her claim being that Danish cinema is now robust enough to survive a 15 per cent reduction in support (Danish cinema currently receives 267 million Danish Crowns – about 36 million Euros – annually in state support). The DFI disagrees with this assessment, and so do experts at the Copenhagen Business School, who argue that the Danish film industry remains unattractive to private investors, and thus vulnerable.

A second challenge that arises in connection with the emergence of New Danish Cinema concerns the balance between what is typically thought of as film as art and film as commercial product. Von Trier's critical remarks about Danish film in 2005 focused on the need for risk-taking as an antidote to various banalities and proprieties. It would be easy to show that, in the context of dominant Danish mentalities, Susanne Bier's *Brothers* (which drew von Trier's fire) takes considerable risks inasmuch as it avoids an ever-popular Danish ironising in favour of a sustained treatment of 'big' issues requiring powerful emotional responses. Yet, it is undeniable that the success of the New Danish Cinema is intimately linked to the preference, clearly exhibited by some of the younger filmmakers, for formulae that can be used to settle many questions in advance. The challenge will be to ensure that initiatives like New Danish Screen actually deliver what they promise: spaces where filmmakers are encouraged to set aside the tried and tested and to push the limits of the cinematic medium.

A third challenge concerns the ethnic composition of the Danish film milieu. With its long history of ethnic and cultural homogeneity, Denmark lacks the kind of multicultural literacy that it needs as a multi-ethnic society. While ethnicity is a recurrent theme in contemporary Danish feature films, these films are for the most part made by Danes with ancestral ties to Denmark, and not by 'new' Danes or Danes with a bi-racial heritage. Indeed, the black Danish actor and satirist turned director, Hella Joof (*Fidibus/Easy Skanking*, 2006; *Oh Happy Day*, 2004; *En kort en lang/Shake It All About*, 2001), is currently the only exception to the mono-racial rule of Danish feature-length filmmaking (although this will change with the release of Omar Shargawi's *Ma Salama Jamil/Go in Peace*). The area of short and documentary filmmaking is considerably more open, and Sami Saif (*Dogville Confessions*, 2003; *Family*, 2001; *The Diary of Ricardo Lopez*, 2000) has at this point emerged as a leading figure. While new Danes are a visible presence in contemporary Danish film as actors, none of them has the kind of star status of a Mads Mikkelsen, Nikolaj Lie Kaas or Ulrich Thomsen. Indeed, when DICAR (Danish International Center for Analytical Reporting) analysed 162 films produced between 1996 and 2004 in an attempt to identify the most regularly employed actors in contemporary Danish film, the result was a strikingly mono-racial group (Kragh 2005). Dominant Danish mentalities favour irony, levelling and humour at the expense of others, and these preferences are very much in evidence in many of the feature films dealing with questions of ethnicity, although here too there are exceptions (Annette K. Olesen's *1:1*, 2006). Danish film would be well served in the long run, as would no doubt Danish society more generally, if some of the problems of access and inclusion that have been taken up so successfully in terms of the small-nation phenomenon could be pursued with equal energy and inventiveness with reference to ethnic minorities within the nation-state.

NOTES

1. The most recent DFI development plan argues that the figure should be revised upwards to twenty-five features per year, complemented by 6–8 co-productions with a non-Danish major, the argument having less to do in this instance with viability per se than with the potential for competing even more effectively with Hollywood products on a national basis (DFI 2006b: 17).

2. See the 'Miracle or Illusion' articles solicited from Derek Malcolm and Hanns-Georg Rodek by *Politiken* in 2006.
3. Von Trier made his pronouncements in June 2005, and in this same period Bille August also chose to criticise Danish films as 'extremely uninteresting'. See August (2005) and, for a discussion of both interventions, the response by Meta Louise Foldager (2005), von Trier's new producer.

WORKS CITED

August, Bille. 2005. 'Return to Hornbæk'. *Politiken*, 25 June.
Danish Film Institute (DFI). 'Entréindtægter i biograferne 1980–2000' ['Gross Box Office Revenue in Danish Cinemas 1980–2000']. www.dfi.dk/talogstatistik/biograftal/entre1980_2000/entre1980_2000.htm.
DFI. 2002. 'Handlingsplan 2003–06'. www.dfi.dk/NR/rdonlyres/5F505DAD-2579-4111-8636-2DC767DC1727/0/Handlingsplan0306.pdf.
DFI. 2006a. 'Facts and Figures 2006: Production and Exhibition Figures for 2005'. www.dfi.dk/NR/rdonlyres/CBOB2FCAA-8CFE-4D55-938A-A255109EFABF/0/ff_2006.pdf.
DFI. 2006b. *Nye mål: Udfordringer og perspektiver for dansk film 2007–2010* [*New Goals: Challenges and Opportunities for Danish Film 2007–2010*]. www.dfi.dk/NR/rdonlyres/87B/C854-89CA-438F-A48E-D619FAFA2876/0/udsendelsesbrev_nye_maal.pdf.
Elster, Jon. 1992. 'Conventions, Creativity, Originality'. In Mette Hjort (ed.), *Rules and Conventions: Literature, Philosophy, Social Theory*. Baltimore, MD: Johns Hopkins University Press. pp. 32–44.
Elster, Jon. 2000. *Ulysses Unbound: Studies in Rationality, Precommitment, and Constraints*. Cambridge: Cambridge University Press.
Filmbyen website. www.filmbyen.com.
Foldager, Meta Louise. 2005. 'Drilleri og dansk film' ['Teasing and Danish Film']. *Politiken*, 2 July.
Frank, Robert H., and Philip J. Cook. 1995. *The Winner-Take-All-Society: How more and more Americans compete for ever fewer and bigger prizes, encouraging economic waste, income inequality, and an impoverished cultural life*. New York: Free Press.
Gundelach Brandstrup, Pil. 2002. 'Director's Cut'. *FILM* 24, www.dfi.dk/tidsskriftetfilm/24/directorscut.htm.
Hirschman, Albert O. 2006. *Exit, Voice, and Loyalty: Responses to Declines in Firms, Organizations, and States*. Cambridge, MA: Harvard University Press.
Hjort, Mette. 2005. *Small Nation, Global Cinema: The New Danish Cinema*. Minneapolis, MN: University of Minnesota Press.
Hjort, Mette. Forthcoming. 'Affinitive and Experimental Transnationalism: The "Advance Party" Initiative'. In Dina Iordanova, David Martin-Jones and Belén Vidal (eds), *Cinema at the Periphery*. Detroit, MI: Wayne State University Press.
Hjort, Mette, and Ib Bondebjerg. 2000. 'Introduction'. In Hjort and Bondebjerg (eds), *The Danish Directors: Dialogues on a Contemporary National Cinema*. Bristol: Intellect. pp. 8–22.
Hjort, Mette, and Scott MacKenzie. 2003. 'Introduction'. In Hjort and MacKenzie (eds), *Purity and Provocation: Dogma 95*. London: British Film Institute. pp. 1–28.
Jacobsen, Kirsten. 2001. *Uden Cigar: Faderen, Sønnen og Filmkøbmanden Peter Aalbæk Jensen* [*Without Cigar: The Father, The Son and the Film Merchant Peter Aalbæk Jensen*]. Copenhagen: Høst & Søn.
Kragh, Nina. 2005. 'Nogle skuespillere er bare bedre end andre' ['Some Actors are Just Better than Others']. *Politiken*, 24 July.

Malcolm, Derek. 2006. 'Op ad bakke i modvind' ['Uphill and Against the Wind']. *Politiken*, 7 January.

Rodek, Hanns-Georg. 2006. 'Der er en præst med i hver anden film' ['There's a Priest in Every Second Film']. *Politiken*, 8 January.

Ross, Andrew. 2000. 'The Mental Labor Problem'. *Social Text*, Vol. 63, No. 2. pp. 1–31.

Skotte, Kim. 2006. 'New Danish Screen'. *FILM* 50, www.dfi.dk/tidsskriftetfilm/50/screen.htm.

Taylor, Charles. 1992. 'The Politics of Recognition'. In Amy Guttman (ed.), *Multiculturalism and 'The Politics of Recognition'*. Princeton, NJ: Princeton University Press. pp. 25–73.

Zeruneith, Ida. 1995. 'Carrots and Candyfloss'. In *Wide-eyed: Films for Children and Young People in the Nordic Countries*. Copenhagen: Tiderne Skifter. pp. 33–48.

2. ICELAND

Björn Norðfjörð

The anti-hero of the novel *101 Reykjavik* travels around the world by browsing the World Wide Web and flipping through his satellite television channels without ever leaving downtown Reykjavik:

> I watch the Pakistani news, mainly to see if they've included Iceland on their world map. The anchor is a ball of hair: hair all over Europe and Greenland. I wait for him to bend his head a little. Iceland isn't there. That's the deal with Iceland. Iceland is the kind of country that sometimes is there and sometimes isn't. (Helgason 2002: 138)

And very much like the country itself, Icelandic cinema is the kind of national cinema that is sometimes there and sometimes is not.

In the voluminous *Oxford History of World Cinema* not a single Icelandic film is mentioned (Nowell-Smith 1996). *Nordic National Cinemas* has a very brief chapter on Icelandic cinema (Soila et al. 1998). However, call it Scandinavian instead of Nordic and you can leave Iceland out of the equation, as in *The Cinema of Scandinavia* (Soila 2005), but then Peter Cowie (1992) includes the country in his study of *Scandinavian Cinema*. In *Cinema Today* Edward Buscombe ends his chapter on Western European cinema with Iceland: 'It seems appropriate to conclude with one of Europe's smallest nations. In an age of globalization it is heartening to find that such countries accord so important a place to national cinema' (Buscombe 2003: 333). And in this very volume Iceland is represented as one of the world's smallest national cinemas – one where the local and the global meet face to face.

ADJUSTING THE SCALES

Until recently, the question of scale has been for the most part unduly neglected in the bourgeoning field of national cinema studies. Attempts at theorising the concept of national cinema have stemmed primarily from results gathered from the studies of the larger national cinemas, and predominantly Western ones, making their general validity suspect, particularly when applied to smaller cinemas. This becomes quite apparent when looking at some of the field's most influential work. In his study of British cinema Andrew Higson lists five distinct economic policies, summarised below, that national cinemas can adopt in response to Hollywood's domination:

1. Distribution and exhibition of Hollywood films.
2. Direct competition with Hollywood.
3. Low-budget film production directed at the home market, or production of art cinema for international consumption.
4. Protective measures in the form of quotas and incentives for national production.
5. International co-operation. (1995: 9–13)

For most small national cinemas such policies are simply not available options, as the following account of prevailing conditions in places such as Iceland makes clear:

1. National film production could never amount to more than a fraction of the exhibition market, always leaving Hollywood or other foreign films as the central film source.
2. The financial resources needed to compete with Hollywood are lacking since the domestic market is too small.
3. Usually, international art cinema must combine with products targeting the home market, since the latter is so small.
4. Without state funding few small national cinemas would be able to operate (making the debate on the feasibility of state involvement mostly irrelevant), but quotas on foreign films are pretty much out of the question considering the low levels of domestic productivity.
5. There is no choice but to seek out international funding (thus further enforcing the international art film as a model).

Leaving aside Higson's first option of not making films, small national cinemas would not exist without combining policies 3 (both options), 4 and 5, while 2 is clearly beyond their capacity. These policies are only available as options to populous and wealthy nation-states, leaving the smaller ones with little choice in these matters.[1]

Similarly there is little room for small national cinemas among the seven varieties of national cinema outlined by Stephen Crofts (1993). They should be thought of as varieties of larger cinemas, as the smaller ones can neither afford to ignore (d) nor imitate (e) Hollywood, let alone support their own totalitarian cinema (f). Regional and ethnic variations (g) are economically implausible, and I fear Third Cinema (b) applies to little of today's cinema. Small national cinemas (and many medium-sized ones) – and thus most national cinemas – are forced to combine in one form or another what Crofts refers to as 'European-model art cinema' (a) and 'Third World and European Commercial Cinemas' (c).[2]

But an awareness of the specificity of small national cinemas must also take into account the diversity within the category in question. In fact, the coinage has been applied to everything from countries producing the occasional feature film to industries producing dozens of films annually. Out of the 102 countries listed in UNESCO's survey of its member states' film production during the years 1988–99 the great majority are classified as small, or producing less than twenty films annually. However, it would seem important to distinguish between countries such as Denmark and Australia (classified as small in the survey although they have more recently surpassed the twenty films criterion, which is clearly a practical demarcation rather than a meaningful definition of the concept) with an infrastructure in place and producing films on a consistent basis, and the occasional forays of local filmmakers from countries mostly or altogether devoid of such infrastructure, resulting in single digit numbers (fifty-four or the majority of the countries listed). It seems to me that a clear distinction between these two is called for, and perhaps the latter ones should be, somewhat logically, referred to as x-small (or extra-small) cinemas.

Furthermore, cinemas can be small in different ways. How can Iceland, a country of only 300,000 inhabitants, produce more films annually than Ukraine (46 million inhabitants), Algeria (33 million) or Chile (16 million) (UNESCO 2001)?[3] The size of a national cinema depends not only on its respective population/audience, but also on its economic situation, on the state's cultural policy (assuming there is one), and, to a certain extent, on language.[4] It is only because of Iceland's relative wealth (the fifth highest GDP per capita and the second most livable country, according to the UN 'Human Development Report' [UNDP 2006]), the state's generous cultural policy, and conversely, the lack of such wealth and/or policy in other countries, that Iceland produces more films than countries with 100 times its population.

None the less, population is a crucial factor, as it delimits the possible expansion of the cinema in question. Thus, places such as Ukraine, Algeria and Chile all have the potential as populous countries to develop strong national cinemas – and thus of making the transition from x-small to medium-size. The former Communist states in Eastern Europe are also relevant in this connection (see, for example, Dina Iordanova's [2007] discussion of Bulgaria elsewhere in this book), as they might well in the future rebuild the film industries that collapsed with the advent of a free market economy. Iceland, however, has no such potential, as the national audience is simply much too small. State support is already considerable, and the funding needed would be highly disproportionate compared to other state-supported cinemas. Unlike in some other small national cinemas, including its Nordic neighbours, even a very successful film cannot recuperate its costs at the local box-office. Furthermore, the Icelandic language hampers co-productions and foreign distribution, making it something of an anomaly even within the other Nordic countries. Thus Iceland would seem to be destined to remain an x-small cinema, struggling to develop an industry out of what are mostly occasional forays into filmmaking.

Friðrik Þór Friðriksson and the Transnational Turn

The first step towards establishing regular film production in Iceland was taken in 1978 with the introduction of the Icelandic Film Fund. The first few films proved to be immensely popular, with many attracting a third of the population or thereabouts; they included *Land and Sons* (*Land og synir*, 1980, Ágúst Guðmundsson), *Fathers' Estate* (*Óðal feðranna*, 1980, Hrafn Gunnlaugsson), *The Twins* (*Jón Oddur og Jón Bjarni*, 1981, Þráinn Bertelsson), *On Top* (*Með allt á hreinu*, 1982, Ágúst Guðmundsson) and *When the Raven Flies* (*Hrafninn flýgur*, 1984, Hrafn Gunnlaugsson). However, optimism soon gave way to despair when audience numbers began to fall rapidly as the novelty of Icelandic films began to wear off. Many filmmakers faced bankruptcy as the Fund's contributions were far too small to bridge the gap between production costs and box-office take. At the end of the decade it would seem as if there were only two options available to Icelandic filmmakers: stop making films altogether (as some did) or search for financing abroad.

It was the good fortune of Icelandic cinema that the 1990s saw an unparalleled explosion of co-productions in Europe with considerable financial support from pan-European funds, some of which were particularly attentive to small nations and their cultural and linguistic specificities. The European Community introduced the MEDIA programme in 1987, which, along with its general goal of strengthening audiovisual industries on the continent, offered protection for minority languages. A year later the European Council established Eurimages, a fund solely geared towards co-productions and particularly attentive to countries with low film productivity. As Anne Jäckel points out, both MEDIA and Eurimages offered indispensable support for small European nations and she pinpoints Iceland as an exemplary beneficiary of both programmes (Jäckel 2003: 78 and 86). And in 1990 the Nordic Film and Television Fund was established, soon becoming the most important monetary source for Icelandic film production along with Eurimages and the Icelandic Film Fund. These transnational funding practices were to transform Icelandic cinema during the following decade.[5]

The films of the 1980s were for the most part local productions, financed, produced and distributed/exhibited solely in Iceland. Furthermore, they were set in Iceland, and they were addressed in Icelandic to Icelanders only. Typically the films were comedies of local appeal (and not easily translated), or they were similar to what Andrew Higson, in the context of British cinema, has defined as the heritage film, the emphasis being on 'the reproduction of literary texts, artifacts, and landscapes which already have a privileged status within the accepted definition of the national heritage' (Higson 1995: 27). All in all, these were quintessential local productions that made little or no effort to appeal to or involve a foreign audience (which was not necessarily the case with the British heritage film [Higson 2003]). But the introduction of European funding was already greatly in evidence in the very first films of the 1990s. The account of King Ólafur Tryggvason's christening of first Norway and then Iceland in *The White Viking* (*Hvíti víkingurinn*, 1991, Hrafn Gunnlaugsson) was a pan-Nordic production, shot in both countries, while *As in Heaven* (*Svo á jörðu sem á himni*, 1992, Kristín Jóhannesdóttir) was a pan-European production depicting the shipwreck of Jean-Baptiste Charcot's *Pourquoi Pas?* off the coast of Iceland in 1936. Most important in this regard, however, was *Children of Nature* (*Börn náttúrunnar*, 1991), and its international success was to put director Friðrik Þór Friðriksson at the forefront of the Icelandic film industry throughout the decade.

As a director Friðriksson was very different from the mavericks who made their first features in the early 1980s. Having organised a student *cinémathèque* and directed experimental films and documentaries prior to his debut feature, *White Whales* (*Skytturnar*, 1987), he began making feature films that were characterised by a global address rarely found in the films of the 1980s. *Children of Nature* is a case in point; its story of an elderly couple escaping their nursing home in Reykjavik for a final return to the home of their youth is not so much about the local city versus country debate, like the earlier films *Land and Sons* and *Fathers' Estate*, but a thematic study of such universal themes as nature, religion, life and death. The Icelandic dialogue is minimal, while great emphasis is put on seeing, hearing and touching. This emphasis on perception, along with formalistic studies of both characters and nature, can be said to take priority over the rather loose narrative build-up. In all these ways the film reveals its debts to the European art film – a debt that is spelled out at the end of the film when Bruno Ganz arrives at the scene as the angel from Wim Wenders' *Wings of Desire* (*Himmel über Berlin*, 1987). Following its success at various international film festivals, culminating with an Oscar nomination for best foreign film, *Children of Nature* soon became the most widely seen Icelandic film abroad. Thus it is very much a transnational film not only in terms of financing (a European co-production supported by Eurimages) and distribution/exhibition, but also in terms of its narrative, with national aspects being addressed to a global audience. In other words, it is not the lack of nationality that ensures *Children of Nature's* appeal to a global audience, but its transparent packaging. Part of what makes the film appealing is its foreignness – its 'Icelandicness' – but only because this element is never allowed to stifle, disorient or put the foreign spectator at a disadvantage. These are the defining characteristics of the transnational for, unlike the international, the transnational does not do away with the national.

Friðriksson further enforced his ties to the auteurist traditions of international art cinema in his next feature, *Movie Days* (*Bíódagar*, 1994) – a film the director himself compared to Federico Fellini's *Amarcord* (1973), Bille August's *Zappa* (1983) and Woody Allen's *Radio Days* (1987). Similar to Giuseppe Tornatore's *Cinema Paradiso* (1988), this is a cinephilic nostalgia film that includes references to, amongst other films, Vsevolod Pudovkin's *Mother* (1926), François Truffaut's *The 400 Blows* (*Les Quatre cents coups*, 1959), Nicholas Ray's *The King of Kings* (1961) and again *Wings of Desire*, whose other angel, played by Otto Sanders, makes a brief appearance. Like its financing, the narrative is very much a transnational one, taking place in the midst of the Cold War, and emphasising its political and cultural impact upon the local community. While Iceland is still at the heart of the narrative, it is framed in a global context that makes it readily accessible to foreign audiences. It was thus only fitting that Iceland should be offered upon a plate like an exotic dish in Friðriksson's next feature, indicating that Icelandic cinema had in only five years been transformed from an inherently local cultural institution to a transnational enterprise.

A multinational production led by US producer Jim Stark, *Cold Fever* (1995) tells the story of a young Japanese businessman, Hirata (Masatoshi Nagase), who travels from Tokyo to a remote corner of Iceland to carry out a ritual ceremony in memory of his deceased parents. It is a rather peculiar film as it takes place mostly in Iceland but has no Icelandic dialogue. However, it is technically not an English language production where English replaces the respective national/local language. It is 'realistic' to the extent that the film depicts foreigners in Iceland speaking amongst themselves, or addressing locals who must answer in English. Furthermore, the early scenes set in Tokyo are all in Japanese. In fact, the very first scene taking place outside Japan, on board a plane about to land in Iceland, begins with an obtrusive passenger asking Hirata: 'Excuse me. Do you speak English?' Having received a hesitant confirmation, the passenger goes on: 'Is this your first visit to Iceland? [. . .] You are going to love it. Everybody does.' The question is equally addressed to the audience, who like arriving tourists are about to be introduced to Iceland: its spectacular nature and curious customs. The film cuts to the first view of Iceland, a harrowing mountain scene covered with snow, by shifting from a narrow television-like frame to cinemascope, further enforcing the island's grandeur and majesty (as compared to the enclosed spaces of Tokyo and Hirata's restricted point of view). This sets the tone for the film, which in terms of narrative and production, typifies a transnational approach in traversing two or more countries, the local making way for the global in terms of financing, distribution/exhibition and address. After *Cold Fever* Icelandic cinema seemed somehow less Icelandic.

If I have focused here primarily on Friðriksson it is not only because he, more than any other director, typifies the 1990s transformation of Icelandic cinema, but also because, due to his international success, he became the industry's spokesperson as Icelandic filmmaking began to revolve more and more around his production company, the Icelandic Film Corporation (whose ironic naming had begun to describe its role rather truthfully). During the latter half of the decade Friðriksson became more involved with producing, and the Corporation had a hand in most of the key films of the period. In addition he acted as an associate or executive producer on foreign productions having to do with Iceland in one form or another, including Lars von Trier's *Dancer in the Dark* (2000), starring Icelandic singer Björk, and Hal Hartley's *No Such Thing* (2001), mostly filmed in Iceland. At home Friðriksson would agitate for further state support, and abroad work towards carving out a space for Icelandic cinema – most dramatically at the Rouen Nordic Film Festival, when he threw his prize statue to the floor in protest over what he viewed as the under-representation of Icelandic films at the festival (Þórsdóttir 1997).

While many films adhered to the transnational imperative typical of Friðriksson's work – particularly striking examples include *Tears of Stone* (*Tár úr Steini*, 1995, Hilmar Oddsson) and *Honour of the House* (*Ungfrúin góða og húsið*, 1999, Guðný Halldórsdóttir) – others were more local in character. As a general rule the lower the budget, the stronger its local emphasis. Noteworthy exceptions are Friðriksson's two adaptations of popular novels, *Devil's Island* (*Djöflaeyjan*, 1996) by Einar Kárason and *Angels of the Universe* (*Englar alheimsins*, 2000) by Einar Már Guðmundsson. The local emphasis in these films constituted something of a U-turn from *Cold Fever*, and they were to prove the most popular films at the local box-office since the mid-1980s. Their success suggested a fundamental dilemma for Icelandic filmmakers; the need for foreign funding called for a transnational approach to filmmaking, while the national audience seemed to have a strong preference for local films. This dilemma became all the more visible when Friðriksson's next two films, *Falcons* (2002) and *Niceland* (2004), were striking flops at the local box-office. In these films, the director chose to revert to the transnationalism of *Cold Fever*, and in the case of *Niceland* he eliminated Iceland altogether from the equation.

A Change of Scenery

At the turn of the century important changes took place regarding both the industry's infrastructure and its leading players – to some extent resulting from, but not resolving, the local/global dilemma. Foreign funding had helped the industry to survive and it had of course been welcome, but its disproportionate contribution, with local sources often supplying no more than a third of production budgets, was something of a concern. The key concern seemed to have less to do with the lack of national inscription in the films themselves, and much more to do with a sense that the high proportion of foreign funding might be unavailable in the future (and might even be frowned upon by contributing countries). As a response, an agreement between the industry and the government was reached in 1998 which involved an extensive restructuring of the national film industry and culminated with the establishment of the Icelandic Film Centre in 2003 and a substantial increase in funding over a period of four years. The allocation for the Centre in 2005 was 374 million ISK, with 313 million ISK allocated for the Fund itself as compared to only 109 million ISK in 1999 (*Fjárlagafrumvarp 2005* 2004).[6] Recent grants allocated to individual feature film productions have generally ranged from 15 to 50 million ISK, with most budgets between 60 and 200 million ISK.

In the new set-up the Fund no longer exists as a separate institution, but is simply a source of finance provided by the state to be distributed by the Centre, whose role as defined by the Icelandic Film Law of 2001 is:

1. To subsidise the production and distribution of Icelandic films.
2. To assist in the promotion, circulation and trading of Icelandic cinema at home and abroad.
3. To strengthen film culture in Iceland.
4. To promote co-operation with foreign film parties. (*Kvikmyndalög* 2001)

If one of these roles has been marginalised, it is most certainly the third one stipulating the strengthening of local film culture. As the exhibition/distribution market has been monopolised by two companies favouring Hollywood films, to the extent that their market share is close to 90 per cent (Karlsson 2003), an art-house theatre has been sorely needed in recent years. This has been somewhat offset by the National Film Archive of Iceland, whose primary role is film preservation, but which also showcases a small selection of classic local and foreign films. Furthermore, the establishment of the Reykjavik International Film Festival in 2004 (whose numerous guests in 2006 included Atom Egoyan and Aleksandr Sokurov) promises to be more than an annual alternative, as it established an art-house theatre in February 2007 – notably named after the student *cinémathèque* formerly run by Friðriksson. In general, though, it is in the realm of culture and education that more input has been needed from the state, whether through the Centre or other venues. Practical film training has been solely provided by the privately run Icelandic Film Academy, but an institution akin to the National Film School of Denmark, with the clear goal of developing filmmakers, is lacking; there is no magazine/journal published on cinema in the country; and book publications are sporadic at best (and stem mostly from the University of Iceland rather than the Centre). In this regard, the infrastructure in, for example, both Denmark and Ireland is more securely rooted in practical training designed to develop new talent, and in fostering an all-round film culture environment benefiting the national cinema. To a certain extent these shortcomings may be among the defining characteristics of x-small cinemas, for they arise in contexts that typically lack either the financial means or the population to develop an all-round film culture.

The central responsibility of the Centre is the distribution of the Fund's annual allowance. The decision-making process is in the hands of its director and specially hired film advisors. Funding is divided between feature productions, documentaries, short subjects and television fiction, and grants can be given to original scripts, script development, production, post-production and marketing (*Reglugerð um Kvikmyndasjóð* 2003). The bulk of the Fund is devoted to supporting the production of feature films, currently 55–60 per cent of its total allocation. To give a concrete example, the Centre received thirty-nine applications in 2003 and gave four promises of funding (www.kvikmyndamidstod.is/frettir/nr/9). Such promises become concrete payments when the producer has completed the film's financing (although not all succeed in this), and often function as 'invitations' to various foreign sources (ranging from private investors to Eurimages); in 2003 six such promises were fulfilled.

Also, increased emphasis has been put on attracting foreign film crews to Iceland, most notably by the 2001 introduction of 12 per cent reimbursements (raised to 14 per cent in 2006) of production costs incurred in the country, and thus following the example of various other nation-states competing for such overseas productions. A glossy brochure, *Film in Iceland*, promotes the country's filmmaking potential with heterogeneous landscape pictures, many taken from actual films or work on location. The accompanying texts praise Iceland's 'astonishing spectrum of scenery', 'incredible daylight' and even its narrative tradition dating back to the medieval sagas (*Film in Iceland* 2001: 2). A strong emphasis is also placed on the recent professionalisation of local filmmaking: 'Icelandic production companies have in recent years produced 5–6 motion pictures per year of high technical standard. This means that Iceland has a good pool of highly professional film crews to work on films and television programmes' (7). Thus, if Icelandic film talent offers an important service for such overseas projects, the latter are equally instrumental not only in developing local film talent, but also in providing work between sporadic local productions. Noteworthy examples include the production companies Saga Film, Truenorth and Pegasus, which along with their local television and feature film productions, also provide assistance to foreign crews shooting everything from automobile commercials to scenes in major Hollywood films like *Die Another Day* (Lee Tamahori, 2002), *Batman Begins* (Christopher Nolan, 2005) and *The Flags of Our Fathers* (Clint Eastwood, 2006). Due to the high expense involved in such Hollywood productions, a handful of scenes can easily surpass the total budget of a local feature.

To use John Hill's helpful (1993) distinction between the cultural category of national cinema proper and the economic category of a national film industry, we could say that in recent years the former has been making way for the latter in defining Icelandic cinema. To some extent it was a strategic discursive move instigated by filmmakers themselves in trying to increase state support by focusing on job creation, foreign investment, tourism and so on. However, the strategy in question can be precarious as it risks erasing the difference between local productions of cultural and social value for the nation (the original motivation for establishing the Fund) and foreign productions simply making use of local talent but ultimately producing films devoid of any such value. On the other hand, as Duncan Petrie has pointed out in writing on Scottish cinema, these two need not be thought of as mutually exclusive: 'While a viable national cinema is necessarily rooted in indigenous forms of cultural expression, these can exist within an industry that also services outside productions drawing upon local technicians, services and facilities' (Petrie 2000: 155). Indeed, for a small national cinema, certainly the x-small ones, whose local productions cannot sustain an industry by themselves, a productive partnership between the two could be said to be vital.[7]

As the industry thus changed face, so did the recognisable faces of Icelandic cinema. If the great success of *Angels of the Universe* in 2000 seemed to confirm Friðriksson's place at the forefront of the industry, many of the Corporation's other productions had little success at home and/or abroad, including the director's own *Falcons* (2002), and the company was declared bankrupt in 2004. Friðriksson's latest feature, *Niceland* (2004), was the first film that he neither scripted nor produced, and in 2006 he was forced to return the Centre's funding promise for his proposed Viking epic, *A Gathering of Foes* (*Óvinafagnaður*), as he could not secure the financing of what would have been Iceland's most expensive film. It is something of an irony (and perhaps an inside joke) that Friðriksson played a successful Icelandic businessman in Lars von Trier's *The Boss of it All* (*Direktøren for det hele*, 2006).

If *Angels of the Universe* was the big success story of 2000, that year also saw the release of three significant debut films: *The Icelandic Dream* (*Íslenski draumurinn*, Róbert I. Douglas), *Fiasco* (*Fíaskó*, Ragnar Bragason) and, most notably, *101 Reykjavik* (Baltasar Kormákur). In fact, if *Angels of the Universe* was the big success story at home, *101 Reykjavik* was the big story abroad. An Icelandic–Danish–Norwegian–French co-production, it was the first film to take advantage of Reykjavik's reputation 'as the hotspot of cosmopolitan nightlife, fashion, youth culture, and sexual freedom' for marketing purposes abroad (Jóhannsdóttir 2006: 112). It told the story of the city-slacker, Hlynur (Hilmir Snær Guðnason), whose life is transformed when his mother Berglind (Hanna María Karlsdóttir) begins a relationship with her Spanish friend Lola (Victoria Abril), whom he later suspects to be carrying his own child. If relying less on the classical European art film in the manner of Friðriksson's work, *101 Reykjavik* is very much indebted to popular trends in European cinema. It is extremely colourful, has stylised camera-work, and boasts a joyful soundtrack by Einar Örn and Damon Albarn (of *Sugarcubes* and *Blur* respectively). Most striking, though, is its playful handling of sexual identities, an approach that recalls Pedro Almodóvar, whose influence is apparent in the casting of Victoria Abril.

The narrative of Hallgrímur Helgason's novel, on which the film is based, has been systematically altered in order to accommodate a foreign audience. Most importantly, the nationality of Lola was changed from Icelandic to Spanish. As a result, extensive portions of the film are in English, and the character becomes a stand-in for foreign audience members as Lola is guided around Reykjavik and introduced to local customs. Thus while the '101' of the novel's title simply referred to the local postal code of downtown Reykjavik, in the film it signals a brief introductory course on Reykjavik for foreigners (as '101' has no such implication in Icelandic). In adapting the play *The Sea* (*Hafið*) by Ólafur Haukur Símonarson in 2002, Kormákur again reverted to this narrative strategy when he changed the Icelandic character Lóa to the French character of Françoise (Hélène de Fougerolles), who is introduced to local specificities in English. His third feature, *A Little Trip to Heaven* (2005), was an Icelandic film in an industrial sense only, for while it was shot in Iceland it was a *noir*-ish thriller set in the American Midwest, starring Forest Whitaker and Julia Stiles. Much like Friðriksson's international productions it was met with little interest at home. In contrast, the astounding local success of Kormákur's fourth feature, *Jar City* (*Mýrin*, 2006), seemed to confirm once again that the national audience preferred local films. Based on the popular crime novel by Arnaldur Indriðason, this film was uncharacteristically local in approach compared to the director's earlier work.

The most popular of the debut films of 2000 in local box-office terms was Róbert I. Douglas' *The Icelandic Dream*; this held mostly local appeal despite including a foreign character – a strategy Douglas repeated in his next feature, *A Man like Me* (*Maður eins og ég*, 2002). His third, *Eleven Men Out* (*Strákarnir okkar*, 2005), was a typical local production although the theme of a gay football team garnered it considerable attention abroad. Ragnar Bragason finally followed up his debut film, *Fiasco*, with the critically acclaimed companion pieces *Children* (*Börn*, 2006) and *Parents* (*Foreldrar*, 2007), whose universal themes and aesthetics transcended their otherwise local setting and narrative. Also belonging to this latest generation of Icelandic filmmakers is Dagur Kári, whose debut film *Noi Albino* (*Nói albínói*, 2002) did remarkably well abroad, without addressing a foreign audience along the lines of *101 Reykjavik*. Nonetheless, it was a somewhat universal story of teenage alienation and rebellion mostly devoid of local specificities despite its village setting in a remote corner of Iceland. Of all Icelandic directors Kári would seem to have the most tenuous relationship to Iceland; educated at the National Film School in Denmark, he directed a second feature, *Voksne mennesker* (*Dark Horse*, 2005), which was for all purposes a Danish production, and his current project, *The Good Heart*, is an English-language film. Most disheartening about this latest generation of Icelandic filmmakers is the lack of women filmmakers in its midst; its only representative, Silja Hauksdóttir, has not yet followed up on her debut film *Dís* (2004), which addressed 101 Reykjavik from a young woman's perspective. This does not bode well for what is already a heavily male-gendered film industry.

The three debut films of 2000 also introduced new production companies to the local industry. *101 Reykjavik* was produced by Kormákur's own Blueeyes Productions which, in addition to his own films, has also produced a couple of other features. While *The Icelandic Dream* was the third production by the Icelandic Film Company, it was the first that was not co-produced with Friðriksson's Corporation. And if Zik Zak's first production, *Fiasco*, also involved the Corporation, only four years were to pass before Friðriksson directed Zik Zak's production of *Niceland*. Zik Zak most clearly reflects the larger changes in the industry, as its co-founders, Skúli Fr. Malmquist and Þórir Sigurjónsson, are producers who have so far shown no intention of directing their own films. Zik Zak is first and foremost a business enterprise, while earlier production firms were established by filmmakers with the express intent of enabling the production of their own films. And with the eventual demise of Friðriksson's Corporation in 2004, the industry has become decentralised as numerous smaller companies produce their own films without the involvement of a single dominant company (although all still rely on funding from the Centre).

LOCAL AND GLOBAL COUNTERCURRENTS

Irrespective of genre, theme and style, most Icelandic filmmakers have in recent years had to confront the issue of local versus global. Certainly, the process may range from explicit to implicit, but in one form or another they all have to make a decision about catering to the local audience or to a foreign one; alternatively they can try to negotiate an in-between position – the transnational approach. It is probably a question that most directors (and certainly producers) face, but it is a quintessential one for filmmakers of small national cinemas. Given the small size of the local market, there is a strong economic incentive to aim for the foreign one (although if there is one industry that offers absolutely no guarantee that any such strategy will return a profit it must surely be film production); yet, the local audience often shows precariously little interest in these very productions. This tension is accentuated by the fact that while foreign funding offers the filmmakers larger budgets and the possibility of international visibility and a career that transcends the local context, the desire to deal with national issues often seems strongest among directors from smaller nations (and in some cases it may well be one of the conditions for securing financial backing for their filmmaking).

These countercurrents are very much in evidence when looking at the volatile history of Icelandic cinema, established as a local institution in the early 1980s before becoming a thoroughly transnational enterprise midway through the 1990s. And while local features have been produced throughout the period, Icelandic cinema's most successful directors – Friðriksson, Kormákur and Kári – all made features that were no longer Icelandic according to the cultural definition that instigated the 1978 establishment of the Icelandic Film Fund. Although one should refrain from deriving conclusive evidence from any cinema's annual output, particularly that of small cinemas, one cannot help but remark, when looking at the films produced in 2006, that Icelandic cinema may have come full circle and returned to its local roots.

Apart from their financing, all four films were for most purposes local productions: shot in Icelandic in Iceland with crews consisting primarily of local talent. All were also local narratives even though two borrowed foreign genre formulae – which, paradoxically, was another novelty of the year. *Thicker than Water* (*Blóðbönd*, Árni Ólafur Ásgeirsson) and *Children*, along with its 2007 companion piece *Parents*, were social dramas in a Scandinavian vein, while *Jar City* and *Cold Trail* (*Köld slóð*, Björn Br. Björnsson) were generic crime films in the Hollywood mould. While *Children* and *Thicker than Water* have garnered notable attention at film festivals, it is too early to say much about their distribution/exhibition abroad. What one can argue, though, is that evading local particularities altogether has been no recipe for success abroad for Icelandic filmmakers, as suggested by the lukewarm interest shown in *Falcons*, *Niceland* and *A Little Trip to Heaven*. What would seem to be more important is to approach local settings and narratives in a manner that can be appreciated by local and foreign audiences alike, in the manner of *Children of Nature*, *101 Reykjavik* or *Noi Albino* (although it should be pointed out that none did spectacularly well at the local box-office). That is, the particular circumstances of Icelandic cinema seem to call for the transnational approach mentioned above.

With elements of transnationality, the social drama and polished aesthetics of both *Thicker than Water* and *Children*, and perhaps also the familiar genre formulae of *Cold Trail* and *Jar City* (the latter the surprise winner at the 2007 Karlovy Vary Film Festival), might very well appeal to foreign audiences. Most notable at the local box-office was the success of *Jar City*, marketed as a Hollywood blockbuster, which sold more tickets than any other Icelandic film since the early 1980s. *Thicker than Water* and *Children*, on the other hand, received a lukewarm reception despite glowing reviews.

To a certain extent the return to a local emphasis has been made possible by changes at the level of pan-European funding. In the wake of criticism levelled at so-called Euro-puddings, requirements regarding multinational involvement have been eased. Another important factor, however, is the increase in funding at the national level. Towards the end of 2006 the government introduced its new four-year plan, raising its annual contribution to the film industry to an eventual 700 million ISK (with 420 million earmarked for feature productions) in 2010, with the explicit goal of guaranteeing that the national contribution would constitute at least half of the budgets in question. These strategies are clearly intended to strengthen the autonomy of Icelandic cinema, but it is difficult to see how making only four films annually – as outlined in the new policy (Gunnarsdóttir 2006) – could suffice to ensure viability or vitality. Instead of making four films budgeted at 210 million ISK, it might be more feasible to produce eight films at half those budgets, so as to offer more opportunities to the local film talent. It took Bragason five years to follow up on his debut film, and one cannot help but wonder how long the local audience will have to wait for the sequel to *Jar City* based upon another of Indriðason's entries in the popular crime series. A decision to aim at a higher level of production would also help to alleviate the problem of a conspicuous absence of women directors in contemporary Icelandic cinema, and would quite simply enhance opportunities for promising filmmakers all around. Conversely, the drawback of such an approach is the possible departure of established directors such as Kormákur and Kári from the local scene in search of higher budgets and an international exposure. However, even the proposed budget of 210 million ISK is unlikely to convince any director to remain within the national realm, while the Centre's contribution to a production like *A Little Trip to Heaven* (where it scarcely mattered considering its high budget) could have contributed to at least two local productions. Perhaps this 'choice' between numbers and relative lavishness is another defining characteristic of x-small cinemas; Iceland can at the very least hardly afford both.

Ultimately the key issue here has to do with visibility. It is not only abroad that Icelandic cinema is one that is sometimes there and sometimes is not. This same tendency is also very much in evidence in Iceland, and while Icelandic cinema's anomalous nature used to be its greatest pull at the box-office, it may have developed into something of a burden over the years. A large section of the local audience seems to view Icelandic films as too strange, too different and ultimately too 'Icelandic' when it comes to making a decision about what to see at the cinema. Seeing an Icelandic film may for many spectators be more like an elevated cultural event and the success of the 2006 crime films may well be explicable in terms of their generic likeness to the Hollywood product. A *New York Times* reporter was astounded when two Icelandic teenage girls opted to leave the theatre when they could not get tickets for *Anacondas: The Hunt for the Blood Orchid* (2004, Dwight H. Little), rather than watch either of the two Icelandic films being offered (George 2004). Eight films may be a far cry from the numbers produced by established national cinemas, and while twice as many as four, it might also be the very outer limit of what such a small nation can realistically hope to produce annually.

This struggle for visibility is in many ways a struggle for existence. If the establishing of the Film Fund in 1978 lay the foundation for a national cinema in Iceland, its existence has by no means been guaranteed. Its history has been a volatile one characterised by abrupt shifts between highs and lows. Arguably, the smaller the nation, the greater the gamble in what is already a notoriously risky business. As Icelandic filmmakers have had to rely on funding from heterogeneous sources to stay afloat, dramatic transformations have resulted in terms of both narratives and modes of address. As such, Icelandic films reflect their small-nation origin, most notably in a striking tension between the local and the global.

NOTES

1. Higson's (1989) highly influential consumption thesis – that national cinema studies should focus on what the national audience is watching rather than the films produced nationally – becomes altogether untenable when applied to small cinemas, as such studies would amount to little else than reception studies of Hollywood films (and other foreign films depending on the nation in question) around the globe. While such studies are, of course, not without value, the consumption thesis strikes me as highly suspect when applied to national cinemas. In one sense such reception studies implicitly enforce Hollywood's hegemonic position, by preferring to analyse the reception of Hollywood films rather than to study locally produced films (and often without interrogating the reasons why local films are not widely screened, if made at all, and therefore not available for reception study). Rarely are films other than Hollywood ones addressed in such studies. See also Eva Jørholt's (2007) critique of the Euro-centricity of much theorising on national cinema in her chapter on Burkina Faso elsewhere in this volume.
2. Note that I discuss the concept of national cinema and the specificity of small ones in more detail in my dissertation on Icelandic cinema (Norðfjörð 2005).
3. According to UNESCO's list, Iceland produced 7 films, Ukraine 6, Algeria 2 and Chile 1. These numbers may in some cases be open to debate. However, their accuracy matters less than the very real discrepancies shown to exist as a general principle amongst film-producing countries (not to mention those countries that produced no films at all). I should also point out that I will only be addressing Icelandic feature film production.

4. Language is one of the three factors outlined by Mette Hjort and Ib Bondebjerg in defining Denmark as a small national cinema:

1. The size of its population is too small to sustain a commercially based, indigenous film industry. 2. The language spoken by the nation in question, Danish, is understood primarily by Danes, making it difficult to expand the market for Danish film through exports. 3. A key problem for the indigenous film industry is the ongoing influx of American films (Hjort and Bondebjerg 2001: 20).

It would thus seem that it is partly due to language that Australian cinema is usually considered a medium-sized cinema while Denmark is classified as a small one. It is not without reason that Tom O'Regan (1996) defines the former as 'a medium-sized *English-language* cinema' (my italics). Note also that, when divided into clusters, the UNESCO survey groups Australia together with Canada, England and the US as forming 'a homogeneous and structured English-language market' (UNESCO 2001). Perhaps size in terms of geography could also be listed as a factor, with Denmark being much smaller than Australia.

5. In this, as in much of what follows, I am drawing to a considerable extent upon my dissertation, which also offers an account of Icelandic cinema throughout the twentieth century (Norðfjörð 2005).
6. At the beginning of 2007 the Euro amounted to approximately 92 ISK and the US dollar was the equivalent of 70 ISK.
7. According to Snorri Þórisson, film producer and CEO of Pegasus, it is simply unviable to run a production company making only local feature films, as advertisements and other work provide steady revenues making up for the inevitable financial risks of producing Icelandic features (Þórisson 2004).

Works Cited

Buscombe, Edward. 2003. *Cinema Today*. New York: Phaidon.

Cowie, Peter. 1992. *Scandinavian Cinema*. London: Tantivy.

Crofts, Stephen. 1993. 'Reconceptualizing National Cinema/s'. In *Quarterly Review of Film or Video*, Vol. II, No. 3. pp. 49–67.

Film in Iceland. 2001. Reykjavik: Invest in Iceland Agency.

Fjárlagafrumvarp 2005. 2004. Reykjavik: Fjármálaráðuneytið.

Friðriksson, Friðrik Þór. 1994. 'Friðrik Þór Friðriksson segist vera ánægður með þá gagnrýni sem *Bíódagar* hafa fengið í fjölmiðlum'. *Morgunblaðið*, 24 July.

George, Jason. 2004. 'In Iceland, Freeze Frame Takes on New Meaning'. *New York Times*, 4 November.

Gunnarsdóttir, Þorgerður Katrín. 2006. 'Efling íslenskrar kvikmyndagerðar'. *Morgunblaðið*, 18 November.

Helgason, Hallgrímur. 2002. *101 Reykjavik*, trans. Brian FitzGibbon. London: Faber & Faber.

Higson, Andrew. 1989. 'The Concept of National Cinema'. *Screen*, Vol. 30, No. 4. pp. 36–46.

Higson, Andrew. 1995. *Waving the Flag: Constructing a National Cinema in Britain*. Oxford: Oxford University Press.

Higson, Andrew. 2003. *English Heritage, English Cinema: Costume Drama since 1980*. Oxford: Oxford University Press.

Hill, John. 1993. 'The Issue of National Cinema and British Film Production'. In Duncan Petrie (ed.), *New Questions of British Cinema*. London: British Film Institute. pp. 10–21.

Hjort, Mette, and Ib Bondebjerg. 2001. 'Danish Cinema: A Small Nation in a Global

Culture.' In Hjort and Bondebjerg (eds), *The Danish Directors: Dialogues on a Contemporary National Cinema*. Bristol: Intellect. pp. 8–22.

Icelandic Film Centre. 2003. 'Úthlutanir 10. júlí 2003.' www.kvikmyndamidstod.is/frettir/nr/9.

Jäckel, Anne. 2003. *European Film Industries*. London: British Film Institute.

Jóhannsdóttir, Heiða. 2006. 'Under the Tourist Gaze: Reykjavík as the City that Never Sleeps'. In Ástráður Eysteinsson (ed.), *The Cultural Reconstruction of Places*. Reykjavik: University of Iceland. pp. 101–10.

Karlsson, Ragnar. 2003. *Media and Culture*. Reykjavik: Statistics Iceland.

Kvikmyndalög. 2001. No. 137, Article 3, 21 December.

Norðfjörð, Björn. 2005. *Icelandic Cinema: A National Practice in a Global Context*. Unpublished dissertation defended at the University of Iowa.

Nowell-Smith, Geoffrey (ed). 1996. *The Oxford History of World Cinema*. Oxford: Oxford University Press.

O'Regan, Tom. 1996. *Australian National Cinema*. London: Routledge.

Petrie, Duncan. 2000. 'The New Scottish Cinema'. In Mette Hjort and Scott Mackenzie (eds), *Cinema and Nation*. London: Routledge. pp. 153–169.

Reglugerð um Kvikmyndasjóð. 2003. No. 229/200, 31 March.

Soila, Tytti (ed.) 2005. *The Cinema of Scandinavia*. London: Wallflower.

Soila, Tytti, Astrid Söderbergh Widding and Gunnar Iversen (eds). 1998. *Nordic National Cinemas*. London: Routledge.

UNDP. 2006. 'Human Development Report 2006'. http://hdr.undp.org/hdr2006/statistics/.

UNESCO. 2001. 'A Survey on National Cinematography'. http://www.unesco.org/culture/industries/cinema/html_eng/prod.shtml.

Þórisson, Snorri. 2004. Personal interview, September.

Þórsdóttir, Þórunn. 1997. '*Djöflaeyjan* verðlaunuð í Rúðuborg: Friðrik braut verðlaunastyttuna í mótmælaskyni'. *Morgunblaðið*, 25 March.

3. IRELAND

Martin McLoone

Between them, the film industries in Ireland and Northern Ireland turn out on average about ten feature films a year and support the production of very many more short films, animations and documentaries. This is achieved through collaboration and co-operation across borders and involves a complex mix of internal sources (state-funded production agencies, the broadcasters, independent producers and the increasing number of schools and colleges that now teach filmmaking) and external provision (larger supra-state funding agencies as well as the international commercial film industry). In this regard the Irish film industry resembles that of most other medium- and small-scale European industries, in that film production is the result of a complex structure of national and transnational funding initiatives in a mixed economy with private capital. As in other European industries, in Ireland state support for film production is designed to promote an indigenous film industry and to develop a more pluralist film culture in a country where cinema screens are dominated by Hollywood films.

Ireland, however, differs from most other small-scale European national film industries in one major respect. Although the native language (Irish Gaelic) is still spoken in small pockets of the country, Ireland reflects its status as a former colony of Britain in the fact that it is now an overwhelmingly English-speaking culture with an Anglophone cinema. There is an Irish language television channel in Ireland (TG4) which produces a range of bread and butter television material as well as some occasionally excellent documentaries, and there are funding schemes in place for Irish language shorts, but the overwhelming majority of productions from Ireland are in English. In this regard, Irish cinema closely resembles the 'non-nation-state' cinemas of Wales and Scotland in being peculiarly exposed to the metropolitan industries of London and Hollywood, with which it shares a language. And yet, somewhat ironically, precisely because Irish cinema is Anglophone, there is always the hope that Irish films will break through into the American market, with the consequent danger that production strategies are geared towards that eventuality. So far, only Neil Jordan's *The Crying Game* (1993) and Jim Sheridan's *My Left Foot* (1989), both largely British-financed, have really done so, but, as is the case with British cinema's long search for the American 'Holy Grail', the temptation is always there to compete with rather than to live with Hollywood cinema and to mould production with the American market in mind.

The development of a film industry in Ireland is itself only one among a number of high-profile cultural indicators of a country that has grown in confidence as its economic well-being has improved. The turnaround in just over two decades has been remarkable, and in this regard the successful development of a film industry mirrors the equally impressive turnaround in Ireland's economic performance over the same period, when from being one of Europe's poorest societies in the 1980s, it has become one of the European Community's most vibrant, high-growth economies – the so-called 'Celtic Tiger' phenomenon. For a culture that emerged from colonial domination only in the early twentieth century and which, during the following fifty years, invested so much political and cultural energy in defining its national difference, Ireland since the early 1990s has embraced the global economy and global culture with some alacrity and no little success. If anything, Irish cinema still operates in the shadow of those other arts that have long been associated with the Irish, including literature and drama which during the last two decades have scored notable high-profile international successes. (Seamus Heaney's Nobel prize for literature in 1994 seemed to add cultural weight to the perception of a booming economy and a vibrant culture.) Moreover, in the field of popular music and dance, Ireland has also enjoyed a level of international success that belies its small population. In other words, to understand both the strengths and the weaknesses of Ireland's film industry today, it is important to see it in this wider cultural, political and historical context – a cultural space where the national meets the international, the local meets the global, and the present responds to a complex and conflicted past (McLoone 2000: 85–131).

Irish History, Irish Film

Two of the most commercially successful films at the Irish box-office in recent years have been Neil Jordan's *Michael Collins* (1996) and Ken Loach's *The Wind that Shakes the Barley* (2006). In its cinema run back in 1996, Jordan's film took over IR£4 million, while by the end of 2006, Loach's film had earned more than 3.7 million Euros. Both productions deal with a controversial and bitterly contested period in twentieth-century Irish history – the War of Independence and the ensuing civil war – and their success suggests that there is an audience for films that directly address complex social, political and historical realities. Indeed, the capacity to address local concerns is surely fundamental to any definition of a national cinema and the popular reaction to these two films suggests that an Irish national cinema is as much a process of national questioning and exploration as it is of celebration. Irish audiences, it would also appear, are prepared to grapple with films that challenge and provoke as well as entertain. However, as exemplars of an exploratory national cinema, both films also present some ontological difficulties. Their respective production profiles, for example, seriously complicate the very notion of the national to begin with.

The budget for *Michael Collins* was $27 million, a huge sum in terms of Irish filmmaking generally, and the epic scale of the film was only possible because of this level of investment from American sources, including the Geffen Company and Warner Bros. The film also features two A-list stars in Liam Neeson and Julia Roberts and was promoted in all respects as a high-profile, Hollywood production. The success of *Michael Collins* with the Irish audience was not, however, repeated in the USA where the film performed very poorly at the box-office (perhaps because Warner Bros. lost confidence in the film after the breakdown of the 1995 IRA ceasefire in Northern Ireland and failed to give it the kind of high-promotion release in the US that its budget would have suggested). Loach's film, on the other hand, is a complex multinational co-production involving Ireland, the UK, Germany, Italy, Spain and Switzerland. Within this complex internationalism, the film's budget of approximately 6.5 million Euros came from state-funded agencies (the Irish Film Board and the UK Film Council), supra-state funding (the MEDIA programme of the European Community), and a mixture of other European sources – state, private and regional – including funding from Ireland's commercial television channel, TV3. It is surely ironic that this complex mix of funding sources facilitated an 'Irish' film written and directed by two of contemporary British cinema's most celebrated creative talents (Loach and writer, Paul Laverty), a film which won the Palme d'Or at Cannes in 2006 'for Britain' and a film which takes its place within the œuvre of one of British cinema's most celebrated and enduring auteurs. *The Wind that Shakes the Barley* may well have connected with Irish audiences in a particularly resonant manner. However, it belongs just as assuredly to the national cinema of Britain as it does to Ireland – even if, as with *Michael Collins*, its success with the Irish audience was not repeated in the film's 'home' territory.

The production details of these two 'Irish' films suggest both the complexity and the ambiguities inherent in discussing the concept of a national cinema in a small, post-colonial, Anglophone culture like Ireland's. This is a culture caught on the cusp of rapid economic and social change, poised between Britain and America, locked into a dependent, if economically beneficial, relationship with its European neighbours and influenced by its own past history of national (and nationalist) struggle. If, however, the complexity of funding arrangements and the ambiguities in the nationality of both films raise fundamental issues about what constitutes the 'Irishness' of an Irish film, then there is less doubt about the manner in which both these films have intervened in an ongoing national debate about 'Irishness' itself.

Loach's film is, in many ways, a riposte to Jordan's and it is interesting that, while both films cover exactly the same years of armed insurrection and civil war (1916–22), for the most part they actually look quite different and offer very different interpretations of the historical events. Both films use these events to address more contemporary issues, of course – *Michael Collins* addresses the peace process in Northern Ireland as it was in the mid-1990s, while *The Wind that Shakes the Barley* carries echoes of the British and American invasion of Iraq and the consequent war there against 'insurgents'. Jordan's humanist message is that violence begets violence and there is always tragedy (and sacrifice) involved in bringing to an end a period of conflict. The film argues that eventually there must be negotiation, compromise and reconciliation, and that purist politics and principled intransigence lead to tragedy. The real tragedy for Ireland was that the new state emerging from colonial domination lost its most charismatic and most visionary leader because of dogmatic intransigence, with profound long-term consequences for the nature of the national project itself, and consequently *Michael Collins* sides unequivocally with the Treaty side in the civil war. Loach's conclusions are very different. His class-based analysis of the civil war argues that ultimately the Irish people were betrayed by their own petty bourgeois leadership, content to take over the roles and functions of the departing British. The negotiations and compromises with the British, which brought about the ceasefire and the Treaty, represented a betrayal of nationalist aims and class principles. For Loach, a foreign oppression was replaced by a native establishment that secured Ireland for capitalism and the existing social order. (By implication, *The Wind that Shakes the Barley* also offers a critique of contemporary Ireland and its global economic success.) The film sides unequivocally with the anti-Treaty forces in the civil war.

The fact that these differing interpretations of history emanate from two films that proved enormously popular with Irish audiences is significant. Both have tapped into and become part of a wider cultural debate in Ireland about the nature of contemporary Irish identity. This continuing debate – in a real sense, a nation talking to itself about its own past – has been a key factor in Irish historical studies since the 1960s and has subsequently influenced debates in cultural studies, sociology and economics. It has also been a recurring theme in Irish literature and drama for almost as long. As Ireland developed from the insular, conservative Catholic culture that emerged after independence in the 1920s into an affluent, increasingly secular European culture from the 1990s on, this debate has intensified, sometimes to the point of acrimony. The Irish cinema that emerged slowly from the 1970s on was itself a product of these wide-ranging economic, social and cultural changes, and quickly became an important cultural channel for mediating the implications of these changes. Irish cinema, in other words, entered the wider cultural debate. In a sense, films like *Michael Collins* and *The Wind that Shakes the Barley* brought the debate out of academia (with its literary/historical bias) and into the main-stream of popular culture. Irish cinema, then, has played an important role in re-imagining Ireland and the Irish, and has visualised on the screen and in a popular idiom many of the transformations, renegotiations and aspirations that have characterised a rapidly changing society. The source of funding or the cre-ative genesis of these two films hardly seemed to have any implications for their cultural and national significance. Although the one is 'Hollywood' and the other is 'British', these films exist within the nexus of Irish film culture and do not carry the same resonance in their respective 'home' territories.

It is important to note, though, that in this process of re-imagining Irish iden-tity, the emerging cinema did not have a blank cinematic canvas to work on, nor did *Michael Collins* and *The Wind that Shakes the Barley* emerge newly minted from their respective industries. The fact that filmmaking in Ireland is a fairly recent phenomenon should not disguise the fact that Ireland and the Irish have maintained a major presence in American and British cinema since the beginnings of the cinema itself. This presence has been manifested in terms of personnel (especially actors and directors), but most specifically in terms of theme, setting and plot. The relatively high profile of Irish themes and stereo-types in American and British cinema has ensured that the representation of Ireland and the Irish has been a major concern for film studies in Ireland and that the traditions of representation, crucial to Ireland's post-colonial identity formation, are a key issue for the emerging national cinema. The importance of these traditions warrants closer consideration.

FILM AND NATIONAL REPRESENTATION

The extraordinarily high levels of emigration from Ireland to the United States during the decades following the Irish famine of the late 1840s meant that by the turn of the century the Irish and Irish–Americans made up a significant percentage of early American cinema audiences, especially in the eastern cities where they tended to congregate. During the early silent era film producers pandered to these audiences with sentimental tales and romantic adventures set in Irish-American communities of the US or in Ireland itself. These early one-, two- and three-reel films attracted a range of Irish and Irish-American actors, who perfected the stereotypes that defined the cinematic image of the Irish for decades. Although many of these films are now lost, their titles remain to evoke the world of Irish ethnic comedies: Biograph's 'Hooligan' one-reelers from 1903, longer comedies and dramas like those made by the Kalem Film Company between 1908 and 1912, and hundreds of films that featured the words 'Ireland' or 'Irish' in their titles from the 1910s onwards. A randomly chosen selection of such titles might include *The Irish Boy* (1910), *The Lad from Old Ireland* (1910), *All for Old Ireland* (1915), *A Wild Irish Rose* (1915), *The Irishman's Flea* (1920), *Luck of the Irish* (1920) or the 'Cohens and the Kellys' cycle (1920s), the last of which was aimed simultaneously at two ethnic audiences (Rockett 1996: 220–9). These films were peopled by amiable drunks and aggressive brawlers, corrupt politicos and honest but dumb cops, Catholic priests and angelic nuns, long-suffering mothers, feisty colleens and vulnerable, naïve maidens. Although established in the very earliest days of silent cinema, these stereotypical characters continued to populate American genre cinema throughout the twentieth century. They were played by a range of character actors and stars who were either native-born Irish, such as Colleen Moore, Maureen O'Hara, Barry Fitzgerald, Peter O'Toole, Richard Harris and in contemporary Hollywood, Liam Neeson, Pierce Brosnan, Patrick Bergin, Aidan Quinn and Colin Farrell, or they had an Irish ancestry upon which to draw when necessary, especially if required to do so by the studio publicity machine: James Cagney, Victor McLaglen, Spencer Tracy, Anthony Quinn and Errol Flynn.

The Irish diaspora also provided some influential pioneers of American film. In the formative years of Hollywood, for example, Irish-born director Rex Ingram (1892–1950) was a particularly noted stylist who made Rudolph Valentino a star with *The Four Horsemen of the Apocalypse* (1921). Herbert Brenon (1880–1958) was one of the most critically acclaimed of silent film directors, although his career foundered with the advent of sound. The most famous and most enduring of the early pioneers was a second-generation Irish–American, John Ford (1894–1973). Ford was one of the great genre directors of Hollywood who lived his Irishness openly in life as well as on the screen. He peopled his westerns and other non-Irish films with many of the stereotypical characters that early cinema had established. More than anyone, he helped to prolong a romantic Irish–American sense of identity, of which the ultimate expression is *The Quiet Man* (1952), in which Ford manages the not inconsiderable achievement of both celebrating and gently undermining the outrageous stereotypes of Ireland and the Irish he helped to create.

The considerable presence of the Irish in early audiences resulted in another historically important development for American cinema. In 1910, the Kalem Film Company became the first American company to shoot on location outside of the United States when it made *The Lad from Old Ireland* in Killarney. The film was produced and directed by Sidney Olcott, an Irish–Canadian who recognised the commercial value of showing authentic Irish locations to a nostalgic and homesick audience in the United States. He brought Kalem back to Ireland for two more summer visits in 1911 and 1912, making a range of one- and two-reel films based on old Irish melodramas or depicting historical moments in Ireland's long nationalist struggle against Britain. These films established the use of Ireland as a theme and as a location for filmmaking by American and British producers, linking Irish cinematic landscapes to nostalgia, romantic escape and the tourist industry, while little effort was made to develop indigenous production.

All this activity created a recognisable cinematic Irish identity, with two traditions in particular being identified (Rockett et al. 1988). In the dominant and most enduring tradition, Ireland has tended to be represented in romantic rural terms with great emphasis placed on its beautiful landscapes and seascapes. John Ford's *The Quiet Man* may well be the screen's most famous and most enduring example of this tendency. However, the romanticisation of Ireland and the Irish landscape is so deeply ingrained in the cinematic cultures of both Britain and America that it frequently re-emerges in both nations' film industries, newly fashioned but little changed. Recent examples of such traditional imagery have been the British production *Waking Ned* (1999) and the American *The Match Maker* (1997). Ireland's long and fractious political relationship with Britain has provided the other recurring cinematic view of Ireland – a land of urban violence and sectarian hatreds where a proclivity to violence seems to form part of the Irish character and to have locked the Irish into an endless and meaningless cycle of murder and revenge. Ford again provided one of the early and most enduring examples of this tendency in his expressionist view of a strife-torn Dublin in *The Informer* (1935). The most celebrated British version of this stricken Ireland is Carol Reed's equally expressionistic Belfast in *Odd Man Out* (1947). In the 1970s and 1980s, when political violence in Northern Ireland escalated, this image appeared with more regularity, sometimes merely as a plot device in otherwise conventional thrillers, such as Phillip Noyce's *Patriot Games* (1992) or Alan J. Pakula's *The Devil's Own* (1997).

Both *Michael Collins* and *The Wind that Shakes the Barley* are, in their different ways, responses to this dual tradition of representation, attempts to re-inscribe history, social context and rationality into the cinematic representation of political violence in Ireland. In Loach's case, as well, his careful evocation of the Irish landscape and use of the thatched cottage are knowing references to both of these cinematic traditions. The grey and black uniforms of the British literally invade and violate this landscape. The lovingly composed shots of the hills and fields of rural Ireland are inhabited by a native population steeped in local traditions and customs – 'natives' who become 'insurgents' only under extreme political and military provocation.

The fact that indigenous filmmaking developed only very slowly meant that these two dominant traditions went largely unchallenged in cinematic terms and therefore tended to circulate as markers of a general Irish identity. What has exacerbated the problem for younger filmmakers is the fact that the nationalist imagining upon which Ireland based its struggle for independence also dovetailed closely with the romantic tendencies of the metropolitan centres. However, as the Irish economy has boomed, effecting a period of rapid change, and as the film industry has been consolidated, these traditional and recurring images of the Irish have marked a point of departure for indigenous filmmakers attempting to forge a recognisably contemporary Irish cinematic identity. The existence of this long tradition goes some way towards explaining the emergence in Ireland not just of a film production sector but also of a critically engaged film culture with links to a broader sphere of cultural activity. Indeed, if anything characterises the concept of a national cinema in a small nation, it is surely the awareness that production in itself is never going to be enough to challenge the hegemony of metropolitan cultures, especially when they share a common language. The promotion of production also requires the promotion of a wider critical film culture and some engagement with historical factors. This truism, as we have seen, was a characteristic of Irish literary and historical studies and it became an underlying theme in the campaigns for the development of a rounded national film culture.

The Development of an Indigenous Cinema

There was one brief period of indigenous filmmaking during the silent period when the Film Company of Ireland made two well-regarded features, *Knocknagow* (1918) and *Willie Reilly and His Colleen Bawn* (1920). Subsequently, except for some semi-amateur films or B-movie quota quickies in the 1930s and government-sponsored informational films in the 1950s, little cinema of any significance was made in Ireland until the mid-1970s. The reasons were mainly economic. Until the 1970s Ireland was a relatively poor country with little capital available for investment in film production. However, there were political and cultural factors as well. The independent Irish state, established in 1922, was built on a nationalism that was conservative in politics, Catholic in religion, and almost xenophobic in its attitude to cultural influences from the outside. Because the political and religious establishment regarded the cinema with suspicion and distaste, it subjected it to the most rigid censorship in Europe from the 1920s until the more liberal 1970s. There also existed a cultural bias against the cinema, which is hardly surprising in a country that celebrates a strong literary and theatrical tradition. (Three Nobel literature awards during the twentieth century, none of which was Joyce, is surely a small nation punching above its weight in literary terms.) In Northern Ireland in the 1930s actor/singer Richard Hayward attempted to start up a small film production industry, but there was little economic or political interest, and after a number of small-scale comedies – *The Luck of the Irish* (1936) and *The Early Bird* (1936) – indigenous feature filmmaking in Ireland ceased to exist for the next four decades (Hill 2006: 19–45).

During these years, Ireland continued to attract both Hollywood and British productions, and in 1958 the Irish government established the Ardmore studios at Bray in County Wicklow to facilitate such inward investment and to encourage further location shooting. These were job-creating strategies in the main and little regard was given to questions of film culture, representation, or the image of Ireland that was being promoted or prolonged. However, the presence of such 'outsider' productions inevitably gave rise to aspirations within Ireland itself for a more indigenous form of filmmaking. In the 1960s and 1970s, an increasingly vocal lobby emerged. It was supported in large measure by two influential directors who remained in Ireland after shooting some of their films there: the American, John Huston, and the Englishman, John Boorman. Huston shot *Moby Dick* in Youghal, Co. Cork, in 1952 and then actually moved to Ireland, disgusted with the House Committee on Un-American Activities (HUAC) hearings in Hollywood. He became an Irish citizen in 1964 and, in 1968, chaired a government-sponsored report on the feasibility of a film industry in Ireland. The subsequent 'Huston Report' was never acted upon but became an important lobby tool for later Irish filmmakers. Boorman retained a residence in Ireland after shooting *Zardoz* in Wicklow in 1972. After completing *Excalibur*, again in Wicklow, in 1980, he became Chair of the first Irish Film Board (Bord Scannán na h-Éireann/ Irish Film Board, BSÉ/IFB) when it was established in 1981.

Indigenous production emerged haltingly in the 1970s through the efforts of a group of young filmmakers (Bob Quinn, Kieran Hickey, Joe Comerford, Thaddeus O'Sullivan, Pat Murphy and Cathal Black) who emerged from art college or through television (Irish public service television, now RTÉ, had been established in 1962). In the 1970s, there was little in the way of public funding for film and independent filmmakers had to struggle to find even the most modest budgets. In their struggle to find funding, this group became an effective lobby on behalf of state funding for film. The Arts Council began the process of public funding by establishing a script award in 1977 – Bob Quinn's anti-romantic vision of the west of Ireland, *Poitín* (1978), was the first recipient – and by 1981 the government finally established the main funding mechanism in BSÉ/IFB. The funding provided by the Board was modest indeed. It was allocated only IR£200,000 for its first year of operation in 1981, half of which was invested in Neil Jordan's first feature film, *Angel* (1982) (and thus was launched the career of Ireland's most high-profile and critically successful filmmaker of the last twenty-five years). But the principle of state funding had finally been established, and although the Board was suspended in 1987 as a cost-cutting exercise at a time of deep recession, it was re-established in 1993 and continues to be the main mechanism for funding independent filmmaking in Ireland.

It is hardly surprising that the generation of Irish filmmakers that emerged in these years would respond to both the dominance of cinematic stereotypes from abroad and the legacies of the nationalist traditions internally. In other words, the films they produced constituted a radical reassessment of Irish identity. This first wave of indigenous filmmakers evinced an avant-garde sensibility and their films were aesthetically as well as politically challenging, an Irish version of 'Third Cinema' political filmmaking (McLoone 2006: 88–99). At the 1984 Cannes Film Festival, two such films (Cathal Black's naturalistic take on Dublin inner-city squatters, *Pigs*, and Pat Murphy's feminist historical drama, *Anne Devlin*) were shown out of competition. Significantly, the one Irish film in competition at that year's festival, winning the Best Actress award for Helen Mirren, was Pat O'Connor's much more commercial and conventional narrative film *Cal*, which was produced by David Puttnam and financed through a combination of British sources (Enigma and Goldcrest) and Hollywood (Warner Bros). If both kinds of film represented an emerging new cinema, there was clearly a contrast in scale, ambition and intention, as well as in budget. Low-budget indigenous film and the kind of slick co-produced commercial cinema that *Cal* represented needed to find a way to coexist, and when BSÉ/IFB was relaunched in 1993, this is precisely what was attempted.

Indeed, in introducing his package of measures to stimulate film culture in Ireland in 1993, the then Minister for Arts, Culture and the Gaeltacht, Michael D. Higgins, identified his project as the integration of 'indigenous energy' and the 'commercial space that tax incentive creates' (Higgins 1995). The tax incentive that Higgins referred to was first introduced by a previous government in 1987 (as Section 35 of that year's finance act) as a replacement for the suspended BSÉ/IFB. When he relaunched the Board in his own 1993 package, he also extended and improved Section 35. Despite periodic fears that it might be scrapped, the scheme has been retained and updated on several occasions since and is now known as Section 481. The scheme encourages both individual and corporate investment in filmmaking by allowing investment to be written off against tax. Although the revisions under Higgins allowed for investment in Irish films, the scheme's major function remains to attract to Ireland large-scale film production from abroad. The most famous success of the scheme (or the most notorious, depending on which side of the Irish Sea is involved) was in 1995 when Higgins himself persuaded Mel Gibson to move his production of *Braveheart* from Scotland to Ireland. Other high-profile productions attracted to Ireland because of the tax incentives were Steven Spielberg's *Saving Private Ryan* (1998), Rob Bowman's *Reign of Fire* in 1992, and Antoine Fuqua's *King Arthur* (2004). The 'trickle-down' impact of these productions can be significant. According to one estimate, *Reign of Fire* received IR£2.7 million through Section 481 but the production then spent a total of IR£35 million on Irish goods and services. The problem with relying solely on such trickle-down economics, however, is also eloquently articulated by the same producer. 'We're a branch office to America in other business fields – why not in film?' (Morgan O'Sullivan interviewed in Duffy 2003: 32).

In fact the Higgins package of 1993 was a total support strategy for all aspects of film production, education and training, and a smaller-scale version of this scheme was established later in Northern Ireland based around the disbursement of British lottery money. Every element of an elaborate infrastructure was put in place: the Film Board for indigenous production; the Screen Commission for location promotion; the Film Institute for cultural exhibition, educational and archival activity; and Screen Training Ireland to co-ordinate all aspects of training. For the first time as well, the state broadcaster, RTÉ, was required to commission a percentage of its production from the independent sector and in response set up the Independent Production Unit (IPU). The package was designed to allow for three levels of film funding and film activity, from mega-budget Hollywood location shoots through mid-budget Irish co-productions and small-scale low-budget indigenous films, including material originated primarily for television. In the Film Board's annual review for 1993, the chief executive, Rod Stoneman, famously described this multiple approach as an attempt to establish a pluralist film culture. 'Let a thousand flowers bloom and a thousand schools of thought contend: we set out to achieve a rich, variegated Irish cinema, with its roots embedded in a vigorous culture. A genuine aspiration towards a radical pluralism' (BSÉ/IFB 1993: 4).

What the Higgins package represented, and Stoneman's formulation articulated, was an attempt to bridge the gap between film as commerce and film as art and culture. For too long in Ireland, film suffered because it was seen either as a form of low-quality entertainment and a distraction dangerous to public morality or as an expensive luxury that the state could not afford. Filmmaking (and cinema attendance) had traditionally lacked cultural legitimacy or economic clout. The Higgins package attempted to address this historic problem, and to some extent it succeeded admirably. In his tenth-year review of the Board's activities, Kevin Rockett notes that, while in 1994, the first full year of the Board's operation, state funding amounted to 2.54 million Euros, by 2003 total investment had reached 65 million Euros. During the ten years from 1993, the Board supported over one hundred feature films and television series and over three hundred short films, documentaries and animation. The value of film production in Ireland rose in this period from a total of 64 million Euros in

1993 to 259 Euros million by 2001, and full-time jobs increased from 845 in 1993 to over 1500 by 2001 (Rockett 2003: ix).

PRODUCTION, DISTRIBUTION, AUDIENCE

The problems associated with Ireland's film industry, though, are almost as variegated as the plural film culture originally envisaged. The main criticism stems from the supposed lack of international impact of indigenous cinema and the relative lack of commercial success outside of Ireland. The fact that Ireland's international profile is overly dependent on the success of just two directors, Neil Jordan and Jim Sheridan (with a lesser profile, perhaps, for Pat O'Connor and Thaddeus O'Sullivan), suggests a cinema of limited appeal and modest achievement. Furthermore, sceptics point out, these directors established their reputations before the introduction of the 1993 funding package and their major films were funded entirely outside of Ireland, without Board involvement or access to tax incentive funding. So, for example, although the original Board launched Jordan's career with *Angel*, his commercial and critical successes – *Company of Wolves* (1984), *Mona Lisa* (1986), *The Crying Game* (1992), *Interview with the Vampire* (1994), *Michael Collins* (1996) and *The Butcher Boy* (1997) – had no Board involvement (although the producers of the latter did avail themselves of the tax incentives). Critics continue to bemoan the fact that there has been no Irish equivalent to the cross-over success of British cinema's *Trainspotting* (1995), *The Full Monty* (1997) or even of an art-house success such as *Bend it like Beckham* (2002).

Despite the success in Ireland of both *Michael Collins* and *The Wind that Shakes the Barley*, the box-office performance of most indigenous Irish films is modest. Indeed, most of the films that have connected with the Irish audience and have played their part in the continuing debate about Ireland's history, Irish identity or the state of contemporary Ireland have been funded and produced outside of the country. This was the case with Peter Mullan's *The Magdalene Sisters* (2002), which was largely Scottish-produced and shot, and *Veronica Guerin* (2003), about the eponymous murdered Irish journalist, which was a big-budget Hollywood movie directed by Joel Schumacher. For the most part, and with some notable exceptions, the small-scale indigenous films promoted by the BSÉ/IFB have performed very poorly at the Irish box-office and have made little impact internationally. Thus in 2001, something of a boom year for low-budget indigenous cinema, nine titles were released in the domestic market. The box-office gross for these nine was a little over IR£2.2 million and just two of these films, Gerry Stembridge's *About Adam* and Kieron J. Walsh's *When Brendan Met Trudy*, accounted for over IR£1.4 million of this. This means that many of the films, with a minuscule box-office take, hardly registered at all with the local audience.

Another criticism of the Irish situation is that, despite the seemingly comprehensive nature of the Higgins funding package, the Irish industry remains stubbornly small-scale in comparison to both other Anglophone cinemas and European film industries. The tax incentive schemes are vulnerable to larger, more competitive regimes so that the scale of inward investment is likely to fluctuate. For example, in 2003, after the UK introduced a similar scheme and the Irish government prevaricated about the future of its own provision, the amount of large-scale location shooting coming to Ireland decreased significantly. The weakness of the dollar made Ireland expensive to shoot in and this further depressed the local film economy. Given the nature of the funding regime, this had a knock-on effect throughout the sector, and by 2005 especially the industry in Ireland, both indigenous and foreign, looked to be in some kind of crisis.

In one sense, though, it could be argued that these criticisms merely reflect the opinions of those whose eyes are on the global rather than the local and whose sense of proportion is scaled to the Anglo-American horizon. In the end, Ireland is a small country and its film and television production sector will always be small-scale compared to its larger neighbours or to the American industry. Furthermore, just as the global film industry goes through periodic troughs and retrenchment, so a small, subsidised cinema like Ireland's is subject to similar fluctuations. The strength of the national funding strategy is surely that production in Ireland is underwritten by state funding so that to some extent it is protected from the worst aspects of a purely market system. Thus, at the end of the 'crisis' year of 2005, the government made extra money available to the Film Board (an extra 1.5 million Euros for 2005 and an increase of 21 per cent in the 2006 budget). A further increase of 2.3 million Euros was awarded during 2006. The extra cash re-energised the industry, and in 2006 production picked up again. Thus the Irish 'spend' for the year is estimated at 175.5 million Euros, up from 96.9 million Euros, and resulting in the production of ten indigenous Irish films and fifteen international film and television productions using Irish locations.

It is surely more realistic to regard the films and television programmes that are produced through national policies and national agencies as being for the home audience in the first instance and commercial success beyond that as a bonus rather than as the defining strategy. The potential audience for any film in Ireland is small. In 2005 there were only 336 screens in the Republic of Ireland with total admissions of just 16.4 million (about one-tenth of the British figure). In Northern Ireland, there were just 156 screens in 2005 and the total admissions of 4.9 million represent about 3 per cent of the UK total. The majority of these screens, as in Britain, are owned and controlled by the major distributors and consequently an Irish film has to work hard to get adequate screen time to make any kind of impact with the audience. There is no network of independent cinemas that might allow films to find an audience outside the parameters of the majors, and with only three art-house cinemas in the whole country, distribution can be a major problem for Irish productions at home just as in Britain.

Seen in this light, the box-office take for *The Wind that Shakes the Barley* is all the more remarkable. Released originally in June of 2006 on only sixty screens, its take of over 3.5 million Euros, representing admissions in excess of 1 million, is very impressive. The total budget for this film was 6.5 million Euros, of which almost 4 million Euros was spent in Ireland, and it subsequently recouped almost all of its Irish spend at the local box-office alone. (This is in marked contrast to the film's relative failure in Britain, on the back of some typically knee-jerk negative press and on an initial print run of less than 100 screens, which is extremely small by UK standards.) Similarly over the years, despite poor performance abroad, Irish independent cinema, initiated and supported by the Film Board, has consistently performed well at the Irish box-office. The 2001 figures for *About Adam* and *When Brendan Met Trudy* look respectable when viewed within the total capacity of the Irish market, and subsequent Irish successes – Pearse Elliot's *Man About Dog* took 2.1 million Euros in 2004 and John Crowley's *InterMission* took 2.8 million Euros in 2003 – merely confirm that if the home market is taken into consideration as the primary criterion, then the strategy of funding for Irish audiences in the first instance has been a significant success.

Of course, all of these films find another audience on television so that even those that performed poorly at the local box-office can pick up a significant audience. So, for example, Joe Comerford's bleak and challenging *High Boot Benny* (1993) failed to get any kind of distribution in Irish cinemas but achieved an audience of 314,000 on its television screening – a 46 per cent audience share and the equivalent to 3.1 million viewers in terms of the British market. Even such an obscure and relatively unseen film like Owen McPolin's *Drinking Crude* (1997), which disappeared as a theatrical release, gained a respectable 170,000 viewers on television, a 38 per cent audience share (Barton 2004: 192). Television and the theatrical release were linked in the funding package established in 1993 and it is important to see the life span of the film extended to include all its dissemination options – rental and retail as well as television. The Irish film industry looks even healthier when these factors are also taken into consideration.

It could also be argued that a perspective fixated on the British or American theatrical market is blind to other trends and audience potential. One obvious problem is that concentration on the Anglophone market risks underestimating the European market. In an interesting editorial in the magazine *Film Ireland*, Tony Keily makes the point that Irish films very often do much better in France, Germany, Spain and especially Italy than they do in Anglophone

Britain, and this is as true for the low-budget independent films as it is for bigger-budgeted co-productions. Thus *The Magdalene Sisters* was a huge and controversial success in Italy (3 million Euros) as well as in Ireland and Paul Greengrass's *Bloody Sunday* (2001) took almost 1 million Euros in Italy, twice what it earned in the US. On the other hand, while Pat Murphy's feminist film *Nora* (2000) achieved only 1000 admissions in its home territory, it accumulated nine times that in Italy. Keily looks at a range of other examples and considers Irish film performance across other European markets and comes to the conclusion that European markets are more open to Irish (therefore art-house, subtitled fare) than Anglophone Ireland is to their films. The European countries are part of the 'home market' and perhaps this should be recognised more readily at an earlier stage of production and marketing planning, rather than focusing on the British or American market (Keily 2003: 5).

Finally, the experience of *The Wind that Shakes the Barley* highlights another factor that may well work in favour of small-scale indigenous film but which is currently lying below the radar of public awareness. The film's distributors, Pathé, went into partnership with the Irish company Digital Cinema Limited (DCL), to release the film digitally on eleven screens throughout the country (simultaneously with the release in 35mm format of forty-nine other prints). DCL and the Irish market are at the forefront of experiments in digital cinema and the ambition is to establish the country with the world's first fully digital cinema network. According to DCL, all the cinemas in this first tranche of digitalisation 'received, at no cost, all the necessary equipment to receive and play digital movies, as well as a comprehensive training and maintenance package'. This is a significant development and it opens up intriguing possibilities for lower-budget indigenous cinema. The real possibility exists that a much more flexible network of screens can be established and that a wider and more diverse range of films will go into theatrical distribution. As DCL argues:

> Digital cinema technology is delivering the inherent advantages of digital presentation systems, including: cost and labour reduction in making prints, cost reduction of film distribution, enhanced quality of film prints, increased security against movie piracy, and easier management. (DCL Press Release 2006)

This is, of course, the perspective of business and industry (DCL works with all the major Hollywood and European distribution companies) and we have been here before with video/DVD and multiplexes without any appreciable improvement in terms of the diversity of films that are shown. None the less, the development of a digital network in Ireland is potentially exciting for Irish cinema. The fact that the world's first digital network is being developed in Ireland merely confirms the country's position at the cusp of global capitalist modernity. The hope is that the existence of a clear strategy for developing and maintaining a national cinema will ensure that there remains a cultural dimension to the industrial development and that Higgins's original 'indigenous energy' will be stimulated and not stifled in the new digital 'commercial space' being created.

Works Cited

Barton, Ruth. 2004. *Irish National Cinema*. London: Routledge.

BSÉ/IFB. 1993. 'Review and Annual Report 1993. Galway.

DCL Press Release. 2006. 'Pathé Distribution Ltd and Digital Cinema Ltd Release "The Wind that Shakes the Barley" Digitally in Ireland', 23 June.

Duffy, Martin. 2003. 'The Business'. *Film Ireland*, 95, Nov/Dec. pp. 32–5.

Higgins, Michael D. 1995. Public interview. National Film Theatre: London, October.

Hill, John. 2006. *Cinema and Northern Ireland*. London: British Film Institute.

Keily, Tony. 2003. 'Editorial 90'. *Film Ireland*, 90, Jan/Feb. p. 5.

McLoone, Martin. 2000. *Irish Film: The Emergence of a Contemporary Cinema*. London: British Film Institute.

McLoone, Martin. 2006. 'National Cinema in Ireland'. In Valentina Vitali and Paul Willemen (eds), *Theorising National Cinema*. London: British Film Institute. pp. 88–99.

Pettitt, Lance. 2000. *Screening Ireland: Film and Television Representation*. Manchester: Manchester University Press.

Rockett, Kevin. 1996. *The Irish Filmography*. Dublin: Red Mountain Media.

Rockett, Kevin. 2003. *Ten Years After: The Irish Film Board 1993–2003*. Galway: BSÉ/IFB.

Rockett, Kevin, L. Gibbons and J. Hill. 1988. *Cinema and Ireland*. London: Routledge.

4. SCOTLAND

Jonathan Murray

'I'm going to be just like you.' These are the final words uttered by anti-hero Mark Renton (Ewan McGregor) in the final scene of *Trainspotting* (Danny Boyle, 1996) as he walks across a bridge in central London armed with nothing but a holdall full of stolen money and a newly unshakable sense of self-belief. His now-famous closing monologue delivered direct to camera, Renton's image blurs then dissolves as he marches ever closer to the lens, threatening to burst through the auditorium's fourth wall. At a textual level, both Mark's warning to the viewer and the manner of its visualisation are indicative of *Trainspotting*'s remarkable ability to satisfy, yet also subvert, the vicarious thrill-seeking that lured so many to its cinematic safari tour of post-industrial, drug-ravaged, late twentieth-century Scotland. Yet an extra-textual resonance also accrues to Renton's self-proclaimed transformation, implying as it does an elision of difference between viewed object and viewing subject.

Trainspotting was a remarkable critical and commercial success, the world's most profitable film of 1996 when profitability is calculated by setting original production costs – £1.7 million – against eventual global box-office receipts, in this instance some $72 million (Dyja 1997; Street 2000). Yet that film was by no means the only encouraging development experienced within Scottish film culture in 1995–6. This brief period witnessed the advent of National Lottery funds to subsidise UK feature film production and the unprecedented inward investment and international publicity generated by visiting Scottish-themed, Hollywood-financed productions *Rob Roy* (Michael Caton-Jones, 1995) and *Braveheart* (Mel Gibson, 1995). This concatenation led many contemporary

Scottish observers to believe that they were living through 'arguably the most dynamic period in one hundred years of Scottish film history' (Bruce 1996: 3). For Eddie Dick, then head of the Scottish Film Production Fund, at that time the country's most significant source of public funding for feature production, 1995 was the year that witnessed an epochal 'change of attitudes here' in Scotland (Hunter 1995: 12). On the one hand, local institutional and infra-structural resources were finally attaining something like the critical mass and quality necessary to attract projects associated with the international commer-cial mainstream to Scotland, so building the experienced (and solvent) talent pool necessary to underwrite and populate a low-budget domestic production culture. On the other, emergent local filmmaking talent was proving ambitious and creatively adroit enough to produce low-budget Scottish feature work capable of competing profitably in the global market place. The 'New Scottish Cinema' (Petrie 2000b) spearheaded by *Trainspotting* was, just like that film's central character, shaking off inherited shackles of deprivation (in this case industrial). Scotland was announcing its intent to become, as quickly as pos-sible, a peer of far better established Anglophone and European cinemas. Thus 1996 was the year in which an infant Scottish national cinema proclaimed to any established international peer that would listen that it was 'going to be just like you'.

In a survey of the decade that has passed since that extraordinary mid-1990s moment of confidence and felt possibility within Scottish film culture, two points demand to be made at the outset. The first is that the optimism of 1995–6 was in significant part borne out. From a near-standing start, over the last decade Scottish cinema *did* become more like the film cultures and industries of comparably small European and Anglophone national cinemas, in terms of the extent, stability and visibility of its feature film output. Year-by-year fluctuations acknowledged, levels of feature production, indigenous and visiting, over the period have proved unprecedented. The twenty-seven-strong contingent of Scottish features, shorts and documentaries at the 2004 Edinburgh International Film Festival represented easily the most substantial local presence in the Festival's history (Murray 2005a: 1). The infrastructure of Scottish cinema expanded, diversified and consolidated itself in the decade since 1996; the online edition of *Film Bang*, the Directory for the Scottish Industry since 1976 (www.filmbang.com), currently lists seventy-three independent production companies active in Scotland, a far greater number than was the case a decade ago. A respectable number of post-*Trainspotting* Scottish films and filmmakers have achieved significant international commercial success and/or critical notice. Amongst others, we might single out David Mackenzie – *The Last Great Wilderness* (2002), *Young Adam* (2003); Peter Mullan – *Orphans* (1999), *The Magdalene Sisters* (2001); and Lynne Ramsay – *Ratcatcher* (1999), *Morvern Callar* (2002). Moreover, in a development all too often ignored by academic commentary on Scottish cinema, native acting talent – including Brian Cox, Robert Carlyle, Alan Cumming, Douglas Henshall, Kelly Macdonald, Ewan McGregor, Peter Mullan, Dougray Scott, Tilda Swinton, to name but a few – established a never-before-experienced collective international visibility in the few years either side of the millennium (McKibbin 2000b).

It is therefore worth recalling from the vantage point of 2006 that as recently as 1993 the HMSO *Charter for the Arts in Scotland* could apprehend only 'a massive hole at the centre of the [local] industry where feature film production should be' (HMSO 1993: 29). Current base levels of indigenous production activity, available finance and career opportunities for domestically based talent, as well as Scottish cinema's all-round national and international visibility, would have seemed quite unimaginable just a decade ago. This fact in turn has consequences for the significance of moving image production as a constituent element of contemporary Scottish culture as a whole. Duncan Petrie, for instance, asserted in 2004 that indigenous film and television were now, alongside the Scottish novel, 'the primary media' through which 'the myths and realities, experiences and dreams of Scotland and its inhabitants have been reflected and asserted, imagined and re-imagined' (Petrie 2004: 1–2) for local and international audiences. Regardless of whether one believes this declaration to be right or wrong, prescient or premature, the most striking fact about it is that until a decade or so ago, it would have been quite simply impossible to make. The crushing material under-development that squashed nearly all Scottish filmmaking aspirations until the very last few years of the twentieth century would surely have precluded it.

Yet the second point that needs to be made about the story of Scottish cinema between the mid-1990s and mid-2000s is that the potted narrative of achievement and consolidation set out above is one that many (maybe even most) participants within Scotland's film production sector would either overlook or reject in 2006. At the time of writing, the best-informed, most responsive (and frequently scurrilous) commentary on Scottish cinema comes from an online blog called filmflam (http://mssmithfilmflam.blogspot.com/), written by one 'Leanne Smith' (this may or may not be a *nom de guerre*) who claims to be a media studies graduate-turned-lap dancer-turned-aspiring Scottish filmmaker. Her inaugural blog of 6 September 2005 is significant because it accurately indicates the tone and perspective that came to dominate internal debates about Scottish cinema in the mid-2000s: 'we need to admit we don't have a film industry in this country. Instead what we have is a kiddy-onny [that is, 'pretend'] Executive [that is, the devolved Scottish government] sponsored set-up' (Smith 2005).

Also writing in autumn 2005, writer/director May Miles Thomas – *One Life Stand* (2000), *Solid Air* (2003) – echoed and developed this pessimistic overview further. She argued that Scotland did not possess 'a truly national cinema' because its film culture lacked the significant degree of industrial and creative independence that would characterise such an entity: 'filmmakers here are increasingly under pressure to conform commercially – and culturally – to other's agendas. To ape London, which apes Hollywood, only on wee budgets' (Miles Thomas 2005). From this internal perspective, post-*Trainspotting* Scottish cinema's Rentonesque rush to be 'just like' other larger, longer-established and more internationally successful national cinemas proved ultimately to be a process of institutionally enforced capitulation, rather than of self-confident, enterprising local assertion and self-becoming.

Moreover, at the time of writing (autumn 2006) the most prominent issue related to Scottish cinema is the decision in January this year by the devolved Scottish government (or Executive, as the government prefers to call itself) to dissolve Scottish Screen. That organisation has since 1997 been the single non-departmental public body (NDPB) for film, television and new media in Scotland. The Executive wishes to establish from some point in 2008 a single publicly funded agency overseeing all aspects of cultural production and provision in Scotland (Murray forthcoming). Scottish Screen was created on the coat tails of the collective euphoria that took hold within Scottish film culture during the immediate post-*Trainspotting* period. Indeed, the creation of a single public body for film in Scotland with a higher, more coherent public profile and significantly more available operational capital than its predecessors was believed important because the goal of a self-sustaining national cinema and film production sector in Scotland seemed achievable for perhaps the first time in cinema history. What is really interesting about the move a decade on to dissolve Scottish Screen, therefore, is that it seems motivated not by the belief that such a national cinema did emerge in Scotland post-1997. Rather, the dissolution of Scotland's flagship public body for moving image and new media industries seems relatable instead to a fundamental, collective scepticism, evinced by the likes of Smith and Miles Thomas, about whether that emergence did, or ever can, take place in that country.

In that regard, what for many is being dissolved along with Scottish Screen is local faith in the aspiration towards a Scottish cinema. Even Scottish Screen's own current CEO (appointed in May 2005), Ken Hay, spent much of 2006 appearing to welcome the imminent dissolution of the institution he heads, and by extension, its decade-long prioritisation of the creation of a Scottish national cinema. Hay announced in a press interview that he had spent his first eleven months in post conducting

> a classic root and branch analysis . . . a re-organisation of Scottish Screen into something fit for purpose . . . if we just concentrate on trying to build a film industry without considering everything else that's going on, then we've got it all wrong. (Phelan 2006)

Formally announcing a new overall operational strategy for Scottish Screen, Hay subsequently stated that 'Scottish Screen's fresh approach to driving forward a successful screen industries sector in Scotland' entailed 'giving a higher level of priority to education, skills and audience development activities' (Scottish Screen 2006). Increasing funding for these areas and decreasing the amount of monies set aside annually for production activities, Hay argued that, 'the difference now is that we are taking seriously the whole of what the screen industry represents in Scotland and not just the production of films' (Miller 2006). By way of contrast, for a forty-five-strong contingent of filmmakers who all have at some point succeeded in producing a feature in Scotland, such developments are anything but welcome, taken to signify that 'Scottish Screen no longer recognises the importance of supporting Scottish film production companies' and 'implying a significant reduction in the number of feature films that will be made in Scotland' (Aitken et al. 2006). To paraphrase Colin Welland, Scotland spent the late 1990s announcing to others that its national cinema was 'coming' on to the international commercial scene in a substantive, sustainable fashion. By contrast, the country has spent much of the 2000s worrying that the intense sense of forward motion experienced in the years just before the millennium was nothing more than collective self-delusion.

The story of Scottish cinema in the decade between 1996 and 2006 is therefore one marked by a glaring paradox. Never in film history have so many commentators been so underwhelmed by so much significant local cinematic achievement. This begs the questions: How did Scottish cinema evolve post-*Trainspotting*? How and why has that process of evolution diverged from or failed to meet the expectations created by the *annus mirabilis* of 1995–6? Between 1980 and 1990, sixteen features and six short projects with significant or majority Scottish creative input, Scottish-specific narrative content and/or domestic funding were produced and subsequently distributed in British cinemas. Between 1990 and 1995, the equivalent figures were seven and nine. Finally, in the aftermath of *Trainspotting*, between 1995 and 2000 quantum acceleration took place, with figures of eighteen features and forty-five shorts for that half-decade alone. Moreover, the latter set of statistics does not include international film shoots locating to Scotland in the same period, a substantial list including *Braveheart*, *Breaking the Waves* (Lars von Trier, 1996) and *Mission Impossible* (Brian De Palma, 1996) (McBain 1990; Petrie 2000a, 2000b: 227–30). This unprecedented expansion – and more fundamentally, normalisation – of feature production in Scotland can be traced to the wholesale creation of an entirely new, or in parts reconstituted, local institutional infrastructure. On the one hand, a set of initiatives and new organisations can be identified that aimed better to attract mobile – especially American – film productions and capital to Scotland. Representative and influential in this regard were bodies or policy initiatives such as Scottish Screen Locations

(1990), the Glasgow Film Fund (1993), Scottish Screen (1997) and Glasgow District Council's Film Charter (1998). In addition, and of at least equal importance, were a range of interventions geared more towards the stimulation and support of indigenous production activity through financial subsidy, specialist training or a combination of the two. Mirroring new inward investment schemes' particularly acute consciousness of the American industry's felt influence and demands, new institutions aiming to nurture domestic activity were often modelled explicitly on pre-existing North American counterparts. Examples of this phenomenon included the screenwriting workshop Movie Makars (1992), the Glasgow Film Fund, the ambitious, pan-European screenwriting and directing laboratory Moonstone International (1997) and Glasgow's Film Charter.

A brief consideration of one of the institutional examples listed above, Moonstone International, helps to illustrate the nature of the local ambition that created a catalyst for the significant expansion and reorganisation of Scotland's film infrastructure during the 1990s. Moonstone was the brainchild of the late John McGrath, a pioneering theatre, film and television writer, producer and director (Taxidou 1996). For McGrath, the economics of scale inherent in producing films within small nations – those with populations (and therefore potential domestic audiences) of under 6 million – necessarily entailed that to achieve any kind of industrial sustainability small national film cultures had systematically to inculcate commercially aware, internationally orientated filmmaking practices in their creative talent. The problem in Scotland was that this had never happened. Moonstone was based on the example of Robert Redford's Sundance Institute, and conceived as an antidote to the fact that, as McGrath saw matters, 'a lot of people in Scotland and Ireland are cut off from mainstream filmmaking . . . there is an international dimension to filmmaking that can be studied' (Hunter 1997: 17). For McGrath, as for most key institutional personnel in mid- and late-1990s Scotland, this international dimension was associated with the American film industry.

Equally significant in the mid- to late 1990s was the advent of National Lottery funding for feature film production in 1995. The Scottish Lottery Fund, administered initially by the Scottish Arts Council (and subsequently by Scottish Screen), quickly became the most significant single financial patron of late 1990s Scottish cinema. By 1998, the Fund had already made production grants worth a total of £13.5 million, with a further £12.75 million forecast between that year and early 2003 (Anon 1998: 3). Ultimately, Lottery funds contributed just over £9.43 million of public monies to fifteen wholly or part Scottish-funded features actually produced between 1995 and mid-2000 (figures derived from Petrie 2000a: 177, 227–8).

Yet despite the unprecedented largesse associated with it, the Lottery's status within late 1990s Scottish film culture proved controversial. One Scottish film to benefit from a £1 million Lottery award was Bill Forsyth's *Gregory's 2 Girls* (1999), a belated sequel to *Gregory's Girl* (1980). Yet in 1997, Forsyth resigned from his position as a member of the Lottery Fund advisory panel after attending only one meeting, accusing fellow members of endemic cronyism in their distribution of funding awards. Forsyth's controversial, very public allegations led to the creation of a Scottish filmmakers' pressure group, Scottish Stand, in June 1997. Leaving aside allegations of nepotism, Scottish Stand complained that the Lottery Fund priced most Scottish filmmakers out of the market, aiming to use its funds to attract mid-budget mobile productions to Scotland at the expense of support for low-budget indigenous productions and producers. Producer Jim Hickey, for example, complained that the Lottery Panel's early predilection for £1 million grants showed that the body 'probably would not use that money to give £150 000 each to six new filmmakers and let them make a low budget feature' (Hunter 1997: 17). *Rob Roy* producer, Peter Broughan, complained about what he saw as a situation in which far larger amounts of public finance for feature production were available in Scotland, such new 'Scottish money being used [however] by people who don't have a commitment to Scotland. All you end up with is a carpetbagging process' (Russell 1997: 13).

It was certainly the case that late 1990s Lottery awards seemed geared deliberately towards moving Scotland away for good from the £2 million budget level that had to that point represented the financial ceiling within a low-budget film industry and culture. Lottery awards of up to as much as £1 million a time quickly inflated typical late 1990s Scottish feature budget levels to two or three times that of those that had financed *Shallow Grave* (Danny Boyle, 1995; £0.9 million) and *Trainspotting* (£1.7 million). And these figures may be usefully compared with the following: *Regeneration* (Gillies Mackinnon, 1997; £3.9 million), *The Winter Guest* (Alan Rickman, 1997; £5 million) and *Complicity* (Gavin Millar, 2000; £4.6 million) (Dyja 1997: 22, 26; Dyja 2001: 24). Equally symptomatic of the Lottery-led push to turn Scotland into a minor player in the international Anglophone mainstream was the commercial and cultural conservatism that led to a slew of literary adaptations and/or projects written by literary celebrities, with adaptations thus dominating in numerical terms the late 1990s Scottish film landscape. This trend was readable as an attempt to create a Scottish cinema that would be 'prestigious' in terms of its dependent link to 'legitimate' literary traditions, and it signalled a move towards the highest possible production values that could realistically be pursued in Scotland at this time. Eight of the first fifteen Lottery-supported Scottish features produced up to the year 2000 were adaptations of pre-existing literary works: *The Slab Boys* (a theatrical trilogy by Byrne himself), *Regeneration* (a novel by Pat Barker), *The Winter Guest* (a play by Sharman Macdonald), *The Life of Stuff* (Simon Donald, 1997; a play by Simon Donald), *The Acid House* (Paul McGuigan, 1998; based on short stories by Irvine Welsh), *My Life*

So Far (Hugh Hudson, 1999; an autobiography by Denis Forman), *Complicity* (a novel by Iain Banks), *House of Mirth* (Terence Davies, 2000; a novel by Edith Wharton). Moreover, five of the fifteen works referred to above were believed to be 'bankable' to some degree because they were scripted by writers whose professional reputations were primarily or solely as novelists and/or play-wrights, not screenwriters: *The Winter Guest* (Sharman Macdonald and Alan Rickman), *The Life of Stuff* (Simon Donald), *Stella Does Tricks* (Coky Giedroyc, 1998; A. L. Kennedy), *The Acid House* (Irvine Welsh), *My Life So Far* (Simon Donald). One statistic that would seem to bear out contemporary anxieties about the exceptionally ambitious, internationally focused late 1990s institutional programme for Scottish cinema is that only 41 per cent of the £9.43 million of Lottery funds allocated to successfully produced features between 1995 and 2000 supported projects developed from original screen-plays produced by dedicated screenwriters (figures derived from Petrie 2000a: 177, 227–8).

By around the turn of the millennium it had become abundantly clear that, despite the exceptional international successes of *Shallow Grave* and *Trainspotting*, the ambitious attempt to move Scotland from a traditional low-budget, public subsidy, art cinema production model to a mid-level budget, public/private partnership, quality mainstream successor model was simply unsustainable. With a few exceptions, namely the Scottish work of Ken Loach – *Carla's Song* (1997), *My Name is Joe* (1998) – and the impressive 1999 debut features from Peter Mullan and Lynne Ramsay – *Orphans* and *Ratcatcher* – post-*Trainspotting* Scottish cinema of the late 1990s was commercially and critically unloved. The Scottish Lottery's Fund's ambitious largesse between 1995 and 2000 came to be seen as flawed by unrealistic levels of expectation, a view further entrenched by the fate of the other major funder of Scottish feature work in the five- or six-year period after *Trainspotting*, the London-based broadcaster Channel 4.

The channel's funding in full of *Trainspotting*'s £1.7 million budget in 1995/6 was at that time the broadcaster's single largest investment in a feature project. Buoyed by that film's remarkable success at the international box-office, Channel 4 became a major patron of late 1990s Scottish cinema. Nine of the eighteen Scottish-produced and themed features released in British cinemas between 1995 and 2000 were part-financed by the broadcaster: *Shallow Grave, Trainspotting, Carla's Song, The Slab Boys, My Name is Joe, The Winter Guest, The Acid House, The Debt Collector* (Anthony Neilson, 1999), *Orphans* and *Gregory's 2 Girls*. Yet by July 2002, Channel 4 announced the closure of the expanded, semi-autonomous FilmFour mini-studio it had established in 1998 in order to integrate and expand to an international scale the broadcaster's film production, distribution and sales activities, an attempt in effect to establish itself as a major player in the international commercial mainstream. Between

2000 and 2001 alone FilmFour incurred unsustainably high operational losses of £8.4 million, primarily because of the commercial failure of £10 million plus commercial feature projects such as *Charlotte Gray* (Gillian Armstrong, 2001) (Pulver 2002). Not without significance in this regard is the fact that the latter movie was itself the brainchild of a Scottish producer, Douglas Rae. Rae's positive mid-1990s experience with Oscar-nominated Scottish heritage movie *Mrs Brown* (John Madden, 1997), a film that explores the relationship between Queen Victoria and her Highland ghillie John Brown, encouraged him to develop costly, commercially ambitious projects such as *Charlotte Gray* working from a UK base.

In many ways, it must be said that for Scottish film culture the early 2000s lacked the high level of public excitement and expectation that had characterised the late 1990s. Yet one positive reason for this fact is that many active within Scottish cinema after the millennium seemed anxious to learn from recent disappointments and to adopt different industrial strategies from those found wanting between 1996 and 2000. Although that latter period had been dominated by overtures towards the international Anglophone commercial mainstream and aspirations towards a Scottish cinema structured along these lines, by 2003, one observer at that year's Edinburgh International Film Festival argued, the Scottish feature work being premiered – *Young Adam*, *16 Years of Alcohol* (Richard Jobson, 2003) and *Wilbur Wants to Kill Himself* (Lone Scherfig, 2002) – was indicative of a national cinema that was 'culturally distinct, yet also chime[s] with the themes and aspirations of a new generation of European film-makers' (Didcock 2003: 11). If the late 1990s infatuation with America had raised expectations without meeting them, the early 2000s witnessed a collective turn to Europe that was aesthetic, thematic and industrial in nature. The Scottish films screened at Edinburgh 2003 were all impeccably 'European art-house' fare. Representative of how Scottish cinema was evolving in the years immediately post-2000, these films manifested a shared desire to explore private experience and complex, extreme psychological states rather than exploit popular genres and conventional narrative forms. *Young Adam*, adapted from Alexander Trocchi's eponymous 1954 novel, centres on the amoral, quasi-existential alienation of a young male drifter whose one remaining, tenuous connection to the social milieu he inhabits depends on random, emotionless sex; *16 Years of Alcohol* explores a young man's attempts to redeem the damage inflicted on his psyche by immersion in an urban upbringing soaked in machismo, gang violence and hard liquor; *Wilbur* . . . is a fey comedy built around a young man who cannot successfully execute his constant suicidal urges.

This renewed Scottish interest in themes and subjects associated with European film traditions also had a significant industrial component. Consider, for instance, the list of Scottish features premiered at the Edinburgh

International Film Festival in 2003 and 2004: *Young Adam, 16 Years . . ., Solid Air, Wilbur . . ., Afterlife* (Alison Peebles, 2003), *Ae Fond Kiss* (Loach, 2004), *Blinded* (Eleanor Yule, 2004), *Dear Frankie* (Shona Auerbach, 2003), *The Purifiers* (Jobson, 2004), *Yasmin* (Kenny Glenaan, 2004). Significantly, five of these ten films are Scottish-European co-productions; producers and funders from eight other European national cinemas had a hand in facilitating this early 2000s 'national' body of Scottish feature work. Most productive of all the post-2000 European connections made by key personnel within Scottish film culture have been those forged with Scandinavian film cultures and industries. Initial, isolated links had already been made with Nordic national cinemas through the general upturn in both visiting and indigenous production in late 1990s Scotland, an upturn that encompassed Lars von Trier's *Breaking the Waves* and a rather less well-known work, *Aberdeen* (Hans Petter Moland, 2000). However, this specific transnational connection broadened and became more formalised in the early twenty-first century primarily because of a direct working relationship established between von Trier's Zentropa and Glasgow-based independent producer Sigma Films (producer Gillian Berrie and writer/director David Mackenzie) in late 2000. A year or so later, four of the five feature projects identified by Scottish Screen as recipients of major Lottery production funding awards in 2002 involved Scandinavian finance and/or creative personnel: *Wilbur . . ., Skaggerak* (Søren Kragh-Jacobsen, 2003), *One Last Chance* (Stewart Svaasand, 2004) and an as yet unmade project, *Little Sisters* (see Garside 2001). Post-Dogme, the attraction of Scottish–Scandinavian partnerships (with a particular emphasis on Denmark) perhaps lay in the perception of late 1990s Danish film as a small national cinema that had achieved sustainable international commercial and critical success through a process of cultivated local differentiation from the international Anglophone mainstream. This stood in stark contrast to the short-term benefits associated with Scotland's contemporaneous bid to become a junior partner within the latter. Certainly, this is the kind of analysis that has been offered up by Sigma Films, the Scottish pioneers of the Scandinavian link. Gillian Berrie, for instance, has argued of her company's signature strategy of producing low-budget digital (*Last Great Wilderness*) or mid-budget quality (*Young Adam*) features targeted at an international art-house market that 'all I'm doing is what they did in Denmark' (Phelan 2004: 8) over the last decade or so.

Staying with the specific link forged between Scottish and Danish cinemas during the early 2000s, I write the conclusion to this essay some twenty-four hours after seeing the latest in the post-2000 tradition of Scottish–European co-production, *Red Road* (Andrea Arnold, 2006), on the first day of that film's British theatrical release. This film tells the story of Jackie, a thirty-something woman still numbed by a bereavement experienced a decade before *Red Road*'s narrative begins. Jackie works as a CCTV operator, monitoring some of the most deprived and dangerous suburban slums of present-day Glasgow (including the notorious Red Road high-rise flats from which the film takes its name). One day at work she happens to catch sight of Clyde, a man recently released from prison and a painful figure from her past. Although the precise nature of the connection between the two is not specified immediately, the greater part of *Red Road*'s narrative is taken up with Jackie's obsessive, unexplained stalking of Clyde by CCTV and in person. Ultimately the two reach an understanding that just may allow each to move beyond traumas that have hitherto haunted the past and dominated the present.

If *Trainspotting* was indicative of the industrial, aesthetic and representational strategies that achieved preferred status within late 1990s Scotland, something very similar may hold for *Red Road* and the late 2000s. To be precise: *Red Road* is a pronouncedly 'European' film in a number of regards. Read as a paradigmatic work of and for its period, Arnold's debut feature seems to indicate that the long-term legacy of the US-inspired upturn of the late 1990s was the creation of a set of basic conditions for existence within which a small European film culture and industry could put down enduring roots within Scotland. Of course, some critics have long proclaimed the general truism that 'in the best of Scottish cinema, the European influence is never far away' (McKibbin 2000a: 35) or have argued that, post-1990, 'the kind of production that has come to epitomise Scottish film-making . . . bears a strong affinity with the tradition of European Art Cinema' (Petrie 2004: 202). What is striking from the vantage point of late 2006, however, is the extent to which such views can now – perhaps for the first time – be accepted as objective observation rather than as a prescriptive and only partially applicable aspiration.

Red Road's 'European-ness', for instance, is multifaceted. A remarkably wordless film, it attempts to find a visual language capable of representing the most extreme aspects of grief, not to mention the (self-)destructive actions the experience of such pain propels individuals towards. Both in its decision to subjugate narrative coherence and variety of incident to a psychological exploration of female interiority and sexuality and in its determination to inhabit rather than explain an especially intolerable individual experience of loss, *Red Road* accords generally with the aims of the European art cinema tradition as conventionally defined. The film also recalls specifically certain particularly celebrated European art films of the last decade or so, including *Morvern Callar, Under the Skin* (Carine Adler, 1996) and *Three Colours: Blue* (Krzysztof Kieślowski, 1993). *Red Road* is also a pronouncedly European film in industrial terms. Its comparatively modest production costs of £1.2 million (even before accounting for long-term price inflation, substantially lower than *Trainspotting*'s £1.7 million) are indicative of the extent to which the inflated hopes (and budgets) of the late 1990s and very early 2000s have subsided. What has replaced them is a contemporary local *mentalité* more concerned with full exploration and exploitation of the low-budget, publicly subsidised financing model that traditionally has dominated in Scotland and is prevalent all over Continental Europe. This is in sharp contrast with the brief, ultimately abortive 1990s and 2000s attempt to transcend the perceived shackles of that model in order to join the international Anglophone commercial mainstream. Moreover, it should also be noted that *Red Road* owes its existence to the kind of Scottish-Scandinavian working relationships which proved a novel and increasingly prominent aspect of film culture in Scotland during the early 2000s. Specifically, this film is part of a projected trilogy of features grouped under the 'Advance Party' banner created by Scotland's Sigma Films, Denmark's Zentropa and the Danish filmmakers Lone Scherfig and Anders Thomas Jensen in late 2002/early 2003 (Glasgow Film Office 2006). Scherfig and Jensen devised a set of characters intended to form the basis for three low-budget digital features each set and shot in Glasgow. *Red Road* is the first of the trilogy to reach cinemas, with Scottish director Morag McKinnon and her Danish counterpart Mikkel Nørgaard directing the other two works in the triptych.

In the official press notes for *Red Road* Scherfig and Jensen explain 'The Rules' governing Advance Party thus: 'the interpersonal relationships of the characters differ from film to film and they may be weighted differently as major or minor characters. The development of the characters in each story or genre does not affect the other scripts' (Verve Pictures 2006). In addition, all three features must be made within a six-week location shoot in Glasgow and using digital technologies. The attraction of the Advance Party initiative, therefore, is that it combines industrial entrepreneurialism with creative challenge. If not quite three-for-the-price-of-one, shared crewing, casting and setting over a carefully delimited six-week shoot spread the costs normally associated with a one-off feature across three projects, keeping budgets down. Moreover, the novelty of the initiative has generated a welcome degree of industry publicity and audience awareness. Having seen one film in the trilogy, cinema-goers are perhaps more likely to watch the later two, maybe because *Red Road* has prompted an interest in and attachment to the characters of these as yet unseen works, or because they hope to see which of the minor characters in this work assume central status in its successors.

On the other hand, Advance Party's self-imposed limitation of working with a single set of prefabricated characters and settings perhaps compels the filmmakers involved to approach considerations of character development and storytelling in an unusually self-conscious, innovatory fashion. This is inevitably a matter of speculation, but one explanation for the strongly elliptical character of *Red Road*'s approach to narrative and character explication might involve the need to circumnavigate specific interpersonal relationships and actions played out within the common ensemble in the scripts for the other two Advance Party features. Or, it may instead be conceived as a way of allowing maximum room for manœuvre to McKinnon and Nørgaard in their respective engagements with the common set of protagonists. Alternatively, the conceit of spreading a common set of characters across three features while privileging different protagonists and experiences in each has the inevitable consequence of distancing directors from the idea(l) of neatly crafted, teleological stories harbouring a stable, socially conventional hierarchy of character identities and viewpoints through which audiences are asked to understand the world. As Hannah McGill notes, Advance Party's signature 'notion of a network of tangential individuals who are ceaselessly affected by the actions of its central couple' might be understood as a creatively and socially democratic act, suggesting as it does that 'every individual, and thus every action, has a history' (McGill 2006: 28) as potentially significant and worthy of exploration and attention as any other.

Red Road is an appropriate film to conclude with, therefore, because it seems indicative of certain key ways in which Scottish cinema has evolved over the last decade or so. Andrea Arnold's film also highlights some of the dominant creative and industrial strategies employed by local filmmakers in response to that process of film industrial and cultural evolution. However, *Red Road* also possesses a third order of significance with regard to the overview of recent Scottish cinema offered here. On the one hand, the film instantiates some of the solutions posed by Scottish filmmakers to the obstacles and opportunities they have faced in the last decade or so. Yet on the other, it highlights, indeed helps simultaneously to create, a set of challenges facing contemporary Scottish film criticism. Those challenges relate to what seems, to the present writer at least, to be the increasing difficulty of analysing contemporary Scottish cinema within established, comfortingly familiar frameworks of nation and national identity involving predominantly the classification of individual films into sets of progressive or regressive, complex or reductive allegories of nation.

In an essay published in 2001 I suggested that 'the task of Scottish film criticism . . . necessitates giving voice to a plurality of social identities and voices emphatically not reducible to, or subsumable by, the national dimension of the society they inhabit' (Murray 2001: 86). Yet my work since then has tended to concentrate on discussion of Scottish films, dating from 1990 up to around the start of the twenty-first century, that can be framed as national allegories (Murray 2002; 2004; 2005b). In 2006, however, I would want to suggest that the national critical model may this time really have had its day. This is not because that model seems suddenly inappropriate for consideration of much Scottish cinema made during the twentieth century; rather, it seems less and less applicable to what is being produced in Scotland during the twenty-first. Yet this fact is one that film criticism has difficulty accepting, as a brief consideration of initial responses to *Red Road* shows. Philip French, for instance, starts a highly complimentary review of the film by emphasising first of all the work's

'Scottishness'. For him *Red Road* is to be understood as the latest entry in the 'realistic . . . at times miserabilist and poetic' tradition that is one of the 'two main streams' in the 'recognisable Scottish national cinema' that has emerged 'over the past 30 years or so' (French 2006). Similarly, Hannah McGill argues that *Red Road* 'fits (un)comfortably into an oft-maligned tradition of slum-bound Scottish miserablism that stretches from Bill Douglas to Lynne Ramsay, David Mackenzie and Peter Mullan' (McGill 2006: 28). Yet the point is that such discomfort is felt (or at least should be felt) solely on the part of the critic, in any attempt to prioritise and privilege an engagement with this film which makes it a work primarily about the articulation, conscious or otherwise, of 'Scotland' and 'Scottishness'. Symptomatic of much recent Scottish feature work, *Red Road* is an exceptionally private, localised film, focusing on one character's intense grief and alienation from the wider socio-cultural milieus she inhabits. What is more, it does not offer a totalising representation of those milieus themselves. If anything, the film seems representative of early twenty-first century Scottish feature work in that it deliberately shies away from the sort of grand, totalising statement about present-day urban Scotland that makes a representative late 1990s film like *Orphans* such a provocative and important work. Viewed in this regard, Jackie's position in the CCTV control room, able apparently to survey, interpret and assess the significance of the actions of everyone and everything at once, recalls nothing so much as the god-like position voluntarily claimed by many Scottish filmmakers in the late 1990s and retained by most critics of Scottish film since. Both constituencies have claimed routinely to portray and understand through their work the 'whole' that they study, whether that of Scottish cinema specifically or Scottish culture and identity more generally. Yet maybe, as in Jackie's case, attempting to be in touch with the story of everything precludes a productive engagement with and understanding of the complex, local detail of anything.

The most celebrated critical utterance about twenty-first century Scottish cinema was Duncan Petrie's (representatively totalising) classification of that emergent film industry and culture as 'a devolved entity' (Petrie 2000a: 186). Yet, in keeping with the sense of collective disappointment that seems to have enveloped the Scottish film community ten years on from *Trainspotting*, Petrie has himself recently revisited this statement in an interview, noting that 'I was very positive, upbeat and optimistic . . . I think that would be slightly tempered now' (King 2005: 164). This brings us back to what was earlier identified as one of the central features of Scottish cinema between the mid-1990s and the mid-2000s: namely, the paradoxical lack of fit between the unprecedented level of local achievement in film cultural and industrial terms over the period and the feeling, on the part of the very people responsible for that achievement, that, ultimately, it was less significant than was hoped and expected in the first few years after 1995/6. I would like to suggest that one way of working through that sense of disappointment, rather than simply acknowledging and/or acquiescing in it, might involve revisiting the question of what exactly a 'devolved' Scottish cinema is devolved from in the first instance. In 2005, for instance, Petrie extended his reconsideration of the 'devolved' tag that he first coined in 2000: 'I now ha[ve] a much clearer sense of what I mean when I say Scottish cinema is devolved: it has its own identity, its own impetus but it is still largely dependent on UK structures' (King 2005: 168). Taking a different tack, I have argued elsewhere that one way in which mid-2000s Scottish cinema might now be understood as devolved relates to the impact of a political debate about cultural provision and funding in Scotland initiated by the current Scottish Executive from the very start of its second term of office in 2003. The point is that this evolving debate seems genuinely and increasingly distinctive from UK-wide equivalents taking place at Westminster in ways that did not seem quite so apparent in the first years after 1999 (Murray forthcoming).

However, there is another potential reconceptualisation of contemporary Scottish cinema's devolved character worth considering here, one suggested by *Red Road* and a host of other post-2000 Scottish films. At the end of the twentieth century the notion of 'devolution' applied to Scottish cinema implied a process of distantiation from specific models of national identity and national cinema: unitary British ones. When Petrie revisited the devolved tag in 2005, his point was not to argue that Scottish cinema was not devolving itself away from these things. Rather, he believed that Scotland had not devolved quite as far away from them in both film industrial and cultural terms as seemed possible or even likely at the end of the 1990s. Yet perhaps over the early years of the 2000s the concept of 'devolution' has come to mean something different. It might now be more accurate to say that, both in terms of international working and co-production arrangements and the representational content of much contemporary local feature work, what Scottish cinema is devolving itself away from is the notion that it must automatically be framed and best understood within any framework of national specificity at all. Watching Mark Renton back in 1996, an essay about Scotland conceived for a volume such as this could only have identified a hypothetical national cinema, one that may or may not have been about to emerge. It is a mark of the collective achievement made in the decade since then that it is possible in 2006 to write something about a national cinema that actually did evolve. By 2016, however, we may well have been forced to follow *Trainspotting*'s hero. Perhaps it is time that Scottish film criticism caught up with where Scottish filmmaking seems already to have gone, crossing the border once and for all, leaving behind the traditional compulsion to ponder obsessively and near-exclusively the state, whether psychological or territorial, of 'Scotland'.

WORKS CITED

Aitken, Catherine et al. 2006. 'Don't Let our Film Industry Go Down the Pan'. *The Herald*, 21 June. p. 14.

Anon. 1998. 'SAC May Spread Cash more Thinly'. *Screen Finance*, 19 February. pp. 1–2.

Bruce, David. 1996. *Scotland the Movie*. Edinburgh: Polygon.

Didcock, Barry. 2003. 'Flowering of Scotland'. *Sunday Herald*, 17 August. p. 11.

Dyja, Eddie (ed.). 1997. *BFI Film and Television Handbook 1998*. London: British Film Institute.

Dyja, Eddie (ed.). 2001. *BFI Film and Television Handbook 2002*. London: British Film Institute.

Film Bang. http://www.filmbang.com.

French, Philip. 2006. 'Red Road'. *Observer*, 29 October. http://film.guardian.co.uk/News_Story/Critic_Review/Observer_Film_of_the_week/0,,1934166,00.html.

Garside, Juliette. 2001. 'Viking Raid on Lottery Film Cash'. *Sunday Herald*, 30 December. p. 5.

Glasgow Film Office. 2006. 'The Advance Party: a Timeline'. http://www.glasgowfilm.org.uk/redroad/advance_party.html.

HMSO. 1993. *Charter for the Arts in Scotland*. Edinburgh: HMSO.

Hunter, Allan. 1995. 'Plaid Influence'. *Screen International*, 11 August. pp. 12–13.

Hunter, Allan. 1997. 'Regeneration'. *Screen International*, 8 August. pp. 17–18.

King, Noel. 2005. 'Not a Million Miles Away'. *Metro* [Aus], Vol. 146, No. 7. pp. 164–9.

McBain, Janet. 1990. 'Scotland in Feature Film: a Filmography'. In Eddie Dick (ed.), *From Limelight to Satellite: A Scottish Film Book*. London/Glasgow: British Film Institute/Scottish Film Council. pp. 233–55.

McGill, Hannah. 2006. 'Mean Streets'. *Sight & Sound*, Vol. 16, No. 11. pp. 26–8.

McKibbin, Tony. 2000a. 'Retouching the Real: Lynne Ramsay's *Ratcatcher*'. *Cencrastus*, No. 65. pp. 35–40.

McKibbin, Tony. 2000b. 'Losing the Close Up: The Scottish Actor in the '90s and beyond'. *Cencrastus*, No. 66. pp. 21–6.

Miles Thomas, May. 2005. 'Cinema Purgatorio'. *Allmedia Scotland*, 24 October. http://www.allmediascotland.com/ams/displayCOMMENTSreply.asp?ID=48.

Miller, Phil. 2006. 'Final Cut for Scottish-funded Films'. *The Herald*, 27 April.

Murray, Jonathan. 2001. 'Contemporary Scottish Film'. *Irish Review*, No. 28. pp. 75–88.

Murray, Jonathan. 2002. 'Keep your Head Down and Save your Breath: "Authentic" Scotlands and British Cinema in *The Brave Don't Cry*'. *Drouth*, No. 6. pp. 7–17.

Murray, Jonathan. 2004. 'Convents or Cowboys?'. In John Hill and Kevin Rockett (eds), *Studies in Irish Film I: National Cinemas and Beyond*. Dublin: Four Courts. pp. 149–60.

Murray, Jonathan. 2005a. *That Thinking Feeling: A Research Guide to Scottish Cinema 1938–2004*. Edinburgh/Glasgow: Edinburgh College of Art/Scottish Screen.

Murray, Jonathan. 2005b. 'Kids in America, Fields of Dreams: Narratives of Transatlantic Influence in 1990s Scottish Cinema'. *Screen*, Vol. 46, No. 2. pp. 217–26.

Murray, Jonathan. Forthcoming. 'Hooray for Holyrood? Devolution and Scottish Film Culture'. In Martin McLoone and Robert Porter (eds), *Off-screen Spaces: Regionalism and Globalised Cultures*. Exeter: University of Exeter Press.

Petrie, Duncan. 2000a. *Screening Scotland*. London: British Film Institute.

Petrie, Duncan. 2000b. 'The New Scottish Cinema'. In Mette Hjort and Scott MacKenzie (eds), *Cinema and Nation*. London: Routledge. pp. 153–69.

Petrie, Duncan. 2004. *Contemporary Scottish Fictions: Film, Television and the Novel*. Edinburgh: Edinburgh University Press.

Phelan, Stephen. 2004. 'Girl on Film'. *Sunday Herald*, 1 February. p. 8.

Phelan, Stephen. 2006. 'Critics Love Them, They Win Awards . . . but can this man help?' *Sunday Herald*, 2 April. http://www.findarticles.com/p/articles/mi_qn4156/is_20060402/ai_n16197371.

Pulver, Andrew. 2002. 'End of an Era'. *Guardian*, 12 July, G2 section. pp. 2–4.

Russell, William. 1997. 'Big Fight over Reel Funding Issue'. *The Herald*, 21 July. p. 13.

Scottish Screen. 2006. 'Statement by Ken Hay'. *eroughcuts*, 50, 28 April (industry newsletter distributed via email).

Smith, Leanne. 2005. filmflam. http://mssmithfilmflam.blogspot.com/.

Street, Sarah. 2000. 'Trainspotting'. In Jill Forbes and Sarah Street (eds), *European Cinema: An Introduction*. Basingstoke: Palgrave. pp. 183–92.

Taxidou, Olga. 1996. 'John McGrath: from Cheviots to Silver Darlings'. In Randall Stevenson and Gavin Wallace (eds), *Scottish Theatre since the '70s*. Edinburgh: Edinburgh University Press. pp. 149–63.

Verve Pictures. 2006. *Red Road* Official Press Notes. http://www.vervepictures.co.uk/redroad.shtml.

5. BULGARIA

Dina Iordanova

The choice of Bulgaria to illustrate the processes taking place in the cinemas of new Europe's smaller countries is not obvious at first blush. All former socialist countries suffered a drop in film production in the early 1990s, but after the initial disarray previous output levels were restored in some places and the production cycle stabilised, reinforced by the introduction of new legislation and well-regulated funding mechanisms. Bulgaria, however, is nowhere near recovering and the crisis persists.

The overall political atmosphere in Bulgaria since 1989 has been one of general political instability and persistent economic crisis. Governments have kept changing and most of them have stood accused of corruption at some point. Most importantly, whereas many other Eastern bloc countries joined the European Union in 2004, Bulgaria's entry has been postponed, as the country is still deemed 'unfit' for Europe.

While these processes represent the worst aspects of volatility, bad management and misguided privatisation, they are widespread across the former Eastern bloc and the example of Bulgarian cinema can also stand in for the situation in other small and persistently failing film industries in countries that continue to suffer the repercussions of isolation and timid provincialism. These industries are rarely written about[1] and part of the interest in considering Bulgaria is the way in which this will extricate the specifics of a national cinema that is not only small but also provincial.

BECOMING 'EUROPEAN' AFTER 1989: PARALLEL INDUSTRIES

Just two decades ago culture and media in the countries of the Eastern bloc were thought to be 'immune' to international commercialisation trends (Mattelart and Mattelart 1984). Today, however, the picture has changed dramatically. The film industries in the countries of the former Soviet bloc rapidly became 'European'; that is, they came to resemble the film industries of small West European countries, replicating all their problems and shortcomings. The current position of Eastern Europe's film industries within the New International Division of Cultural Labour (Miller et al. 2001) is characterised by free movement of screen capital to cheap production locations and containment of labour mobility, brokered on the exploitation of skills and facilities developed under state socialism.

Filmmaking in state-socialist Eastern Europe (1948–89) represented probably the best case of a tightly vertically integrated film industry. Film production and distribution here worked within a specific framework of cultural administration. Each country had a government body in charge of filmmaking; film financing was centralised and generous, and came exclusively from the state; the state-owned studios and other production facilities employed permanent teams of salaried workers. Once completed, films were distributed nationwide by the state-run distribution organisation, first shown within the system of state-owned theatres and eventually screened on national television. The capital-intensive nature of film production requires that 'any film industry must either address an international market or a very large domestic one in order to amortise production cost' (Willemen 2006: 35). Hence, a system of exchange of feature films between the Eastern bloc countries was in place, and films made in the countries of the region were getting guaranteed international exposure. The break-up of the bloc also meant the collapse of a consolidated distribution market that was never replaced by a similarly sized market in any of the new configurations.[2] Profit was not a goal; it was enough for the films to return the investment, and most of them did as they were made on relatively small budgets and seen by large audiences domestically. Driven by an underlying intent to rationalise, streamline and facilitate the production-distribution-exhibition cycle, this model successfully maintained consistently high production outputs, comparable to (and sometimes exceeding) the cinematic outputs of similarly sized countries in Western Europe.

After 1989 cinema was no longer 'the most important art' and the new governments were neither willing nor able to continue underwriting filmmaking in full. The state's involvement in running the cultural industries came to a halt; new legislation was introduced to regulate 'hands off' and *'laissez-faire'*-type approaches to culture. The film industries underwent volatile structural changes throughout the region and were subjected to often contradictory undertakings in administration and finance. At first there was crisis, which found expression in crumbling production routines, an abrupt decrease in state funding, a sharp increase in unemployment among skilled personnel, and a considerable decline in documentary and animation output. There was also a concurrent crisis in distribution and exhibition. Earlier concerns over freedom of expression rapidly vanished, and worries over the constraints of a market economy emerged. Financing for film production changed profoundly, moving from the unit-based studio system to producer-driven piece-meal projects. The scarce state subsidies, competitive in some countries or automatic in others, turned into a hotly contested territory. The involvement of national television networks in film production and exhibition became of vital importance, as did funding linked to international co-productions and the expanding sector of private financing. Most studios were partially or fully privatised and thus engaged in competition, for example, to attract foreign film crews to shoot on location. A range of new small production companies proliferated, competing for advertising business from the West or offering services to runaway productions.

Filmmakers from each one of the countries in the region turned to the West as the only desired partner. The reasons were twofold: economic and political. In strictly economic terms, the capitalist economies of the West and the transitional economies of the East developed a relationship of 'haves' and 'have-nots', as the funds needed to keep cinema going could only come from the solvent West. Politically, reorientation to the West was now at the top of the agenda for all East European countries, and former partnerships within the Eastern bloc were thus quickly abandoned in favour of new alliances with the West. Today, two clearly distinct 'parallel' film industries, functioning pretty much independently from each other, exist side by side in the countries of Eastern Europe: the international service industry linked to global Hollywood and the domestic industry.

On the one hand, there is a well-developed and often profitable operation in place to attract and service large-scale international productions, with a streamlined system of studios, service companies, facilities and below-the-line personnel. On the other hand, there is the sphere of domestic filmmaking, with a much smaller technical and production base that is set up ad hoc on a per project basis; the local creative 'above-the-line' talent is engaged mostly here. This second sphere had earlier been central but is now marginalised and squeezed to open up space for the lucrative international productions operation; it has come to function as a parallel and secondary film industry. It is in the context of this second industry that films claiming to represent the national identity discourse are made today. In theory, the two industries could benefit from more integration as the presence of large international productions could underwrite the sustainability of the local industry. In reality, at least for the time being, they are almost fully detached from each other.

Table 5.1 Parallel industries

	International service industry	National cinema
Production	Studio and other production assets are foreign-owned and maintained mostly for the sake of attracting international runaway business. Reliance on foreign-financed (big-budget) productions. Below-the-line personnel mostly engaged on an on-going basis; occasional opportunities for input from local creative talent.	Handled by small companies on a per project basis; no ownership of production assets. Small composite budgets and reliance on grants as no full recoupment is likely. Studio space and teams secured ad hoc where needed. Creative personnel closely engaged with their own projects but also contracted to work occasionally within the international service industry.
Distribution	Mostly Hollywood subsidiaries, engaged in distributing Hollywood product, both to theatrical and ancillary markets.	No access to the operation of big distribution companies; occasional deals with small local or international distributors; reliance on guerrilla distribution.
Exhibition	Theatre owners mostly work in blanket-booking mode with Hollywood subsidiaries.	Individual deals with theatres for occasional showings. Heavy reliance on TV exposure and festival screenings.
Audiences	Mostly engaged with Hollywood product, which is synonymous with cinema to most cinema-goers.	Ignorant about domestic cinema as a consistent process. Pleased to see the occasional domestic film but would not seek it out. Occasional instances of domestic blockbusters.

WHATEVER HAPPENED TO BULGARIAN CINEMA?

In the past, Bulgaria's film industry was comparable in size to the industries of similarly sized countries like Belgium, Switzerland, Hungary and Austria in terms of facilities and outputs. Today the country ranks at the very lowest end of European cinema in just about every respect – production, spectatorship, assets.

Film production started in Bulgaria around the 1930s but only developed properly under state socialism in the aftermath of World War II (Micheli 1971; Brossard 1986; Holloway 1986; 1989). At its peak in the early 1980s, the industry employed about 2,500 highly qualified workers engaged around the film studio Boyana and a number of production units and companies making features, documentaries and animation. Bulgarian films played at big festivals and were distributed internationally, mostly to other countries in the Eastern bloc. The annual domestic production output was shown at the national cinema festival in Varna.

Nearly 600 feature films were produced during the forty-five years of state socialism (1945–89), peaking at around twenty-five features annually in the mid-1980s. In addition, about twenty television films, as well as 400 shorts and animated films, were made annually during the same period. Since 1989, with varying degrees of success, the yearly number of feature films has been around four or five a year (compatible to the outputs of the late 1940s); the total output of Bulgarian films for the fifteen-year period between 1990 and 2005 is slightly over sixty (or less than 30 per cent of the earlier production capacity). Not a single Bulgarian feature title was released in 1999.

On recent occasions when critics were asked to name the best Bulgarian films of all times, most proposed films from the 1960s and 1970s; not a single film made after 1985 has ever made it into the top ten. Ironically, it seems that Bulgarian cinema's identity remains confined to the past, when filmmakers had to be politically conformist but still enjoyed a chance to be prolific.

In the aftermath of 1989, the film industry was characterised by suppressed government funding, empty studios eager to attract foreign film crews, disappearance of domestic films from the wide screen, and armies of idle film professionals. The production of animated and short films shrunk substantially.

Reforms started with the March 1991 closing of TSO Bulgarian Cinema which was directly funded from the state budget. In June 1991, a National Film Centre (NFC) was created as an alternative to centralised film production; funding powers were re-allocated from the Ministry of Culture to the NFC, which established a public commission to disburse the scarce state funding to selected film projects and put in place various bylaws and regulations for producers. In 1992, the Boyana studio, previously owned by the state, was transformed into a state-run shareholding company, Boyana Film EAD. The same period saw the liquidation of state-owned distribution enterprises such as Rasprostranenie na filmi (internal film distribution) and Bulgaria Film (international sales and distribution).

It was not until 2003 that a long-awaited Film Industry Act was passed, raising hopes for more effective regulation in the area of state support for the cinema industry, including distribution and promotion, and intellectual property rights issues. Once again, the NFC was appointed as the executive administrative body for cinema within the Ministry of Culture with a responsibility for support for production, distribution and exhibition.

During an interview at the goEast film festival in Wiesbaden in April 2006, Professor Bojidar Manov, leader of the Bulgarian film critics and an important figure in FIPRESCI (the international federation of film critics) compared Bulgarian cinema to a person who is struggling to recover from a massive stroke. Every sign of progress and improvement, every step forward is celebrated as a huge achievement, yet no one ever mentions that the person remains a shadow of his or her former self.

Similar views are frequently expressed in the pages of the trade magazine *Kino*. Producer and critic Pavlina Jelena argues that the filmmaking community in Bulgaria has failed to secure a respectable place for cinema in the new system of culture management, resulting in serious challenges to the very existence of the nation's cinema (Jeleva 2005). Consequently, the main feature of Bulgarian cinema nowadays is its isolationism, linked to a muted process of lowering artistic criteria and to nostalgia for a romanticised past, which effectively inhibits forward-looking strategies. The prevalent admiration for petty achievements, Jeleva insists, makes new undertakings even pettier and muffles all ambitious attempts to express national identity adequately in cinema.

Back in the 1970s and 1980s, Bulgaria's cinema had come to be known and respected for its poetic character (Holloway 1986; 1989), for its lyrical and sensitive approach to love and affection, for its elegiac and graceful treatment of universal existential themes, and for its tongue-in-cheek assessment of history's volatilities. This sensitivity and insightfulness was no longer present in the majority of the films released throughout the 1990s.

In post-Communism, cineastes had to develop new survival skills focused on fundraising and guerrilla distribution, a challenge met well by some but not others. As a result, some veteran filmmakers were only able to complete a film or two before sinking into oblivion while others simply disappeared from the scene. The shrinking funds triggered generational conflict between established filmmakers who were embittered over the new market realities but nevertheless continued to fight hard, and younger filmmakers who had no choice but to enter the scene in these difficult times and to try to break through in a situation of vanishing opportunities, resulting in petty confrontations. An example is the altercation between newcomer Dimitar Petkov (director of *Devil's Tail/ Opashkata na dyavola*, 2001) and veteran Nikolai Volev (director of *Devil's Mirror/Ogledaloto na dyavola*, 2001). Petkov accused Volev of deliberately changing the name of his film in order to mislead viewers and take advantage of the promotion and success of *Devil's Tail*. Both films performed just as feebly.

Those belonging to the middle generation, whose work had peaked during the '*perestroika*' period of the 1980s, are commonly referred to as a 'lost generation'. Only a few really new directors came to the stage in the 1990s and it is only very recently that younger directors have managed to release films at all. Emerging cineastes face a difficult situation; due to non-existent distribution their names never become known nation-wide; only actors who work in television are known across the country today.

In a context of limited opportunities for professional realisation, seeking employment abroad becomes a solution that functions as a kind of remedial blood-letting; if the dilemma is between a less than optimal career abroad (or even a change of career paths) or staying idle at home, emigration seems to be the more viable alternative. According to a *Financial Times* estimate, by July 2006 more than 750,000 people (about 10 per cent of Bulgaria's population) had left the country to seek work abroad. It is not possible to provide figures for the numbers of creative personnel who have migrated, however. Many film professionals simply use the newly acquired freedom of movement to go for 'spells' abroad rather than establishing themselves permanently outside Bulgaria. They then shuttle back and forth between Bulgaria and whichever country they find enabling. Veteran actor Stefan Danailov, for example, played in some popular Italian gangster TV series throughout the 1990s; he is now back home where he serves as Bulgaria's culture minister. Younger directors go back and forth between opportunities in countries like Italy or Germany, where they are usually engaged in low-profile television work, and film-related work in Bulgaria, where they keep pushing poorly financed feature projects.

In the Bulgarian media, the outmigration of talent is lamented as a significant 'loss' and a 'brain drain', even though it has created a sizeable and lively Bulgarian artistic diaspora. No Bulgarians seem to have achieved genuine celebrity abroad yet, but some – like cameraman Emil Hristov, actor Hristo Shopov (who played Pontius Pilate in Mel Gibson's *The Passion of Christ*), writer Doriana Leondeff (who works regularly with director Silvio Soldini in Italy) or art director Evgeni Ganev (who created the cool city graphics of Sylvain Chomet's acclaimed animation, *Belleville Rendez-vous*) – have done well for themselves by establishing comfortable positions in a range of countries.

More than a decade ago Andrew Horton (1995) outlined several tendencies that he had observed in the cinema of former Yugoslavia, including a proliferation of smaller production companies working in conjunction with larger studios on a film-by-film basis; increased collaboration between film and television production and the development of a made-for-video film market of cheap, swiftly shot genre movies; and an increased number of international co-productions. Most of these elements also apply to Bulgaria. During that transitional period many filmmakers found themselves unprepared to deal with the new funding situation and the previously non-existent figure of the producer obtained definitive importance as a result, as did a number of rapidly proliferating small production companies. Film financing became a more complex affair involving the juggling of a composite budget that could fall apart at any moment, depending as it did on contributions from amongst a wide range of sources: scarce state subsidies, private investors, European funding bodies such as Eurimages and MEDIA, co-production partners and television.

Film grants are now awarded once or twice annually by a commission that has been distributing funds ranging between one and a half million Euros in the mid-1990s to around 3–4 million Euros in the mid-2000s. The declared goal is to secure budgetary financing for five feature films annually (the average budget of which is estimated at 600,000 Euros), ten full-length documentaries and up to 120 minutes of animation production (about fifteen animated films). The intention has always been to cover the bigger part of the budget of the successful projects, but in reality the subsidy often has not stretched much farther than 50 per cent, with the rest of the financing coming either from television networks or from private sponsors. Thus, who receives funding and who gets the chance to do creative work is an important issue, and it cannot be denied that there are instances of preferential treatment. Struggles over alleged unfairness in funding awards re-emerge in the media nearly every year. In order to put financing together, producers are compelled to seek assistance from television networks, and to enter into international partnerships. Bulgaria has been an active member of Eurimages since 1993 and Bulgarian companies have benefited from funding awards, most often in joint ventures with associates from neighbouring countries such as Turkey or Greece, more often as minority rather than majority partners. The country joined MEDIA in 2002, and has since been contributing about 137,000 Euros per annum, a contribution that has been assessed as worthwhile provided that the projects financed through MEDIA bring back grants exceeding membership contributions several times over. The country's filmmakers also benefit from financing through the Balkan Film Fund, which encourages regional co-productions.

Under state socialism, the cycle of production, distribution and exhibition was run in an integrated manner, with all components co-ordinated centrally. Even though the system was charged with producing dull politically correct films, it was effectively safeguarded from the drawbacks of excessive commercialism. It was an arrangement comparable to the classical studio system where the big Hollywood studios exhibited their films in a system of theatres they owned. And like the 1948 anti-trust decree that forced the studios to break up their well-consolidated mechanism, the break-up of the fully vertically integrated state-socialist system enhanced distribution as a key intermediary operation within the film industry cycle.

The centralised control over distribution and exhibition networks, as well as over the television medium, had made it easy to keep the audience from

Table 5.2 Cinemas, screenings and spectators in Bulgaria, 1960–99

Year	Cinemas	Screenings	Spectators	Bulgaria's population
1960	1,515	743,300	112,100,000	7,867,000
1965	2,403	1,027,500	126,400,000	8,201,000
1970	3,170	983,300	112,600,000	8,490,000
1975	3,689	988,600	114,300,000	8,722,000
1980	3,453	988,400	95,851,000	8,862,000
1995	232	136,000	4,676,000	
1996	219	112,600	3,641,000	8,340,900
1997	216	97,400	3,186,000	8,283,200
1998	205	100,100	3,204,000	8,230,400
1999	191	84,300	1,922,000	8,190,900

Source: http://www.titra.net/

fragmenting; people were to be exposed to whatever was on offer. There were instances of interference and censorship, yet, ironically, the percentage of censored films was significantly smaller than the percentage of those films that never get into distribution today, in the context of open-market conditions.

The abolition of a centralised management of culture divorced domestic film production from exhibition and distribution. The well-integrated and centralised vertical distribution network of what used to be the Eastern bloc rapidly disintegrated. By the end of the decade it was replaced by a more or less uniform system of Western-controlled subsidiaries whose main rule of engagement was full loyalty to the Hollywood product. While Bulgaria's distribution today carries an overwhelming percentage of Hollywood fare (currently about 85 per cent), the distribution of Bulgarian features internationally is at a record low.

Exhibition practices have also changed since 1989. In the context of an overall decline in admissions (as growing ticket prices became unaffordable for many), the centrally run system of state-owned theatres was abolished, and after a rushed privatisation in the late 1990s, many cinemas across the country closed or were converted into restaurants or bingo halls. In the 1980s more than 3,000 cinemas functioned across the country, many in villages. By the end of the century, cinema screenings no longer took place in villages and smaller towns. Statistics show that by 1999 one screen catered for nearly 43,000 people in the country (as opposed to one screen per 2,600 in 1980).

A $4.5 million sale of cinemas in the capital Sofia (20,000 sq m of exhibition facilities run centrally by Sofia Film until then) took place in 2001. A special clause in the sale's contract specified that exhibition activity should be continued for at least five years, which was particularly contentious as most cinemas were situated in prime real estate locations where space retails at 1,000 Euros per square meter. Heavy penalties were to be imposed for re-selling or re-purposing. None the less, the buyers did not comply with the obligations and, amidst protests from industry members, just three years later Sofia's cinemas were re-sold to developers for 25 million Euros. Even though they had to pay penalties of 7 million lev (3.5 million Euro), the buyers still made a profit of 8 million Euros. This effectively resulted in the liquidation of cinema exhibition activities in many parts of the capital. Some say that what happened in Sofia was the end of a cycle that began in the provinces and left the country without theatres; there has been extensive talk in the media about the damaging impact that the disappearance of cinemas has had on the nation's cultural memory. *Kino* magazine and some newspapers have been running nostalgic pieces chron-icling the history of well-known cinemas, the demise of which now appears to be a turned page in recent cultural history.

A new multiplex, Arena 1, which can accommodate nearly 3,000 spectators, opened in Sofia in 2003 and immediately gathered about 70 per cent of the audience in the city. It is run by one of the Hollywood subsidiaries (Alexandra Group). Several other multiplexes have since opened in newly built shopping centres, and these are all owned by foreign companies or Hollywood sub-sidiaries. There is also a significant growth in ancillary markets (video, DVD, cable/digital TV), most of which are dominated by foreign-owned companies.

The most problematic aspect of the crisis resulting from the changes in the dis-tribution and exhibition business is that the domestic, locally produced Bulgarian cinema has turned into a cinema without an audience. In the early 1990s viewers could no longer be taken for granted and filmmakers were faced with accelerating audience segmentation. Filmmakers could not identify whom they were addressing in their works. If they tried to appeal to a mass taste, they faced the overwhelming competition of imported mass culture. If they tried to address a more sophisticated audience, they were doomed to failure, as in the mass-market economy distributors and exhibitors have little interest in research-ing and targeting scattered pockets of potential viewers. One producer even claimed that most films in Bulgaria are now made for an audience of about thirty people – usually the filmmakers' own friends. Films are typically unable to recoup the monies that are invested in them, even in those cases where the budget is commensurate with the size of the country's population.

During the communist period of non-box-office orientation, however, local films were able to make their money back and sometimes even turn in a profit (it is claimed that about 30 per cent of the funds that the socialist state invested in filmmaking was simply re-investment of distribution revenues); nowadays such a scenario is out of the question. The widest-seen Bulgarian film of recent years, a city-girl-escaping-to-an-idyllic-village story, *Mila from Mars* (Zorntisa-Sophia, 2004), scored an audience of 20,000. The most successful film of 2005,

Stolen Eyes (Radoslav Spassov), which addressed the painful memories of state-sponsored ethnic confrontations between Christians and Muslims in Bulgaria's recent history, was seen by about 10,000 spectators in Sofia and the film's director was quoted as planning to organise the distribution in the provinces himself, personally taking a copy of the film on a tour from town to town. *Lady Z* (Georgi Dyulgerov, 2005), a hard-hitting story of a socially ostracised teenage girl, which was acclaimed at festivals and won the prestigious Heart of Sarajevo award, was seen by slightly over 4,000 people during the three months of its release in Sofia; once again, the arrangements for distribution across the country were left entirely to the producers as none of the big commercial distributors were interested in committing to distributing the picture. Indeed, many new Bulgarian productions have had only a single screening – to see them, one needs to be in Sofia when they just happen to be shown for specialised audiences. The full production of Bulgarian filmmaking can only be seen during the Golden Rose festival in Varna, an industry gathering of insiders that takes place biennially and showcases features, documentaries and animation. There is no national distributorship that looks into sales of Bulgarian cinema abroad (Bulgarian cinema is usually not represented at film markets), so if a film does manage to break through to international distribution circuits, it is due to the efforts of the team behind it.

Indeed, television is the last resort for Bulgaria's own cinematic products. Over several years, Channel 1 of Bulgarian television aired a programme, called *Ponedelnik 8½*, which featured older Bulgarian films, preceded by documentaries discussing the process of making the film and the respective period in the film industry. Developed under the overall direction of Evgeny Mikhailov, CEO of *Boyana Film*, the programme attracted a good-sized audience and for a while was the only mass forum for Bulgarian cinema. In the aftermath of 1989, public space was overtaken by cheap American entertainment product, often of the straight-to-video kind. Bulgarian films had all but disappeared. Those growing up in the 1990s would not normally see on the screen people talking in their own language or living in the same cities, a situation leading to low national self-esteem and an inferiority complex. Showing Bulgarian films that addressed the concerns of local people and featured life in their respective communities, that tackled important historical episodes (for example, the forced collectivisation of land in the 1950s) or addressed controversial issues specific to the country (such as the mass migration from villages to cities during the period of rushed industrialisation, resulting in a depopulation of villages) alleviated the budding unease over the loss of distinct identity. According to Petrova, the programme successfully targeted the younger generation of Bulgarians, encouraging them to regain national self-esteem by teaching 'a new appreciation of national cultural production' and respectively offering 'an antidote to the Western cultural production and information flow that has inundated Bulgaria in the post-communist period' (Petrova 2003: 27). The recently launched satellite channel TV Bulgaria aimed at diasporic Bulgarians also screens Bulgarian films, just as it features the cinema show, *Kino po noti*.

The Sale of Boyana Film Studio

Most of the studios in Eastern Europe, including Jadran and Avala in Yugoslavia, Buftea in Romania, Koliba in Slovakia, the four Polish studios, and the three Mafilm studios in Hungary, were built during the 1950s. However, the largest and oldest studio in the region, Barrandov in Prague (second in size only to the Italian Cinecittà and somewhat bigger than the East German DEFA, near Berlin) dates, like DEFA, from the pre-war era and possessed the most advanced production facilities. These studios were meant to serve mostly the needs of the national film industries, in addition to co-productions from within the Eastern bloc. However, a number of Western films were also shot in countries like Romania or Yugoslavia, even at the height of the Cold War.

But with the disappearance of centralised funding for cinema in the post-Communist era, the studios rapidly lost business. It soon became obvious that they would be better off if they emphasised the rental of facilities instead of waiting for the resurrection of a sustainable domestic production cycle. With maintenance budgets reduced to bare minimums, armies of idle employees (many of whom were soon made redundant) and equipment that was rapidly becoming out of date, the studios throughout Eastern Europe entered into a fierce competition with each other as they sought to attract 'runaway' productions. Compared with the West, these studios were still able to offer much lower production costs, and the goal thus became one of ensuring that local, below-the-line personnel and facilities were used. Various degrees of privatisation were carried out, often on direct recommendation from the International Monetary Fund. In the most successful cases the privatisation of the studios was accompanied by the establishment of independent satellite film service companies, and these brought a steady stream of international business to the studios.

Boyana, the Bulgarian studio, was no different. Like the other studios, it was built in the 1950s on a large piece of nationalised land on the perimeter of the Vitosha mountain near Sofia, overlooking the city. Besides feature film production, the studio was home to smaller administrative film production units for documentary, TV and animated films. During its peak times in the 1980s, Boyana had an annual output of around twenty-five feature films and attracted a small but significant number of international productions.

Like all other Bulgarian businesses, Boyana was hit by financial difficulties in the early 1990s. In 1992 it was turned into an independent state-run unit, Boyana Film EAD, engaged in servicing productions for, and working in close collaboration with, national TV; like many other studios in the region, this

Bulgarian studio had no choice but to cut the number of employees drastically. For more than a decade, Boyana Film's CEO was Evgeny Mikhailov, a former film director, who is credited with saving the studio from being cut into pieces by restitution of the land to previous owners, and with updating the technical equipment.

Mikhailov managed to bring a relatively steady flow of foreign productions to Boyana, but his international connections were limited. Even though Boyana provided a variety of services – budgeting, contractual security on the projects, recruiting staff, casting, post-production labs – it was more often rented for the inexpensive facilities and labour rather than for the full range of services on offer, with foreign productions organising their own extras and casting and with post-production completed elsewhere.

There were high hopes that, with the entry of countries like Hungary and the Czech Republic into the European Union (EU) in 2004, and the likely disappearance of the cost advantages there, Hollywood's interest in Prague and Budapest as shooting locations would decline and many productions would move south-east to cheaper locations like Bulgaria or Romania. This 'portable industry' of highly mobile transnational filmmaking enterprises could bring significant benefits to the local industry. For the time being, however, no radical change has come about, and Boyana cannot be said to have benefited drastically from the 'portability' of the runaway business.

Boyana's turn to be privatised came in 2002, when an initial valuation was commissioned by the national Privatisation Agency. The valuation set the price at 50 million lev (about 25 million Euros or $30 million). The price included the studio's entire land (30,000 sq m), its three sound stages (2,000 sq m), various other production facilities, a Kodak-equipped film laboratory and an animation unit, as well as an extensive stock of wardrobe and props.

Bids were invited in mid-2004. At this time, the valuation was reduced by 80 per cent, down to 10 million lev (5 million Euros). The reasons for the reduction were not clear; media reports alleged evidence of significant conflict of interest and corruption. The future owner was expected to commit to preserving the site as a production venue for at least ten more years, to producing at least two Bulgarian films a year during the first three years, and to making further investments in the studio for approximately 6 million Euros in the first four years after the sale (Goldsmith and O'Regan 2005: 143). Four offers were received by the deadline (25 February 2005): from Bavaria Film (Germany), Ealing Studios (UK), Nu Image (USA) and Dragon International (an international consortium which was eliminated for procedural reasons).

The winning bid was Nu Image's; they offered 12,223,937 lev for 95 per cent of the shares (6,250,000 Euros or $7.6 million). Of these, 65 per cent of the shares were to be paid for in cash while the remaining 30 per cent could be paid for in privatisation vouchers (which could be purchased at a fraction of the full value of the lev). The buyer was to make further investments of another $36 million in order to bring the facilities up to date to meet the needs of Hollywood producers. The ownership transfer was to take place on condition that the buyer mortgaged the studio's land to the Bulgarian state for the next twenty years, the point being to guarantee the continuation of filmmaking activities.

Based in Los Angeles, Nu Image had been making films in Bulgaria since 1999 and had produced nearly fifty B-features there. It claims to have brought in at least half of Boyana's existing business. The company's main owner, Israeli-born Avi Lerner, is a producer of the ilk of Cannon Films' Menahem Golan and Yoram Globus. Starting off as a concession stand worker at a drive-in in Tel Aviv, Lerner engaged in production in South Africa, established a branch in Hollywood in the early 1990s (forming Nu Image and Millennium Pictures with partners), and sought to diversify into Eastern Europe. While most of the nearly 200 films for which he is credited as producer are in the low-budget action-adventure genre, Lerner is in the process of moving out of the B-movies area into higher-budget mainstream studio fare.

In line with Lerner's intentions, Nu Image's representative in Bulgaria, David Varod, has been insisting that the company will aim to bring high-profile and high-budget productions to Boyana. According to Varod, the studio is 'in very bad shape, and the infrastructure is a mess', so he has lots of work to do before he can make it a profitable enterprise. His plans are to expand the current 2,000 sq m of stages up to 20,000 sq m. For the time being, the production slate in Boyana is dominated by Nu Image's own action-thrillers, but efforts are under way to attract other productions as well and there is talk of an annual turnover of $100 million (indeed, parts of Brian de Palma's *Black Dahlia* were recently shot here).

Nu Image's contract for Boyana was signed in August 2005 but the full transfer of ownership was significantly delayed. The local film community raised fears that Nu Image would turn to foreign productions at the expense of domestic projects or that they would liquidate the studio altogether and sell it off as valuable real estate. Members of the community were particularly bitter over the fact that the studio was being sold at a price equalling a fraction of the budget of an average Hollywood film.

A group of film directors led the opposition. They attempted to expose corruption, described the privatisation as a 'robbery' and claimed that the film industry's assets (built over many years) were being given away for 'a hand down', with contempt for the nation's 'emotional and spiritual memory' (Spassov 2006).[3] The leadership of Boyana Film EAD collectively resigned in October 2005; they made calls for a special parliamentary commission to investigate alleged irregularities surrounding the privatisation. This was, however, gradually put on hold as it was believed such hearings could interfere with Bulgaria's impending EU integration plans. The last resort of the protesters was to approach the European Parliament, but their undertaking did not meet with much success.

Nu Image denied all allegations – the terms of the sale were not tailored to favour them in any way; they were not planning to dispose of filmmaking activity at *Boyana* nor did they intend to sell the studio's land; they would use it for filmmaking and would not change the type of activities for the stipulated period; and they would fully support the making of two Bulgarian features a year and up to 20 minutes of animation. Local producers 'should wake up' and understand that what Nu Image offers is the best that they can get, insisted David Varod (in Schwinke 2006a). None the less, up until the summer of 2006, the transfer of powers had not yet taken place and there were bureaucratic complications. Some of the scheduled shoots had to be cancelled, bringing losses for Nu Image.[4]

Even though most objections were based on projected fears rather than valid concerns, the controversy was justified. The speculation that the studio's land would be sold off for a profit, a move that would spell the end of the country's film industry, was rooted in past disappointments. Some of Bulgaria's largest assets, companies like Bulgartabak or Balkan Airlines, were sold in shady deals that effectively led to their liquidation soon after the sale. The most relevant and recent example of a worrisome transaction was the previously mentioned sale of Sofia's cinemas, a deal in which the new owners opted to sell off and pay the penalty for not maintaining exhibition activity (and still made a hefty profit). The fact that the sale was to a company whose own survival as a Hollywood player is not secure, reinforced the spectre of Boyana's land being sold as prime real estate. For the time being, however, keeping Boyana functioning through Nu Image is the only reasonable option on the table. As far as the domestic production ecology is concerned, Boyana's sale was the final step in shaping the parallel industries where the production of national films is no longer a default feature of the national studio. The servicing of large runaway productions from Hollywood and elsewhere has become the default arrangement, whereas work on domestic productions will need to be negotiated on a per project basis.

In the final analysis, how a studio participates in the international production ecology is determined not so much by strict economic factors as by the perception of its 'symbolic importance' in the eyes of investors; and being located in what is perceived as an isolated provincial corner of Europe, Boyana loses out. Being based 'in a country that nobody really knows', as Nu Image's David Varod put it (Schwinke 2006a), a lot of convincing and promoting is necessary to secure the international business that Boyana requires to thrive.

Bulgaria's New Parallel Industries

Like other Eastern European countries earlier, Bulgaria has been 'carpetbagger heaven' (Millea 1997) for the greater part of two decades. In the context of overall political volatility and short-lived governments, assets are being sold off in a rushed and often heavily disputed manner. The public discourse is one of lamenting the loss of what is now seen as a previously prosperous national industry. Problems are often blamed on the loss of assets and the transfer of control to foreign carpetbaggers. In a representative newspaper piece, veteran cameraman and director Radoslav Spassov, for example, expressed dismay over the government's indifference and bitterly commented that the cycle of the US takeover of whatever was left of Bulgaria's film industry was now almost complete. With the sale of Boyana (including all its inventory and equipment), he claimed that 95 per cent of the means of production had now been passed to American hands. In his estimate, 85 per cent of the distribution sector, 80 per cent of the cinema exhibition and 97 per cent of the media promotions are also American-controlled (Spassov 2006).

Spassov is right to speak of foreign dominance over film and media, but control is not entirely in US hands. In reality the ownership situation is more complex, with a number of other interests – entrepreneurs from Israel, Greece, Turkey, Germany, former Yugoslavia and elsewhere – being drawn into the motley landscape of new media ownership. There is a range of bigger and smaller-sized players, but also medium-size investors and even swindlers looking out for new ventures. They all co-exist side by side and sometimes enter into improbable interactions of a 'wild West' variety.

It is all part and parcel of the transition and there is not necessarily any need to subscribe to the tragic stance often taken by local industry figures. It is clear that in the global division of labour there are losers and there are winners, and that Bulgaria's national film industry will never return to what is now seen as a blissful period of sheltered prosperity.

NOTES

1. Such a category would include not only the national cinemas of countries like Slovakia, Romania, Albania, a range of other former Soviet or Yugoslav republics (for example, Ukraine, Georgia, Bosnia, Croatia, Macedonia, Serbia and so on), but also other 'provincial' cinemas across the globe, in Africa, Asia and Latin America.
2. Along with the break-up of Yugoslavia, for example, filmmakers here saw the break-up of a consolidated distribution space. They often complain today that, whereas their films were previously shown automatically across all six federative republics, nowadays their outputs remain confined to tiny domestic markets.
3. Opponents of the sale protested against the low sale price of $7.6 million and insisted that the earlier $50 million estimate was more realistic. The studio is situated on 300,000 sq m of land, the cost of which is estimated at 100 Euros per square meter and growing; thus the land alone is worth at least 30 million Euros, they claimed. The 14,000 sq m of buildings could be sold for another 7 million Euros, the recently acquired equipment for about 2 million Euros, and then there is the cost of 60,000 costumes, 3,000 pieces of weaponry and tens of thousands of props.
4. The loud public controversy surrounding Boyana's privatisation was very similar to the critiques expressed in the Czech Republic when the Barrandov studio was

privatised a decade earlier. Like Boyana, Barrandov was privatised under the government stipulation that it should continue as a film production studio. Just as in the Boyana case, Czech film directors insisted that the studio's actual market value was up to five times higher and that the price had been artificially lowered simply because the preferred purchaser's available capital was far from sufficient to cover the studio's real value. Back then, fears were voiced that privatising Barrandov would bring the Czech film industry to an end and that the studio's land would be parcelled up and sold as real estate. Unlike Boyana, however, in the Barrandov case the alleged price lowering had been effected in order to keep the studio in domestic hands (Clark 1992); Barrandov is still Czech-owned. Had Boyana hired competent Hollywood representation and consultants, had it encouraged satellite production companies to grow alongside it (as was the case in Hungary and the Czech Republic), the studio would have been able to get a much better share of international business. Domestic ownership does not, however, seem to have been a priority.

WORKS CITED

Brossard, Jean-Pierre. 1986. *Aspects nouveaux du cinéma bulgare*. La Chaux-de-Fonds: Cinédiff.

Clark, John. 1992. 'Czech Barrandov Studios to go Private'. *Daily Variety*, 6 July. p. 14.

Fainaru, Dan. 2005. 'Lady Zee'. *Screen International*, 28– September, 1513. p. 35.

Goldsmith, Ben and Timothy O'Regan. 2005. *The Film Studio: Film Production in the Global Economy*. Boulder, CO: Rowman & Littlefield.

Holloway, Ronald. 1986. *The Bulgarian Cinema*. Rutherford, NJ: Fairleigh Dickinson University Press.

Holloway, Ronald. 1989. 'Bulgaria: The Cinema of Poetics'. In D. J. Goulding (ed.), *Post New Wave Cinema in the Soviet Union and Eastern Europe*. Bloomington, IN: Indiana University Press. pp. 215–48.

Horton, Andrew. 1995. 'Only Crooks Can Get Ahead: Post-Yugoslav Cinema/ TV/Video in the 1990s'. In S. P. Ramet and L. S. Adamovic (eds), *Beyond Yugoslavia. Politics, Economics and Culture in a Shattered Community*. Boulder, CO: Westview. pp. 413–31.

Iordanova, Dina. 1997. 'Canaries and Birds of Prey: the New Season of Bulgarian Cinema'. In J. Bell (ed.), *Bulgaria in Transition*. Boulder, CO: Westview. pp. 255–81.

Iordanova, Dina. 1999. 'East Europe's Cinema Industries since 1989: Financing Structure and Studios'. *Javnost/The Public*, Vol. 4, No. 2. pp. 45–60.

Iordanova, Dina. 2002. 'Feature Filmmaking within the New Europe: Moving Funds and Images Across the East-West Divide'. *Media, Culture and Society*, Vol. 24, No. 4. pp. 517–37.

Iordanova, Dina. 2003. *Cinema of the Other Europe: The Industry and Artistry of East Central European Film*. London: Wallflower.

Iordanova, Dina (ed.). 2006. *Kinokultura Special Issue 5: Bulgarian Cinema*. http://www.kinokultura.com/specials/5/bulgarian.shtml.

Iordanova, Dina. 2007. 'Bulgarian Cinema: Optimism in Moderation'. In C. Portuges and P. Hames (eds), *East European Cinemas since 1989*. Philadelphia, PA: Temple University Press.

Jeleva, Pavlina. 2005. 'European Cinema – A Perspective without an Alternative' ['Evropeyskoto kino – perspective bez alternative']. *Kino*, Vol. 3. pp. 25–9.

Mattelart, Armand and Michelle Mattelart. 1984. *International Image Markets: In Search of an Alternative Perspective*. London: Comedia.

Micheli, Sergio. 1971. *Il Cinema bulgaro*. Padua: Marsilio.

Millea, Martin. 1997. 'Czech Privatization: The Case of Filmove Studio Barrandov'. *Journal of International Affairs*, Winter, Vol. 50, No. 2. pp. 489–504.

Miller, Toby, Nitin Govil, John McMurria and Richard Maxwell. 2001. *Global Hollywood*. London: British Film Institute.

Petrova, Velina. 2003. 'Are We Going to Have a Race of Angels? Post-Communist Interpretation of Bulgarian Dissident Cinema'. *Berkeley Journal of Sociology*, Vol. 47. pp. 27–48.

Schwinke, Theodor. 2006a. 'Nu Image acquires Boyana Film Studios in Bulgaria'. *Screen Daily*, 16 January.

Schwinke, Theodor. 2006b. 'The Battle of Bulgaria'. *Screen International*, 17 February. p. 15.

Spassov, Radoslav. 2006. 'Dream Factory or Factory for Wooden Clogs?' ['Fabrika za sanishta ili fabrika za nalumi']. *Trud*, 16 March, p. 16.

Taylor, Richard, Julian Graffi, Nancy Wood and Dina Iordanova (eds). 2000. *BFI Companion to Eastern European and Russian Cinema*. London: British Film Institute.

Willemen, Paul. 2006. 'The National Revisited'. In Valentina Vitali and Paul Willemen (eds), *Theorizing National Cinemas*. London: British Film Institute. pp. 29–44.

Young, Deborah. 2005. 'Lady Z'. *Variety*, 30 August. http://www.variety.com/review/VE1117928020?categoryid=31&cs=1&s=h&p=0.

PART TWO

ASIA AND OCEANIA

6. HONG KONG

Ackbar Abbas

HONG KONG AS A 'PARA-SITE'

Can there be a national cinema in the absence of a nation-state (however small) and, more importantly, without the aspiration for a nation-state? This is the question posed by the Hong Kong cinema, which has become one of the world's more important cinemas, while Hong Kong itself has never been and will never be an independent nation-state. Before 1997 an economically developed British Crown Colony whose gross domestic product exceeded that of many small nations, and now a Special Administrative Region of China with an assurance that its status will remain unchanged for fifty years, Hong Kong has always been a political anomaly, a special case. However, it is arguably its ambiguous position *vis-à-vis* nationalism and self-determination that has been instrumental in stimulating the emergence of a successful international cinema: a cinema that has produced a string of outstanding films, a growing roster of auteurs like Wong Kar-wai, Ann Hui, Stanley Kwan and Fruit Chan, and some would even say a distinctive cinematic style. It is precisely the paradoxical nature of the Hong Kong case that allows us to raise certain kinds of critical questions about 'the cinema of small nations', including: Can 'statelessness' generate a 'national cinema'? And if so, how can we understand the 'national' in cinema?

Statelessness can take different forms. Perhaps the most poignant and embattled example of a stateless national cinema is Palestinian, which not coincidentally displays a number of broad similarities to the Hong Kong cinema, despite the many political and historical differences between them. In the introductory essay to *Dreams of a Nation: On Palestinian Cinema*, the editor Hamid Dabashi speaks of 'the spectacular rise of a national cinema . . . precisely at a moment when the nation that is producing it is itself negated and denied . . . That paradox does not only preface the case of Palestinian cinema, it occasions it and gives it a unique and unsettling disposition' (Dabashi 2006: 8–9). Hence, Dabashi can go on to note that 'at the creative core of Palestinian cinema' is 'the over-riding presence of an absence' (10). This play between presence/absence is reiterated in a different way by the late Edward Said in his preface to the volume when he points to the necessity on the part of Palestinians to 'stand against invisibility' on the one hand, and to 'stand against the stereotype in the media' on the other (for example, the stereotype of the 'Palestinian terrorist') (3). The parallels with the Hong Kong cinema in these respects are quite striking. We also saw the emergence of a new Hong Kong cinema in the 1980s and 1990s at a moment when Hong Kong as we knew it was threatened by what elsewhere I have called 'disappearance'. A cinema emerged when the political status of the city was most in doubt. There is also a play of presence and absence, in that disappearance connotes not simply a vanishing without a trace, an absence, but an elusive and problematic presence: like, for example, the colonial ghosts that remain after the colonial body has departed.

There is nevertheless an obvious but crucial difference between the two cinemas, seen in their relation to nationhood and colonialism. For Palestinians, the crucial date is 1948 (an event they call *Nakba* or 'Catastrophe'), when the state of Israel was formed and Palestinians lost their homeland. Nationalism became a form of resistance to colonialism as bitter wars were fought and are still being fought. The Hong Kong case is less brutal but also more paradoxical. It is marked not by wars and conflicts which exist only as a fading memory, but by something else: a conflicted attitude towards nationalism and colonialism. For Hong Kong, the crucial date is not 1843, when it was ceded to Britain as a Crown Colony through an 'unequal treaty', but 1997, when the city was due to be re-inscribed into the Chinese nation. It is this re-inscription (which has since taken place) that, for a number of historical reasons, produced and is still producing not euphoria but anxiety. One factor was suspicion of 'Communism', which was what many middle-class Chinese fled from in 1949, to the safe haven of a British colony. This was one reason why the return of the colony to China was greeted with fear and trembling in some quarters. There were, however, more complex reasons for anxiety, hinted at by the fact that for Hong Kong the main issue was never colonialism or nationalism, in spite of the rhetoric from all sides. The main issue was whether the status quo could be preserved: the anomalous status quo of a city that was somehow both dependent and autonomous at the same time. Historically, there was for Hong Kong no possibility of, and hence little interest in, independence. Hong Kong could never have been a city-nation like Singapore, only a 'hyphenation'. It therefore accepted its colonial status as a *sine qua non* and turned towards the international arena, making a career of dependency by fully exploiting its position as a port-city. Hong Kong was less a site than a 'para-site'; but it was its geopolitical position as para-site that enabled it to become an international city with a measure of autonomy. In this it was aided and abetted by a British colonialism that in the latter half of the twentieth century was moving away from imperialist towards globalist paradigms: a colonialism that was sometimes barely recognisable as such.

The major anxiety then was over whether the internationalism and relative autonomy of the port-city would be smothered by re-inscription into the motherland, the Chinese nation-state. It seemed for a while that the choice (not that a choice was in fact available) was between the colonial/'democratic' and the national/'autocratic': a choice of nightmares. The stakes were raised considerably after the Tiananmen Massacre of 4 June 1989. Given the complexity of the situation, terms like the national, the colonial and the democratic began to change their valencies and take on ambiguous overtones. Take the 'democracy movement' in Hong Kong, which clearly got its major impetus from horror over Tiananmen. Even today, the movement targets the Tiananmen Massacre rather than British colonialism. Its leaders include not only grass-roots activists but also a number of British-trained, and some would say Anglophile, lawyers, even though their loyalty to Hong Kong is not in doubt. In other words, at least part of the subtext of 'democracy' (there are, of course, other aspects) is lingering anxiety over national re-inscription.

As if these ambivalences towards colonialism and nationalism were not enough, the situation was further complicated by a third factor: China's recent embrace of globalisation. It could be backdated to Deng Xiaoping's 'open door policy' that took effect when he became paramount leader after the end of the Cultural Revolution. The policy stalled over Tiananmen, but moved rapidly forward again in the early 1990s, driven by 'the socialist market economy'. The effect of this new openness on Hong Kong was palpable and swift. The anxieties of the 1980s were now tempered by the scent of new opportunities. This explains why the sense of doom and gloom evoked by the prospect of 1997 in the 1980s and which reached a nadir in June 1989 could so unpredictably modulate into one of doom and boom in the 1990s. In the lead-up to 1997, the Hong Kong property and stock markets reached historical highs, and the 'red chip stock' rivalled in popularity the 'blue chip stock'.

However, as the period after 1997 shows, China's rapid integration into the global economy (emblematised by its membership in the World Trade Organization and its emergence as an economic superpower) produced not just new opportunities but also a different set of anxieties for Hong Kong. Though it still has the advantage, thanks to its colonial past, of easy access to global networks, the end of Chinese isolationism means that there will be many more global cities in China with equally easy access to information, services and foreign investments. Hong Kong had to reassess and abandon its in-between position as the only global city in the world that is also a colony; it had to abandon all the advantages of the para-site and of hyphenation. As if to drive this very point home, barely two days after the Handover, on 2 July 1997, Thailand devalued the baht, unleashing a chain of events now known as the Asian economic crisis. This crisis arrived in full-blown form in Hong Kong fourteen months later, when a number of hedge-fund managers made a play against the Hong Kong currency and the stock market. The crisis was eventually averted, but there is nevertheless deep irony in the fact that such a past master of hedging, a city that has so successfully used its mediate position between China and the world to profit from asymmetries and instabilities, should itself be a target of hedge funds. This shows that there is a new game in town where as a player Hong Kong no longer holds all the trump cards.

A New Hong Kong Cinema

It was during this period, roughly from the 1970s onwards, when Hong Kong's relation to colonialism, nationalism and globalisation was decisively shifting, that we saw the emergence of what could clearly be called a new Hong Kong cinema. In what sense can it also be called a 'national' cinema?

It has often been pointed out that major national cinemas emerge in response to traumatic historical events like wars and revolutions: Soviet Formalism, Italian Neo-Realism, the French New Wave, New German cinema and Palestinian cinema are some examples that have been cited. The case of the new Hong Kong cinema is different in several important respects. To begin with, it is a cinema formed not in the aftermath of a major political upheaval, but in the anticipation of one. The traumas it responds to are not so much actual and physical, like military invasion and loss of a homeland, as virtual and nebulous (though no less real), involving a change of status and a rearrangement of internal grids, while all the time appearances remain more or less intact. Moreover, these changes are marked not by violent upheavals and displacements, but by a series of small dislocations and readjustments, many of which are neither traumatic nor even discernible. While Palestine has to live through a brutally clear scenario of war, Hong Kong lives through a confused and confusing 'obscenario' of peace. Almost nowhere can we find large-scale images of violence and gross injustice (except for the image of Tiananmen); on the other hand, what we do find almost everywhere is a space, distorted and disfigured, where the real violence is tacit. This may be one reason (there are, of course, a host of others) why the image of Tiananmen is so important for so many Hong Kong people; it is as if some image of real violence were almost a kind of necessary relief from the brooding sense of tacit violence everywhere.

And there is a second difference: if there is an oneiric dimension to the Hong Kong cinema, it is not filled by 'dreams of a nation'. In this respect, it is unlike the Palestinian cinema or even the mainland Chinese cinema. Many Chinese films, from Chen Kaige's *Yellow Earth* to Zhang Yimou's *Hero*, embrace the epic mode and construct allegories of nation-building. Such national allegories are entirely alien to the Hong Kong cinema. It is impossible for there to be a Hong Kong epic entitled 'Fragrant Harbour'! Rather what we do find in the Hong Kong cinematic imaginary is the nation in fragments, the nation as a jigsaw puzzle of the mind with some essential pieces missing. Is this not the implication of the formula 'one country, two systems'? The formula suggests that even the strong Chinese commitment to a unified China has to acknowledge the fragmented and heterogeneous nature of nationalism in the global era.

A third point follows from this. Globalisation, as we know, does not mean that nation-states are disappearing; if anything, more nation-states are coming into being because of it – witness the breaking up of the Soviet Union into Russia and a number of smaller nation-states. It seems therefore that what the nation in fragments is producing as an entirely unexpected corollary is the fragment as nation: that is, the 'small nation' that exists as a nodal point in the global network, where strategic position can compensate for smallness of scale. The fragment as nation allows us to define, tentatively, in what sense it is possible to think about the Hong Kong cinema as a 'national' cinema: in the sense that it is a cinema that perceives the nation from the point of view of the fragment. Its relation to nationhood is unorthodox. It does not see the nation as a finished or achieved entity, but catches it at a moment when the nature of nationhood itself is changing, under pressure from globalisation. What comes out of the fragment as nation are not metaphors but metonymies of nationhood: metonymies that signify in an indirect and often tenuous way, to the point where their relationship to nationhood can become all but disconnected.

This brings us to a fourth point, the question of cinematic style in different kinds of national cinema. Here again a comparison of Hong Kong with Palestinian cinema is illuminating. Hamid Dabashi spoke of 'the presence of an absence' in Palestinian cinema, by which he means the making present or re-presentation through cinematic art of the absent nation. In the Hong Kong cinema we will have to speak of 'the absence of a presence', the elusiveness and absence of the nation, in spite of political assurance to the contrary of how Hong Kong is part of China. Hence what is most 'real', what is most 'present' in the Hong Kong cinema is paradoxically an experience of the negative or the absent, the experience of some elusive or ambivalent space that lies always just beyond our grasp or just beneath our articulations. The nation as absent presence is the negative horizon of the Hong Kong cinema. Though such a negative space defeats direct representation, it is nevertheless discernible through the way it skews social and affective relations, and influences both the style and content of particular films.

The Hong Kong cinema is not a cinema of order, measure and balance; its penchant is for the excessive and extravagant, as if only exaggeration and hyperbole could have a chance of making visible the capillary movements of a skewed space. Throughout the history of new Hong Kong cinema, for every successful film made (that is, a film that somehow catches the paradoxical nature of negative space), there is a much larger number of failures that fall short or go too far: films that seem to caricature themselves by the over-use of clichés, melodramatic plots, sentimentality and generic repetition. In short, the Hong Kong cinema is baroque in style, in the carefully defined sense that Borges gives to that term in his 'Preface to the 1954 Edition' of A Universal History of Iniquity: 'I would define the baroque as that style that deliberately exhausts (or tries to exhaust) its own possibilities and that borders on self-caricature.' In the baroque style extravagance not readiness is all. 'Gallows and pirates fill its pages and that word *iniquity* strikes awe in the title, but under all the storm and lightning, there is nothing' (Borges 1998: 4–5). With a very slight shift of perspective, Borges's lines could be read as a commentary on the Hong Kong cinema, with its ghosts, gangsters, kung-fu masters and urban misfits who parade in spectacular fashion across the screen, matching the toughs, knife-fighters, thugs and *compadres* that flit across Borges's work. And in both cases, underneath it all 'there is nothing', only the absent presence of an entity called 'Argentina' or 'Hong Kong': an entity that can only be deduced from style and content, not reduced to them. And nothing is more baroque than the notion of a Hong Kong national cinema.

When we turn to the analysis of particular Hong Kong films, what we can use as a kind of radioactive thread through the labyrinth is precisely the unresolved issue of the nation, shading on one side into colonialism and on the other into globalisation. What the Hong Kong cinema stages, both before and after 1997, is not the appearance of the nation, but its dis-appearance, its absent presence. The nation is like the fantasmic kernel of the Hong Kong political imaginary; coming too close to it results in the aphanisis (that is, the fading and disintegration) of the subject and the subject's perceptions. The Hong Kong films where the disappearance of the nation is staged cover a wide spectrum from minority art-house productions at one end, to blockbusters and potboilers on the other. We will have to submit all of these to the same kind of careful analysis, following Benjamin's recommendation that 'the everyday [be treated] as impenetrable, the impenetrable as everyday' (Benjamin 1978: 190). In fact, among the types, it may be the kitschy blockbuster or pot-boiler that gives a more direct and immediate representation of the fantasies of nationhood in the Hong Kong cinema.

We can begin with the popular success of Bruce Lee's early films like *Big Boss* (1971) and *Fists of Fury* (1972). What we find in these films is a level of authentic-looking action never seen before in the Hong Kong cinema or in any other cinema, together with an all too familiar discourse on nationalism as resistance to colonialism. Body-building as a discourse on national reconstruction and anti-colonial resistance is a theme that goes back as far as the Boxer Rebellion. Hence some of the key scenes in these films, besides the fight sequences, come when Lee strips down to exercise, displaying like a revelation the finely sculpted Chinese body: *Ecce Homo* is at the same time *Ecce Natio*. The complication is that Lee's own 'anti-colonial' sentiments may have been fuelled not so much by his experience of Hong Kong, where he was a child star, as by his experience of the US, where he was passed over for important roles on American television because he was Chinese. After all, in the 1960s and early 1970s, colonialism in Hong Kong had already begun to take on benign-looking characteristics. It was the moment when both the city and Bruce Lee could embark on their international careers. Hence Lee could not direct his anti-colonial fists of fury against present-day Hong Kong. He had to set his films in the past, in pre-revolutionary Shanghai, serve up old memories, *rechauffés*, of colonialist slights and insults, and turn his animus against a traditional and recognisable enemy, the Japanese. It is as if, in these films, the true identity of the antagonist were occluded, and we had a cardboard figure in its place, as if the nationalist hero in all the beautifully choreographed action sequences were only a blindsided 'dancer in the dark'. In the end, both nationalism and colonialism are represented through proxy and stereotyped figures: in other words, not represented at all. Nevertheless, in *Fists of Fury*, we do find a faint awareness that there is a problem. After the hero has punched and kicked himself into a corner, and we have begun to wonder how the plot could be resolved, the film stops abruptly on a freeze frame of Lee executing a high kick, a shot that leaves both the hero and the political issues suspended in mid-air.

By way of contrast, let us consider very briefly Wong Kar-wai's *Ashes of Time* (1994), his only excursion to date into the martial arts genre. In Wong's film, what we encounter at every turn are problematic spaces of both action and affect. Take, for example, the fight sequence that opens the film. We no longer see a choreography of bodies in motion but a *chiaroscuro* of light and colour into which figures and actions have dissolved. The heroic space of action found in Bruce Lee is now a blind space – because of an excess, not a lack, of light. One of the four heroes of *Ashes of Time* is in fact going blind. Affective space is also skewed; the 'heroes' are more or less neurotics, living on *ressentiment* and projecting their private obsessions back on to the space around them. At no point is nationalism or colonialism directly presented, but it is as if the problematic space in which these terms are situated has somehow seeped through to the kung-fu genre.

It is, of course, not only in the kung-fu genre that questions of the nation and colonialism are important. We also find these problematic issues approached in a different way in a film like Ann Hui's *Song of the Exile* (1990), set in the domestic space of the middle-class Hong Kong family. The film begins as a story of misunderstanding between a mother and daughter who never got along with each other. The key peripeteia occurs when the daughter learns that her mother is in fact Japanese, and that she met her father during Japan's last days in Manchuria. This leads to the daughter, Hueyin, re-examining and reframing her memories of the mother in a series of flashbacks and, even more interestingly, flashbacks of flashbacks. She begins to understand why her grandparents, staunch nationalists, were so hostile to the foreign daughter-in-law, and to see that her mother's reticence in the old days, which contrasted sharply with her behaviour in the present, came from her ignorance of the language. Within the domestic setting, we find not only a quasi-colonial situation but also its radical defamiliarisation, with the Japanese, the traditional figure of the oppressor, cast in the role of the oppressed. The quietly subversive point here is that colonialism cannot be confined to the practices of any one nation. The film's other radical insight is that nationalism too is not always a form of resistance to oppression. It could itself become a form of oppression, of oneself and of others, especially if it is coupled with an ethnocentric mindset and a fixation on the past. One example is the mother's younger brother, a former Japanese war pilot whose life is damaged not so much by the war as by his refusal to accept that the war was over a long time ago. Another example are the grandparents themselves in their display of prejudice against their daughter-in-law. Out of national sentiment they eventually return to mainland China, only to fall victim to the Cultural Revolution.

Ann Hui's film could therefore be read as offering a double critique of the conventional pieties about the nation and colonialism embraced by the older generation, to set up the question of what Hong Kong could be in the present (that is, in the 1990s). After the stories of exiles and émigrés, parents and grandparents, comes the story of Hueyin, the Hong Kong 'native'. If Hong Kong is neither 'nation' nor 'colony', then what could it be? Perhaps an historical experiment, along the lines of one country, two systems: an experiment that has some chance but no guarantee of success? This unpredictability may be what is signified by the film's most puzzling and shocking image which comes towards the end, when Hueyin visits her grandparents in Guangzhou. They have adopted a mentally retarded child, and as the grandmother feeds him, he viciously bites her hand for no apparent reason. Though the image could be read in a number of ways, one of them is the sense it conveys, through the inexplicable behaviour of the retarded child, of the unpredictability of history.

It was also this sense of the unpredictable that made the coming re-inscription of Hong Kong into the larger Chinese nation so fraught with anxiety. One film that played on these anxieties is *Wicked City*, released in 1992 by Tsui Hark's Film Workshop. It is a sci-fi horror film with allegorical overtones, a shameless pot-boiler so bad that it deserves to be a camp classic. The story concerns the conflict between a group of raptors (half-human, half-reptile) bent on dominating the world by addicting humankind to a nasty drug called Happiness, and the humans who try to stop them. The allegory is simplistic and transparent; 1997 when Hong Kong returns to China is also when the raptors are most likely to invade. The most obvious stylistic feature of the film is the blatant way in which it plagiarises and adapts scenes from Hollywood blockbusters. For example, the raptors are a more crude and gothic version of the cyborgs in *Bladerunner* and *Terminator*. Windy, the raptor heroine, is an obvious copy of Rachel, the cyborg heroine of *Bladerunner*. The ending comes straight out of another blockbuster, *Casablanca*. The hero sends the heroine away to safety with the head raptor who loves her, while he walks away in classic Hollywood fashion with the police inspector. The climactic scene with the 747 jet-liner pitted against the China Bank Building (at the time, the tallest building in Hong Kong) reminds us more than a little of *King Kong*. What, we might ask, makes this fantasia constructed out of clichés worth a second look?

One answer, as I suggested earlier, is that the pot-boiler, exactly because it is not bound by the need for consistency or 'good form', can reveal more directly its own fears and desires about the nation. This is the value of what Siegfried Kracauer called 'the mass ornament': 'No matter how low one gauges the value of the mass ornament, its degree of reality is still higher than that of artistic productions which cultivate outdated noble sentiments in obsolete form' (Kracauer 1995: 79). This warns us against being too dismissive of *Wicked City*, in spite of its crudities. It opens up the possibility that the plagiarising style of the film comes less from lack of originality than from a sense that the Hong Kong 'national' cinema can draw on the themes and materials of international cinema as its own. In other words, what we are seeing here is a more or less conscious breaking down of boundaries between the national and the international, just as in the film's sci-fi plot the boundaries between human, animal and machine keep breaking down, as one transforms into the other. To put the argument in the most general terms: what lies behind the clichés is an endorsement of what advocates of globalisation call 'a borderless world'. This is also the view that sustains *Wicked City*, especially if we remember its fascination with technology and machinery which are the pre-conditions of such a world. This vision of a borderless world ameliorates the anxiety of national re-inscription conjured up by the allegory of raptor invasion. *Wicked City*, in spite of its title, is not a pessimistic film.

At the other end of the spectrum from *Wicked City* is Wong Kar-wai's second film, *Days of Being Wild* (1990), arguably the single most important film of the new Hong Kong cinema. Unlike *Wicked City*, political allegory is noticeably absent from Wong's film. Not only is allegory avoided, it is also voided, as the film focuses exclusively on patterns of affective relations. Nevertheless, it is in the way that affective relations are presented – as skewed and enigmatic – that the Hong Kong political situation and the problematics of the fragment as nation can be shown to have left their traces. We find again and again, in every Wong Kar-wai film since *Days of Being Wild*, a curious pattern of connection and disconnection. There seems to be some kind of invisible barrier between people, and affective relations characteristically take the form of proximity without reciprocity. Lovers are close but apart, at once connected and disconnected. Even the space of intimacy is not intimate, as something always seems to stand in the way of reciprocity: something like a serial structure of repetition that imposes itself. Thus we find: A loves B but B loves C, and C has a previous commitment to D so cannot reciprocate, and so on and on. It is as if we were seeing an inhuman algebra of love at work. The ciphers can acquire names and faces. Thus in *Days of Being Wild*, the policeman loves Su Lizhen, who loves Yuddy, the main character, who is obsessed with finding his biological mother. In another series, Yuddy's friend, nicknamed 'Fly', loves Mimi, the dance-hall hostess, who loves Yuddy, who has his mind on other things. Most of the film is taken up with permutating the sets of possible relations among these main characters; but in the end, it is the serial structure that dominates and disconnects the characters. It is almost as if Wong's film were constructed to exemplify the famous Lacanian formula, 'there is no sexual relationship': a formula that has to be understood not literally, but in the sense that there is in love no symmetry or reciprocity, because the object of desire is always a partial-object of fantasy.[1]

Every series seems to lead to and end with Yuddy, apparently the one self-sufficient and narcissistic figure in a world of the emotionally needy. But, as becomes only too clear, Yuddy is the most needy and dependent of all: an abandoned child raised by a foster mother who has supported him financially all his life, a man obsessed with knowing the identity of his biological mother. When he finally locates her in the Philippines, she refuses to see him. The series, then, has no stable centre, just as Yuddy's image of himself is highly ambiguous. He identifies with the image of the legless bird that cannot stand still but must keep flying to survive. For Yuddy, the legless bird is primarily an image of movement, freedom and autonomy, but it is just as clearly an image of castration, lack and dependency. At this point, we begin to see how Wong's portrayal of affective relations re-introduces, strictly on its own terms, the double-bind of autonomy and dependence that arises when we think about the fragment as nation.

If there is neither reciprocity nor a stable centre in affective relations, the inevitable outcome, it seems, would have to be disappointment. Wong's film is full of images of disappointment. Take the meeting between Yuddy and Lizhen at the beginning of the film. The meeting took place at one minute to three in the afternoon of 16 April 1960. This public minute that recurs every day becomes a special moment in the lovers' private time, like a daily appointment with the origin of desire. But in Wong's film all appointments are disappointments. Passion passes elsewhere and private time is swallowed up once again and becomes indistinguishable from public time, no matter how wilfully the lovers themselves try not to forget. Thus the affective series goes on in a regular alternation of desire and disappointment – until it reaches a point where the series reverses itself. At this point, we no longer find a banal and predictable pattern of desire followed by disappointment, but something more paradoxical: a pattern of desire generated by disappointment. Disappointment itself becomes a source and resource of the erotic: an erotics of disappointment. Such an erotics, though implicit in *Days of Being Wild* (as we saw, the disappointing Yuddy is also the object of fantasy), is much more rigorously worked out in later films like *In the Mood for Love* and *2046* which are almost like sequels, or better still, part of an ongoing series. For example, in *In the Mood for Love* we again meet Su Lizhen, still played by Maggie Cheung. She is now married and her husband is having an affair, while Lizhen herself is attracted to the character played by Tony Leung, whose wife is also having an affair. The relation that develops between Maggie and Tony is based on the impossible premise that they do not want to be like their adulterous spouses. The result is that what brings them together ('we do not want to be like them') is also what keeps them apart. Unlike affairs that end in disappointment, this is an affair that begins in disappointment. However, it should be noted that such relationships cannot be understood simply as the result of affective aberrations or perverse personal choices. It takes only a small step to go from an erotics to a politics of disappointment, and to see that this strange mood of love finds a resonance in the mood of a politics where the autonomy of the nation is constituted not through the overcoming of dependency but through learning how to enjoy it, just as *jouissance* in Wong's films is achieved not by overcoming but by traversing disappointment.

Another kind of politics is presented in one of the great successes of post-1997 Hong Kong cinema, Alan Mak and Andrew Lau's trilogy, *Infernal Affairs*: the politics of information and disinformation, of secrecy and confusion; a politics that neither large nor small nations today can ignore. I will restrict the discussion to Part One of the trilogy, released in 2002.

The story concerns the contrasting responses of two secret agents or informers to the space of information. Tony Leung plays the police agent Chan who infiltrates the triads, while Andy Lau plays the triad agent Lau who infiltrates the police. As secret agents, both Chan and Lau live under aliases – that is, pieces of information about personal identity; but they inhabit their aliases and relate to information in different ways. Chan wants to hold on stubbornly to the belief that affect and identity are not just bits of information. He wants to maintain that his alias is false, and that his true identity is that he is a cop; but the only proof of this is in a secret computer file in the police department (that is, in information) that Lau hacks into and deletes. This belief in a reality and a personal identity beyond information makes Chan capable of friendship, fidelity and love; for example, we see him develop a genuine camaraderie with some of the triad gang members. But it also introduces the moral issues of divided loyalties and the betrayal of friends. In a final attempt to prove his identity, he forces a meeting with Lau – and gets shot in the head.

In contrast to Chan, Lau only acknowledges the truth of information, however arbitrary. He brackets identity, lives in his alias and would kill to preserve it. Eventually, he even kills the triad boss he works for, the only person who knows his identity. Murder is the deleting of information; there is nothing personal to it. The kinds of moral and affective concern still so important for Chan, like love and fidelity, have all but disappeared, and with them all sense of moral ambiguity. Hence he can act with resolution, because resolution has now been transcoded into a mere technological concept, resolution as the degree of pixelation on a TV screen. Significantly, Lau's one outside interest is in hi-fi equipment, suggesting that the only fidelity that counts is high fidelity. The film ends with him killing Chan and another officer who witnessed the killing, and when the police arrive, he shows his ID card and declares: 'I am a cop.' Information as identity allows him to get away with murder. This ending is a scandalous one for the commercial cinema, and the directors Mak and Lau have provided an alternative ending where Lau is arrested by the police. Yet it is this first ending that carries the logic of information, because it indicates what a dystopic future might look like: not a hell situated in an afterlife where sinners are tortured by fire, but a hell situated in this life, where things just go on, a cool hell or 'air-conditioned nightmare' where information is processed.

The omnipresence of information produces what might be called the info-nation, a state of things that many may find easier to accept and live with than the precarious position of the absent presence of the nation. The danger, though, is that the info-nation subsumes everything under the requirements of its own logic, and threatens to colonise even the past by turning our memories into statistics and bits of information. Hence the need among small nations and hyphenations like Hong Kong for a politics of memory. This seems to me to be the main interest of the last film I want to discuss, Fruit Chan's *Made in Hong Kong*, released in the crucial year 1997.

At one level, the film tells the story of delinquents and abandoned children who live in Hong Kong's housing estates. There is Autumn Moon, the narrator, whose father has deserted him; his friend, the half-wit orphan Sylvester; Ping, the girl with a terminal disease with whom Moon falls in love; and finally Susan, the student who commits suicide out of unrequited love. These pathetic characters are not so much made as unmade in Hong Kong. What makes the film more than a naturalistic story of the determinism of environment is an important structural twist near the end; we find that after Moon the narrator has shot himself in the head, the narration continues as before. This suggests that the whole story, which up to this point we have assumed is unfolding in the present, has from the very beginning been a posthumous narration; events that seem to be taking place in the present have to be understood as already past. This doubling of the narration – a 'live' narration which is also point for point a memory – unsettles what appears at first to be the deterministic dead-end space with no exits of *Made in Hong Kong*. It disconnects the brutal and specific *facts* of the world that the characters are forced to recall on a daily basis ('that's what life in the housing estates is like and don't you forget it') from the *memory* of something no more definite than a 'promise of happiness': a ghostly promise whose terms are not understood, but which nevertheless remains to haunt those who can hear it.

This 'promise' is paradoxically embodied in the dead girl Susan, whom the three friends have never met. Her story is not a happy one, yet the rare moments of happiness and camaraderie in the film are all associated with her, like the scene in the hills of Hong Kong where they visit her grave. They decide to fulfil her final wish and deliver her suicide letter to her parents. When the letter is opened, it is found to contain additional comments in the margins from both Ping and Moon. The letter, with its parerga, becomes not just a letter addressed to Susan's parents but a kind of joint letter from abandoned children who become delinquent, to delinquent parents who run away to give themselves the second chance that their children never get. 'For the young,' Moon says in the language of filmmaking, 'there is no "take two".' However, it is ultimately not a question of juvenile delinquency or adult delinquency, but a question of delinquencies of memory. Susan's parents show no indication of understanding the joint letter, which becomes, in all senses of the phrase, a dead letter. This scene is followed by a broadcast over the radio of an old speech by Mao to the youth of China, telling them that the world belongs to the young. 'Mao' stands not just for a particular political system but for all the parents and politicians who say one thing and do another: delinquents of memory bequeathing us 'a receipt for deceit'. On the other hand, there is Moon and his group of ill-fated friends, who in the face of deaths and frustrations nevertheless hold on to some memory of other possible ways of life 'made in Hong Kong'. In a last posthumous voice-over, Moon tells us that there is one thing he knows: that Ping, Sylvester, Susan and himself are now happy.

As even such a brief discussion shows, the lesson of the Hong Kong cinema for an understanding of national cinemas big and small lies in the fact that it cannot be a national cinema. It is a cinema that emerged out of the impossibility of a nation-state: specifically, of nationhood understood as a search for independence, and for autonomy as its corollary. What we find in the Hong Kong case, both before and after 1997, is the paradox of autonomy without independence, where nationalism is bracketed by colonialism on one side and by globalisation on the other; hence the need, among other things, for a politics of memory. On the other hand, the Hong Kong cinema can cast a cold and critical eye on the aspirations typically associated with nationhood – precisely because they make no sense in a Hong Kong context. It can show us that the idea of a nation is not unlike the psychoanalytic notion of the subject; both threaten to dissolve and disappear when we come too close to them (aphanisis), though neither absolutely vanishes without a trace. What the Hong Kong cinema stages is such a disappearance of the nation at a moment when nationhood is everywhere vigorously asserted; and nationhood is asserted especially at moments of crisis – witness the surge of American patriotism after the 9/11 attacks. What we are seeing today, then, in spite of all the talk about a 'borderless world', is not so much nationhood in crisis as nationhood as a response to crisis; and emerging from the maelstrom is the idea of the nation as a unified and inviolable entity, to be defended at all costs. Given such an explosive scenario, the indefensibility of nationhood in Hong Kong does not look so negative after all. At least, it encourages us to look for possibilities elsewhere, one example of which is the new Hong Kong cinema itself; not capable of being a national cinema, it becomes a cinema of the fragment as nation.

NOTE

1. A concise discussion of Lacan's formula can be found in Evans 1996.

WORKS CITED

Benjamin, Walter. 1978. 'Surrealism'. In Peter Demetz (ed.), *Reflections: Essays, Aphorisms and Autobiographical Writings*, trans. Edmund Jephcott. New York: Harcourt Brace Jovanovich. pp. 177–92.

Borges, Jorge Luis. 1998. *Collected Fictions: Jorge Luis Borges*, trans. Andrew Hurley. New York: Viking.

Dabashi, Hamid (ed.). 2006. *Dreams of a Nation: On Palestinian Cinema*. London: Verso.

Evans, Dylan. 1996. *An Introductory Dictionary of Lacanian Psychoanalysis*. London: Routledge. pp. 181–2.

Kracauer, Siegfried. 1995. *The Mass Ornament*, trans. Thomas Y. Levin. Cambridge, MA: Harvard University Press.

7. SINGAPORE

See Kam Tan and Jeremy Fernando

[T]he idea of 'national cinema' has given way to 'transnational film studies' . . . [I]nstead of following the rush to abandon the national altogether, we [ask] what happens to the national in transnational film studies. We [call] for the final abandonment of the old national cinemas model, which assumed nation-states were stable and coherent and that films [of a particular nation-state] expressed singular national identity. (Berry and Farquhar 2006: 195)

INTRODUCTION: CONFLICTING NATIONALISMS

Singapore on screen testifies to the fact that this small nation has both benefited from, and paid the price for, its historical position as the premier port in South East Asia. As the gateway between 'east' and 'west' and even 'north' and 'south', the city-state has long been territory to and for the global traffic in people, ideas, images, cultures and capital, including film. Singapore cinema thus has simultaneously local, national and transnational dimensions, similar to the country's multiracial, multicultural, multi-religious and multi-linguistic environments. The inherent contradictions result in considerable complexity. In this chapter we limit our discussion to Singapore cinema of the last two decades or so, a period that coincides with this cinema's revitalisation.

One key ideological tendency informing new Singapore cinema is a form of cultural nationalism that strives to be locally attached. It characteristically yields content about, as film scholar Tom O'Regan has observed in a different context, 'the local people-among-themselves framing their histories, their stories, their lifeways, their locations' – content that carries auras of cultural resonance and national distinction (O'Regan 2002: 139, 155–6). Alongside and in tension with cultural nationalism is a second tendency: technocratic nationalism, which rests on the official notion that Singapore is first and foremost a globally connected market place of ideas and commodities. In this regard, Singapore's legacy as an entrepot port is crucial, and consequently, conceptions of film as merchandise for transnational transaction become dominant, while questions of culture, or of cinema as having cultural currency, have taken a back seat. However seemingly opposed, these two kinds of nationalism are not always mutually exclusive. Technocrat nationalists have as much of a vested interest in the nation's self-image as cultural nationalists; both are concerned with the matter of national specificity in Singaporean films. The key thing to note is that they differ starkly in terms of approaches, perspectives and emphases.

In his 1999 National Day Rally speech former Prime Minister Goh Chok Tong (1999–2004) identified two types of Singaporeans, which correspond to the two forms of nationalism identified above (Goh 1999, accessed 1 January 2003). For Goh, one type was essentially cosmopolitan, encompassing Singaporeans who 'speak English but are bilingual',[1] and 'have skills that command good incomes – banking, IT, engineering, science and technology'. They also 'produce goods and services for the global market', 'use Singapore as a base to operate in the region', and finally 'can work and be comfortable anywhere in the world'. In short, they are the elites. Goh's other type, the 'heartlanders', were by contrast less adaptable and high-flying, making their living primarily in the country:

> Their orientation and interests are local rather than international. Their skills are not marketable beyond Singapore. They speak Singlish. They include taxi-drivers, stallholders, provision shop owners, production workers and contractors . . . If they emigrate to America, they will probably settle in Chinatown, open a Chinese restaurant and call it 'eating house'. (ibid.)

The binary logic informing Goh's privileging of the cosmopolitan over the heartlander reflects institutionalised social divisions along the lines of class, language, education and occupation in contemporary Singaporean society. This elitist bias towards the cosmopolitan, as the chief purveyor of the country's national and cultural identities, lies at the core of technocratic nationalism: 'Singapore is Singapore only because our national spirit is a cosmopolitan one,' as George Yeo, Goh's Minister of Information and the Arts (1991–9), once famously pronounced (Yeo; cited in Kong 2000: 415–16). This technocratic nationalist cosmopolitanism has indeed been a major guiding force for the Goh Government's push to transform Singapore into a regional/international hub for commerce and the arts since the early 1990s, and remains evident in the corresponding efforts by Lee Hsien Loong's successor government (2004–) to remake the island-state into a 'global city of the arts' (Lee 2005; accessed 1 July 2006).

The third tendency is what we would like to call 'ambivalent nationalism'; new Singapore films displaying this tendency involve local participation, whether on- or off-camera, but require no significant local knowledge or engagement. Some are fictional films and *The Song of the Stork/Vu Khuc Con Co* (2001), a Singapore–Vietnam co-production about the impact of the Vietnam War on Vietnamese society, with Singapore national Jonathan Foo as director, and *Miss Wonton* (2001), a US production featuring Singapore national Meng Ong as director, would be representative examples. Others include documentaries such as Gough Lewis's *Sex: The Annabel Chong Story* (1999) and Evans Chan's *Sorceress of the New Piano* (2004). The former focuses on the titular personality, a Singaporean university student in Los Angeles, who becomes a notorious porn star, while the latter is about Margaret Leng Tan, a Singaporean avant-garde musician based in New York.

THE PARABLE OF *MONEY NO ENOUGH* AND *FOREVER FEVER*

In 1998, in spite of the Asian financial crises that unsettled much of East and South East Asia, euphoria descended on Singapore's struggling filmmaking community when two independent films, Jack Neo's *Money No Enough* and Glen Goei's *Forever Fever*, made local film history. The first, a biting satire about money-obsessed Singaporeans starring TV comedian Jack Neo (and his team), became the country's top-grossing local film of all time, earning S$5.84 million (US$3.60 million) at the box-office.[2] *Forever Fever*, on the other hand, became the first local film to break into the international film scene. Miramax bought it for distribution in the United States, Canada and Britain, releasing it under the new title of *That's the Way I Like It*, while other global film distributors released it in Europe, Australia, New Zealand, Japan and elsewhere. The film reportedly earned S$4.5 million (US$2.78 million) in world-wide distribution rights alone.

Despite being a phenomenal hit at home, *Money No Enough* was less successful in finding an audience abroad. This is perhaps not surprising since the film, considered by some locals as 'a very true-blue Singaporean movie' (www.imdb.com, accessed 1 July 2006), requires a significantly higher level of specific local knowledge on the part of the audience. Therefore, if *Money No Enough* strongly corresponds to cultural nationalism, the allure of global cosmopolitanism that endeared *Forever Fever* to a wider audience outside Singapore locates this film somewhere between cultural and ambivalent nationalism, while its global success as a film commodity would fit with the agenda of technocratic nationalism.

Set in the late 1970s, *Forever Fever/That's the Way I like It* straddles the local and global simultaneously. It was written and directed by Glen Goei, a theatre figure with international credentials, while its cinematographer, Brian Breheny (whose credits include *The Adventures of Priscilla, Queen of the Desert*) was recruited in Australia, where sound-mixing for the film was also done. The central protagonist Hock (played by Adrian Pang) is a grocery clerk; he both indexes and personifies the film's affinity vis-à-vis transnational pop-capital of the 1970s and, by extension, the country's connectivity with the transnational economy of the global popular. An avid fan of Bruce Lee, Hock becomes enchanted by a John Travolta look-alike screen character from John Badham's *Saturday Night Fever* (1977), who appears in the film-within-the-film, also called *Forever Fever*. He then starts to kung-fu-groove to the disco music of the Bee Gees and others, and goes on to win the dance competition at a popular discotheque. Thus the local boy becomes a transnational and transcultural mimic by association with the global popular, helping to enhance the film's transnational appeal (Berry and Farquhar 2006: 212–22). Made on a budget of S$1.2 million (US$0.75 million), nearly twice the production cost of *Money No Enough*, it however earned only about S$0.8 million (US$0.5 million) at the domestic box-office, a mere 13 per cent of what the latter generated.

Like *Forever Fever*, *Money No Enough* also features the theme of the triumphant underdog; the film's three protagonists – an office worker, a building contractor and a coffee-stall assistant – all become successful entrepreneurs. Directed and scripted by local TV celebrity Jack Neo (who also stars in the film), it has a noticeably stronger local flavour and focus than *Forever Fever*, being set in the HDB heartland where the vast majority of working-class Singaporeans reside.[3] The film narrates the problems and pains of these average everyday people, within familial and brotherhood-friendship contexts, and celebrates their triumphs. Most distinctively, it employs highly localised humour, mostly of the 'Ah Beng and Ah Lian' type, making it a vehicle for parodic self-referencing in a more sustained way than *Forever Fever*. In Singapore, 'Ah Beng' and his female counterpart, 'Ah Lian', are caricatures of shallow, superficial, materialistic and anti-intellectual urban Chinese–Singaporeans. They strive hard to be trendy or in step with the whims of (transnational) fads and fashions, but from the point of view of the cosmopolitan, they ultimately fail to make the grade, or worse, are embarrassing testimonies of 'good taste' gone horribly wrong. In terms of appearance and mannerisms, they often seem oafish and loud, even – as the monikers 'Ah Beng' and 'Ah Lian' so readily conjure up – hickish. When it comes to music and other pop-culture matter, they generally have a distinct preference for 'things' associated with the Chinese–Singapore, Taiwan and Hong Kong pop scenes.

Money No Enough also displays a richer sociolect smorgasbord, from standard English or Mandarin to Singlish – a homegrown language that Singapore officialdom has consistently dismissed and vilified as the tongue of the uneducated and the uncultured, and accordingly sought to eradicate, along with Chinese dialects such as Hokkein which also features in the film. This, together with humour of the 'Ah Beng' and 'Ah Lian' kind, imbues *Money No Enough* with a significantly stronger sense of national specificity of the culturalist kind. Although celebrated at home, such local idiosyncrasies had the effect of limiting *Money No Enough*'s circulation abroad.

While marking the locations and dislocations of the local-global continuum, *Money No Enough* and *Forever Fever* hastened the 'revival' of contemporary Singapore cinema in the late 1990s. For a time, their combined success generated much local media-hype, engendering a brief flurry of investor interest that resulted in a record number of eight new feature films the following year. The 'revival' can be attributed to various factors (cf. Uhde and Uhde 2000: 59–80 and Toh 2001): the growing call from cultural nationalists for government support for the local art scene, including filmmaking; initiatives of private individuals like Eric Khoo of Zhao Wei Films; and the novelty factor of local film productions including those attracting the attention of international film festivals such as Khoo's *Mee Pok Man* (1995) and *12 Storey/Shi Er Lou* (1997). Films that manifested a high degree of local specificity in casting, characters, stories and situations, such as Khoo's films, Ong Keng Sen's *Army Daze* (1996) and Philip Lim's *Teenage Textbook* (1997), generally found modest local box-office success. Films featuring little local participation, however, mostly bombed at the local box-office. Examples include *Bugis Street/Yao Jie Huanghou* (Yon Yan, 1996), a Singapore-Hong Kong co-production about transvestite sex-workers in late colonial Singapore; *Tiger's Whip* (Victor Khoo, 1998), a locally funded comedy about an American who comes to town in search of a magic cure for his shrinking manhood; and finally *Medium Rare* (Stan Barrett and Arthur Smith, 1991) and *God or Dog/Dabayao Shatongan* (Hugo Ng, 1997), both loosely based on real-life occultist Adrian Lim and his murderous crimes. It would seem that local audiences generally stayed away from films that sought to eroticise, exoticise or demonise Singapore.

The 'revival' coincided with the government's efforts to boost the country's service sectors from the late 1980s onwards, which led to the establishment of the Ministry of Information and the Arts (MITA; later renamed Ministry of Information, Communication and the Arts in 1999 and taking the acronym of MICA in 2004), as the chief architect of arts-related policies. In the area of cinema and mass media, MITA/MICA has continuously maintained the push for Singapore to become an Asian cine-hub, with state-of-the-art production and post-production facilities. In the wake of MITA, tertiary institutions started to offer media-related programmes for the first time, including film, video and TV studies. An age-based film classification system was formulated and put into place,[4] allowing for more product variety, which in turn led to the mushrooming of cineplexes throughout the island with Golden Village (jointly owned by Hong Kong's Golden Harvest, Australia's Village Roadshow Entertainment) and local film distributors and exhibitors such as the Shaw Organisation, Cathay Organisation and Eng Wah Organisation the main players. Meanwhile the government's 'pioneer status' tax-break attracted film and media entrepreneurs seeking production opportunities, co-production deals and post-production facilities (Birch 1996: 185–211; Uhde and Uhde 2000: 59–80; Teh 1993a, 1993b, 1993c; Kerk 1994a, 1994b; Lum 1994; Wee 1996; Toh 1996). With the impending handover of Hong Kong to China in 1997, the authorities additionally looked forward to catching the 'flight' of filmmaking capital from Britain's last colonial outpost in the Far East, including key film talent and production personnel (Khoo; cited Marchetti 2006: 152). As Yvonne Ng sardonically puts it, 'The authorities, ever pragmatic, decided there was economic value in artistic activity [including filmmaking]' (www.kinema.uwaterloo.ca, accessed 1 July 2006). The centrality of state technocrats' economic agendas as such has led Lily Kong to coin the term 'cultural economic policies', as a way of highlighting the economic imperatives in the state's cultural policies for 'the arts' (Kong 2000: 413ff).

Raintree Pictures and Singapore's Technocratic Universe

We seek to be a global city . . . [that is] lively, vibrant, and fun to live and work in . . . We want Singapore to have the X-factor – that buzz that you get in London, Paris or New York . . . [I]f we become a backwater, just one of many ordinary cities in Asia, instead of being a cosmopolitan hub of the region, then many good jobs will be lost, and all Singaporeans will suffer. We cannot afford that. (Lee 2005, accessed 1 July 2006)

Founded in 1998, in the midst of the Asian financial crises, Raintree Pictures (also known as Mediacorp Raintree Pictures) marks a culminating point of public initiatives with respect to contemporary Singapore filmmaking, as would the Singapore Film Commission (SFC), also established in the same year. These and subsequent developments, such as MITA's *Renaissance City Report* (2000) and the Media Development Authority (MDA)'s *Media 21 Report* (2003), are in tandem with the government's push to develop Singapore as a regional cinehub in the global market place.

Raintree Pictures is the filmmaking arm of the state-controlled national broadcaster, the Media Corporation of Singapore (MediaCorp). It is now the country's foremost film studio, accounting for about 34 per cent of the nation's total output since 1991, the year *Medium Rare* – the first 'revival' film – hit the screens. The studio is the biggest recipient of state funding for filmmaking. At the local box-office, Raintree retains 60 per cent of receipts, giving it a position that other local production houses can only wish for (Ong 2005). The studio's output covers the range of genres including comedies, thrillers, horror films, social drama and others and to date its corpus comprises eleven 'local' and eight 'regional' productions, with one 'transregional' one, and more are churning in the pipeline. The last, an action-thriller called *One Last Dance*, involves a trans-Pacific passage, featuring Max Makowski (US) as director and starring Francis Ng (Hong Kong), Ti Lung (Hong Kong), Vivian Hsu (Taiwan) and Harvey Keitel (US). Of its productions so far, only *The Eye/Gui Yan* (2002), a horror flick, has come close to making a mark in the global market place. This Singapore-Hong Kong co-production was partly financed by Raintree Pictures. *The Eye* features low local involvement. It was shot mainly in Thailand and Hong Kong where the story-line unfolds; it is directed by Hong Kong directors, Oxide and Danny Pang, and stars Angelica Chan of Taiwan, with local actors all cast in minor roles. These factors notwithstanding, *The Eye* none the less fits with Raintree Pictures' strategy to produce 'borderless films for the international viewer', featuring 'the right mix of local and regional talents' that can 'travel beyond Asia' (Corporate Profile, accessed 1 January 2005).

Raintree's 'local' film paradigm displays the highest level of local participation. Its 'local' films predominantly and typically draw on talent and resources from the Singaporean filmmaking community, including the national broadcaster TCS[5] with which it is affiliated. As a result, they feature a preponderance of local personnel and talent, in front of and behind the camera. Directed and written by local talent, the films are almost invariably shot in Singapore, and if not, frame their story within a Singaporean context. Finally, Raintree Pictures commonly seeks out a local producer as collaborator and, in this regard, J Team Productions has been Raintree Pictures' most preferred co-producer, collaborating on *I Not Stupid I & II /Hai Zi Bu Ben 1 & 2* (2002, 2006), *Homerun/Pao Ba Hai Zi* (2003), *The Best Bet/Hu Ran Fa Cai* (2003) and *I Do I Do/Ai Dou Ai Dou* (2005). All of these films are scripted, directed by and star Jack Neo of *Money No Enough* fame, who frequently works in TCS's Chinese variety shows and now owns J Team Productions.

With regard to their 'regional' film paradigm, Raintree Pictures typically co-produces and co-finances projects with Hong Kong production houses such as Applause Pictures (for example, *The Eye*), Media Asia (*Infernal Affairs II/Wu Jian Dao 2*, 2003) and Milkyway Image (*Turn Left Turn Right/Xiang Zuo Zou Xiang You Zou*, 2003, also made in conjunction with Warner Bros Asia). Invariably shot outside Singapore and written by non-Singaporeans, these films contain translocal stories set in Thailand, Hong Kong or Taiwan. They typically use Hong Kong directors such as Oxide and Danny Pang (*The Eye*), Lau Wai-Leung and Mak Siu-Fai (*Infernal Affairs II*), and Johnnie To and Wai Ka-fai (*Turn Left Turn Right*), while their casting characteristically manifests an overwhelming East Asian presence, with Singaporean actors, if cast at all, playing second fiddle to their regional counterparts.[6] Such regional collaborations have the advantage of at least one 'ready-made second market' (Nayar 2003), but the greater the translocal connections, the more muddled local and national distinctions become.

Financing varies from production to production. It would seem that Raintree Pictures usually allocates around S$1 million (US$0.58million) per local (co-)production, while the studio's stake in regional co-productions is significantly higher – for example, the investment in *AD 2000* (2000) and *Turn Left Turn Right* (2003) was S$3 million and S$3.1 million (US$1.73 and 1.79 million), or about 50 and 30 per cent of the total production cost, respectively (Ong 2005). However, the extent to which Raintree Pictures has creative control over its regional co-productions is unclear and in all probability, its influence is not significant. On the other hand, the studio seems to have a firmer hold over its local (co-)investments (ibid.).

While Daniel Yun, CEO of Raintree Pictures, believes that, as a type, local films have a useful social function in that they can 'create debate . . . debunk myths about Singaporeans, and . . . tell the truth – even when it's a little unpalatable as in [*I Not*] *Stupid*', his priority appears to lie with 'pan-Asian' films:

> I'm looking at Asia – and beyond – as a market . . . It's a blinkered point of view to think of a Singapore film only as one that's by and for Singaporeans. We [Singaporeans] have to broaden our view. I'd say a film is Singaporean if at least a quarter of the investment is from here and/or there's a meaningful involvement in front of or behind the camera. (ibid)

This type of partial participation strategy is a defining trait of Raintree Pictures' translocal co-productions. It is also in tandem with the government's position that 'Made-by-Singapore' media products need not be 'entirely made in Singapore or made for the Singapore audience only' (Lim; cited in Lee 2003).

SITES OF STRUGGLE

In the arena of contemporary Singapore cinema, the struggles between cultural and technocratic nationalism have many fronts. We will focus on three key areas with respect to Singapore's mediascape: film and politics, film and language, and film and censorship.

Politics

In technocrat nationalist Singapore, the locals have long learned that it does not pay to be on the 'wrong' side of the PAP (People's Action Party), which has ruled the country continuously since coming to power in 1965. The government has consistently, relentlessly and perennially remained hostile to all opposition.

Over the years, political opponents have variously faced harassment, been sued for defamation, been bankrupted and have even been jailed, with some having to resort to permanent self-exile. For James Gomez, this has created a climate of fear and paranoia (Gomez 2000).[7] The overwhelming majority of the population therefore avoids politics, and most filmmakers are quick to disassociate themselves from any suggestion that their work is, or can be read as, political. An example would be Eric Khoo, whose films are notorious for showing the underbelly of affluent Singapore (Tan et al. 2003). As Gina Marchetti discovered, Khoo insists that his films, rather than being political, offer 'slice[s] of life' for viewers to take 'home and try to think a bit more', if they so wish (Marchetti 2006: 153). This turn of phrase points to the location and dislocation of the political in contemporary Singaporean society.

Martyn See's attempt to make state repression visible in *Singapore Rebel* (2005) prompted an outright ban on the grounds that this short documentary breached the Films Act pertaining to party political films – a term encompassing all audio-visual formats that advance the cause of any particular political party in the country (Hussain 2005). This policy was formulated and implemented in 1998, with offenders – anyone convicted of importing, making, reproducing, exhibiting, or possessing for the purpose of distributing, party political films – risking a fine of up to S$100,000 (US$58,000) or a prison-term of up to two years. The censors considered See's film about opposition leader Dr Chee Soon Juan, biased and partisan and thus a 'party political film'. See was called in for questioning by the police, and asked to surrender his video camera and any unused footage for the documentary. But ultimately no charges were laid against him. See, on the other hand, has maintained firmly that his film is about Dr Chee the private citizen and thus non-partisan. MICA made no distinction between Chee the private citizen and Chee the leader of Singapore Democratic Party (SDP), reiterating the official rationale for the ban:

> Party political films are disallowed because they are an undesirable medium for political debate in Singapore. They can present political issues in a sensational manner, evoking emotional rather than rational reactions, without affording the opportunity for a meaningful rebuttal or explanation to audience and viewers. (Cherian George; cited in See, accessed 1 July 2006)

The controversy over See's documentary is not an isolated incident (Agence France-Presse 2005),[8] the banning of the film demonstrating the hegemony of technocrat nationalist agendas over Singapore's political life. If members of opposition parties appear to be invisible in Singapore's public sphere, this is because they have been largely denied equal access to the media, from press to broadcasting. There is no hindrance, on the other hand, for programmes featuring members of the PAP-led government, whether locally made or foreign-produced; they have been regularly passed as 'current affair' items on local TV. Members of opposition parties indeed live a precarious, albeit defiant, existence in the margins of technocratic nationalism.

Language

An analogue to this is the controversy over Singlish, which in technocrat nationalist Singapore has a lowly status akin to Chinese dialects. Former PM Goh, who spearheaded the annually held Speak Good English Movement (SGEM) in 2000, argued that Singlish is 'poor English . . . (it) reflects badly on us . . . and makes us seem less intelligent or competent' (Agence France-Presse 2000). In short, it tarnishes Singapore's national image. However, cultural nationalists support this street language precisely because it bears the irrevocable mark of local ingenuity and industry. Like English, Chinese dialects are imported languages which primarily came along with emigrants from southern China who lived or settled in the British colony of Singapore (1819–1963); they were already part of the language-scape when Singapore became an independent nation some four decades ago. Today, they are largely the tongue of the working class, including the 'Ah Bengs' and 'Ah Lians'. Singlish, on the other hand, is the product in colonial Singapore of the encounter between English and Malay (the language of the colony's indigenous population), Mandarin (standard Chinese), Chinese regional dialects and other immigrant languages, including those used by Indian settlers. Over time, creolisation occurred and Singlish stabilised as an independent English creole, a street language, which the different races then picked up 'natively'; this situation persists to the present day (Ho and Platt 1993; Platt and Weber 1980).

While never a broadcasting language, Singlish started to appear in the media-scape in the 1990s through local films like *Army Daze* and local sitcoms like *Phua Chu Kang*, perhaps taking a cue from the theatre scene where Singlish was making a comeback for young audiences. Chinese dialects, similarly officially marginalised languages, have also become part of the film revival. Though uneven, the manifestation of such languages in film, theatre and TV enthralls local audiences, especially cultural nationalists, with the allusion of a 'homely flavour' (Ha, accessed 1 July 2006). This accounts for their increased use in Singapore's popular culture in recent years. They contain the promise and delight of forbidden fruits and consuming them amounts to gestures of defiance, little acts of rebellion. Perhaps more pertinently, they speak the language of localism, a defining moment for the Singapore of the cultural nationalist imaginary.

While officially Singlish remains *lingua non grata* in the broadcast media, along with the Chinese dialects, it continues to find breathing space in local films. But obstacles continue to exist, as Colin Goh found out when he submitted his directorial debut,[9] *Talking Cock*[10] – *The Movie* (2002), for censorship clearance. This comedy about the lives of ordinary Singaporeans celebrates Singlish culture. The film censors responded with the R(A) classification at first, but upon appeal lowered it to 'NC16' which effectively excludes viewers under the age of 16. For a film that does not have a single sex scene, any violence or any other unsuitable content for the young, both classifications seem disproportionately high and may have been intended as a message to producers that the Board of Film Censors does not condone 'excessive use of Singlish' (Tan 2002).

In addition to taking a swipe at the official government stance on Singlish, Jack Neo's film *I Not Stupid* utilises subtle humour and pathos to develop a style of social commentary involving oblique criticism of official government policy and attitudes – most particularly, the elitist education system that places undue pressure on Singaporean children to achieve academically. The most damning sign indicting the system is a 12-year-old contemplating suicide after receiving a fail grade for a class paper. The film also mocks benevolent authoritarianism, with the overbearing Mrs Khoo (played by Selena Tan) as an allegory for the PAP nanny state. As Neo says in an interview, 'Just as [the] mother [character] wants to run her kids' lives, the Singaporean government has been slow to let its own children grow up' (Neo; cited in Walsh 2002).

By Singaporean standards, *I Not Stupid* is a bold film. And while it is conceivable that Singapore officialdom would have found the satire a 'little unpalatable' (Yun; cited in Nayar 2003), relief came when former PM Goh openly praised the production some six months after its release, at his National Day Rally Speech of 2002 (Goh 2002, accessed 1 January 2003). *I Not Stupid* has since spawned a TV series and a film sequel of the same name, co-produced with TCS and Raintree Pictures respectively, while Jack Neo went on to become the first cultural medallion (film) recipient in 2005. The extent to which the original film, the sequel and the TV series, or for that matter Neo's cultural medallion, are constitutive of a successful form of state co-option remains a moot point. For one thing, Jack Neo made the following clear in an interview, while promoting *I Not Stupid Too* in Hong Kong: 'I have my own philosophy, my own thinking,' he says. 'I will never stop pinpointing my problems and I will put it in a movie' (Neo; cited in Tsui 2006: 4). Moreover, if Daniel Yun's strategy with regard to the principle of 'get[ting] permission [from the authorities] afterwards' strengthens the logic of the gatekeeper for state-funded productions, and if this logic completes a process of self-regulation, then those spinoffs that *I Not Stupid* has engendered would seem to point to the presence of sustained dissent within the constraints of the nanny state's media environment (cf. Fernando 2006). Beyond the local market, government control is less certain – for example, both *I Not Stupid* and *I Not Stupid Too* have a Cantonese export version. While this fulfils the technocrats' dream of 'made-by-Singapore' media products generating export revenue, it also challenges the government's stance that media products not made in Standard English or Mandarin have little or no transnational currency. In any case, since the release of *I Not Stupid* the Ministry of Education has reportedly put a halt to the divisive streaming system for primary school students (Neo; cited, in Tsui 2006: 4).

In addition to *I Not Stupid*, Jack Neo's comedies generally have an acerbic satirical edge. They include *Money No Enough* (about money-obsessed Singaporeans), *One More Chance* (about people with criminal records and social ostracism), *The Best Bet* (about gambling addicts) and *Homerun* (about nostalgia for Singapore's lost innocence), as well as *I Not Stupid Too* (about the importance of showing mutual appreciation and kindness, offered as a building block for people bonding in school, at work and at home). Mostly co-produced with Raintree Pictures, these are all genre films sharing the moralising theme of the triumphant underdog. This happy ending that typically occurs places Neo in the realm of 'court jester' in that he seems to know where and when to draw the line for his satire, so as to give the mocked ample room to save face. The particular 'win-win' situation, together with the fact that Neo is the most bankable film and TV personality in Singapore, endears him to powerful politicians and other technocrat nationalists.

'Very Personal Films'

This official endorsement constitutes the crucial point of divergence between Neo's films and other locally engaged productions, especially those independent films that keep an unblinking critical eye on contemporary Singapore society (Tan et al. 2003; Chua and Yeo 2003). They include Eric Khoo's *Mee Pok Man* (1995), *12 Storey* (1997) and *Be With Me* (2005), and Royston Tan's *15 – The Movie/Shi Wu* (2004) and *4.30* (2006). These socially critical films have been dubbed 'very personal films' by Daniel Yun (Nayar 2003), suggesting a highly subjective and emotional perspective on the part of the filmmakers concerned. In ideological terms, this has the effect of relegating the social issues that the films frequently raise – be they about dysfunctional families, alienated individuals, disenchanted youth, street gangs, disabled people or alternative lifestyles – to the realm of personal concerns. The label thus works to 'neuter' the films' symbolic potency as social critique. (Unlike party political films, there is no legal proscription against 'very personal films'.) The neutralising capacity that the label has is a standard tool for technocrat nationalists to manage the nation's public sphere and regulate the boundaries of political participation.

As it turns out, 'very personal films' tend to travel well on international film festival circuits, occasionally winning awards. This is largely because they do not abide by the genre film format. Simultaneous with this is their character-istic attempt to break into new terrain through formal experimentation and stylistic innovation. They courageously take on risqué subject matter that main-stream commercial producers, such as Raintree Pictures and J Team Productions, would typically eschew (Tan et al. 2003; Lee 2000): for instance, necrophilia (*Mee Pok Man*), child abuse (*Mee Pok Man, 12 Storey*),[11] incest (*12 Storey*),[12] lesbianism (*12 Storey, Be With Me*),[13] bisexuality (*Be With Me*), euthanasia (*Be With Me*), real-life teenage gangsters (*15 – The Movie*), loneli-ness and boredom (*4.30*), and Singlish culture (*Talking Cock – The Movie*). This gives these films the aura of alternative filmmaking, occasionally bringing them into contact with highbrow art cinema.

Negotiating the Local and the Global

It would be premature to suggest that the most challenging examples of Singaporean cinema are made only with the international film festival circuits in mind, or that their producers are 'festival filmmaker[s]' (Berry and Farquhar 2006: 217). In Singapore, where such films make an important contribution to public discourse, the filmmakers continue to walk a thin line with regard to various forms of censorship. One recent example is provided by Royston Tan's *15 – The Movie*, a docu-drama about drug culture and real-life delinquent gangsters. This film gained notoriety, both locally and internationally, when the police labelled it 'a threat to national security' (Aglionby 2004). At first, the censors banned *15 – The Movie* and relented only after Tan agreed to make certain prescribed cuts. Even then the R(A) classification ensured that the film was unavailable for retail distribution and public broadcasting. In the mean-time, Tan ploughed his frustrations into a twelve-minute musical film entitled *Cut* (2005). Made on a minuscule budget of about S$15,000 (US$8,800) (Tan's own savings), *Cut* features a cast of 180, including the who's who of Singapore's creative community such as director Eric Khoo, actress Beatrice Chia and fashion photographer Geoff Ang. The short has a simple plot; a chance encounter between a film buff and a censorship board official in a super-market leads to a rant on films the board has cut and then a song thanking the board for 'saving the country' by making the cuts (Han 2006; Lloyd-Smith 2004; Wong 2004). Finally, the acerbic spoof highlights the perversity of the censorship system in that, unlike *15 — The Movie, Cut* has no nudity, rude language, teenage gangsters or drug scenes. Therefore Tan ensured that the film remained within the 'PG' classification as there was nothing for the censors to cut.

In contrast Eric Khoo's *Be With Me* (2005) is no spoof. It is not a 'talk-cock' film. Nor is it a party political film. Rather, it recounts the life-story of Theresa Chan, a deaf and blind woman who plays herself, interweaving her narrative with stories of fictitious characters. The film received the 'M18' classification, presumably for featuring adult themes such as lesbian and bisexual behaviour. The censors also objected to the image of two women locked in an embrace in the original publicity poster, so Khoo replaced one of the women with an androgynous-looking male, but retained the original design for overseas use. Human speech is almost superfluous in *Be With Me*. People hardly speak or talk to each other; they seem to have nothing to say, and if they do, the exchange amounts to a perfunctory word or two – for example, 'You're fired!', 'How much?' and '*Chia*!' (the Hokkein expression for the command 'Eat!'). The people in the film tend to live alone; intra-familial communication looks strained for the most part. Technology takes over from human speech as a major form of communication, and this applies to the able and disabled alike. A social worker files his reports through a computer, and when not spending time with his perennially quiet father, periodically calls him on the phone. Young schoolgirls exchange words of love in cyber chat rooms or via the SMS, while Theresa writes her autobiography on an old-fashioned typewriter. When the camera is not trained on the typewriter, excerpts of Theresa's memoirs appear as (English) subtitles, sometimes functioning as segues that connect the jumps between situations or locations. She thinks and writes in (standard) English, and remembers the few Cantonese words that she learned as a child.

Be With Me received rave reviews and won numerous festival awards. For a while, it was even a possible Oscar hope (the first for Singapore) in the 'Best Foreign Film' category until the Academy of Motion Picture Arts and Sciences decided that it featured too much English to qualify. On this matter, the country's most ardent promoters of standard English, most enthusiastic supporters of globalisation and foremost advocates of a global market for contemporary Singaporean films have chosen to remain silent, turning a deaf ear and a blind eye to the Academy's unfortunate yet highly ironic decision. But the irony did not escape blogger Brian who posted a tongue-in-cheek comment in the cyber world: 'And poor Singapore', he writes, 'The country has a hard enough time already trying to settle on its official language(s) and now the Oscars come in and try to define it for them' (Brian; cited in Hendrix 2005).

NOTES

1. In the discourse of Singapore officialdom, a bilingual person is one who is fluent either in any two of the country's official languages – Mandarin, English, Malay and Indian – or in combination with internationally recognised languages such as Japanese, French and German, to the exclusion of Chinese dialects and Singlish.
2. In terms of all-time top-grossing movies, this film is third to the two Hollywood blockbusters, *Titanic* (James Cameron, USA: Paramount Pictures, 1997) and *Jurassic Park 2: The Lost World* (Steven Spielberg, USA: Universal Pictures, 1997). See, for example, 'Singapore's Top 5 Grossing Movies of All Time': http://www.sfc.org.sg/statistics/statistic_top5.shtm (accessed 3 March 2006).

3. HDB is the acronym for the Housing Development Board, the national provider of public housing.
4. Since its introduction and implementation in 1991, the classificatory system has been revised numerous times. Nowadays, it has the following five categories: 'G' (General Audience), 'PG' (Parental Guidance), 'NC16' (No Children under 16), 'M18' (Mature – for persons 18 years of age and above) and 'R21' (Restricted to persons 21 years of age and above), previously known as 'R(A)' (Restricted with Artistic Merits). Since March 2004, 'NC16' and 'M18' videos can be purchased at retail outlets, in addition to those with the 'G' or 'PG' classification. R21 videos are still banned. The term 'video' here is shorthand for all films in the video format, inclusive of VCDs and DVDs.
5. TCS is the acronym for the Television Corporation of Singapore, the television arm of Mediacorp.
6. A notable exception in this regard would be *The Truth about Sam and Jane* (Derek Yee). Co-produced by Raintree Pictures (Singapore) and Film Unlimited (Hong Kong) in 1999, it stars local TV personality Fann Wong.
7. Gomez has been disqualified from running in the General Elections once, in 2002. In 2006, he was accused of criminal intimidation of an elections official.
8. In 2001, *Vision of Persistence*, a 15-minute film about long-time opposition politician J. B. Jeyaretnam, was banned because it was deemed a party political film.
9. Colin Goh, founder of the Singaporean website, www.talkingcock.com, is a foremost proponent of Singlish culture. This website satirises current affairs and politics, while pushing for free speech in Singapore. He is also the author of the bestseller, *Coxord Singlish Dictionary*, which chronicles the comic eccentricities of Singapore's argot.
10. 'Talking cock' is a Singlish expression for idle talk or nonsensical chatter. It derives from the Hokkein expression, *kong lan jiao weh*, which transliterally means to speak (*kong*) cock (*lang jiao*) speech (*weh*), with *lan jiao* referring to the male genitalia (as in cock).
11. The theme of child abuse also appears in *The Tree/Hai Zi Shu* (Daisy Chan). Produced by Raintree Pictures in 2001, the film stars local Chinese queen of TV drama Zoe Tay. A father abuses his adopted son sexually; he is exposed and eventually arrested by the police. In *Mee Pok Man* and *12 Storey*, the abuse likewise occurs at home. It is not sexual in nature, but the abusers – a father and an adopted mother respectively – escape the law, leaving psychological trauma for the grown-up child.
12. The film portrays incest implicitly. It contains the suggestion that older brother Meng desires younger sister Trixie sexually and has raped her.
13. In *Be With Me*, this theme is overt, while it is implicit in *12 Storey*.

Works Cited

n.d. *Corporate Profile* and *Our Movies*. http://www.mediacorpraintree.com/about_us/abt_us.htm.
n.d. *I Not Stupid The Official Website*. http://www.inotstupid.com/.
n.d. *Jack Neo*. http://en.wikipedia.org/wiki/Jack_Neo.
n.d. *Qian Bu Gou Yong (Money No Enough)*, directed by Jack Neo. Singapore: Raintree Productions, 1998. http://www.imdb.com/title/tt0125468/.
n.d. 'Singapore's Top 5 Grossing Movies of All Time'. http://www.sfc.org.sg/statistics/statistic_top5.shtm.
n.d. *Zhao Wei Films*. http://www.zhaowei.com/index2.htm.
n.d. 'Singapore Action Flick to Hit America—Homegrown Movie'. *Straits Times*. http://www.mediacorpraintree.com/press/20001109b.htm.

Agence France-Presse. 2000. 'PM Goh Calls on Citizens to Do away with Singlish'. 29 April. http://www.singapore-window.org/sw00/000429af.htm.

Agence France-Presse. 2005. 'Local Film Makers Go "GaGa" in Battle to Present Alternative Singapore'. 20 June. http://singapore-window.org/sw05/050620af.htm.

Aglionby, John. 2004. 'Police Censor Fly-on-wall Tale of Gang Life: Acclaimed Film Dubbed a Threat to Singapore's National Security'. *Guardian*, 5 January. http://film.guardian.co.uk/censorship/news/0,,1116357,00.html.

Berry, Chris and Mary Farquhar. 2006. *China on Screen: Cinema and Nation*. New York: Columbia University Press.

Birch, David. 1996. 'Film and Cinema in Singapore: Cultural Policy as Control'. In Albert Moran (ed.), *Film Policy: International, National and Regional Perspectives*. London: Routledge. pp. 185–211.

Chua, Beng Huat. 2003. *Life is Not Complete Without Shopping: Consumption Culture in Singapore*. Singapore: Singapore University Press.

Chua, Beng Huat and Yeo Wei Wei. 2003. 'Cinematic Critique from the Margins and the Mainstream'. In Chua Beng Huat, *Life is Not Complete Without Shopping: Consumption Culture in Singapore*. Singapore: Singapore University Press. pp. 184ff.

Fernando, Jeremy. 2006. 'The Spectre of the National that Haunts Singapore (Cinema), Or, You Can Only See Ghosts if You are Blind'. *Border lands e-journal* Vol. 5, No. 3. http:// www.borderlandsejournal.adelaide.edu.au/vol5no3_2006/fernando_spectre.htm.

Goh, Chok Tong. 1999. *The Primer Minister National Day Rally Speech: First-World Economy, World-Class Home*. http://app.internet.gov.sg/data/sprinter/pr/archives/1999082202.htm.

Goh, Chok Tong. 2002. *Remaking Singapore – Changing Mindsets*. 18 August. http://www.gov.sg/nd/ND02.htm.

Gomez, James. 2000. *Self-Censorship: Singapore's Shame*. Singapore: Think Centre.

Ha, Kelvin. n.d. *God or Dog: Hugo Ng's Film on Adrian Lim*. http://inkpot.com/film/godordog.html.

Han, Bernice. 2006. 'Take A Big Breath, You'll Survive'. *Standard*, 27 July. http://www.thestandard.com.hk/news_print.asp?art_id=23671&sid=9022393.

Hendrix, Grady. 2005. 'Brian's Comment'. In *Kaiju Shakedown: Variety.com's Asian Film Blog*, 22 December. http://www.kaijushakedown.com/2005/12/singapore_film_.html.

Ho, Mian Lian and John Talbot Platt. 1993. *Dynamics of a Contact Continuum: Singapore English*. New York: Oxford University Press.

Hussain, Zakir. 2005. 'Film Probe: Activist Called for Interview'. *Straits Times*, 22 September.

Kerk, Corinne. 1994a. 'Reviving the Local Film'. *Business Times*, 2 April. LexisNexis™ Academic. p. 4.

Kerk, Corinne. 1994b. 'Warner Proposes $30 Million Fund Here to Finance Chinese Language Cinema'. *Straits Times*, 12 August. LexisNexis™ Academic.

Kong, Lily. 2000. 'Cultural Policy in Singapore: Negotiating Economic and Socio-Cultural Agendas'. *Geoforum* 31. pp. 409–24.

Lee, Hsien Loong. 2005. *Proposal to Develop Integrated Resort*, 18 April. http://app.sprinter.gov.sg/data/pr/2005041803.htm.

Lee, Michael. 2000. 'Dead Man Gazing: Posthumous Voyeurism in *12 Storeys*, or "Splacing" Singapore's Official and Unofficial Discourse'. *Asian Cinema*, Fall/Winter. pp. 115–24.

Lee, Samuel. 2003. 'Stepping Out'. *Straits Times*, 4 August. Life Section, LexisNexis™ Academic.

Lloyd-Smith, Jake. 2004. 'Government Film Censorship has Asia's Equivalent to Michael Moore in an Outrage'. *Houston Chronicle*, 24 July. http://www.singapore-window.org/sw04/040724hc.htm.

Lum, Magdalene. 1994. 'Why they are so Gung-ho about Movie-making'. *Straits Times*, 25 August. LexisNexis™ Academic.

Marchetti, Gina. 2006. *From Tian'anmen to Times Square: Transnational China and the Chinese Diaspora on Global Screens 1989–1997*. Philadelphia, PA: Temple University Press.

Nayar, Parvathi. 2003. 'Mr Yun-inverse'. *Business Times*, 10 May. LexisNexis™ Academic.

Ng, Yvonne. n.d. 'Singapore Cinema: In Search of Identity'. http://www.kinema.uwaterloo.ca/yvo011.htm.

Ong, Sor Fen. 2005. 'Scream King'. *Straits Times*, 22 August. Life Section. LexisNexis™ Academic.

O'Regan, Tom. 2002. 'A National Cinema'. In Graeme Turner (ed.), *The Film Cultures Reader*. London: Routledge. pp. 139–56.

Platt, John Talbot and Heidi Weber. 1980. *English in Singapore and Malaysia: Status, Features, Functions*. Kuala Lumpur: Oxford University Press.

See, Martyn. (Blog). 'No political films Please, We're Singaporeans'. http://singaporerebel.blogspot.com/.

Tan, Hwee Hwee. 2002. 'A War of Words Over "Singlish"'. *Time Asia Magazine*, 29 July. http://www.time.com/time/asia/magazine/article/0,13673,501020729-322685,00.html.

Tan, See Kam, Michael Lee and Annette Aw. 2003. 'Contemporary Singapore Filmmaking: History, Policies and Eric Khoo'. *Jump Cut 46*, Summer. http://www.ejumpcut.org/archive/jc46.2003/12storeys/index.html.

Teh, Hooi Ling. 1993a. 'Plans to Produce Two Films a Year'. *Business Times*, 6 September. LexisNexis™ Academic. p. 2.

Teh, Hooi Ling. 1993b. 'Ho Bee Makes Aggressive Thrust into Movie World'. *Business Times*, 6 September. LexisNexis™ Academic. p. 2.

Teh, Hooi Ling. 1993c. 'Japanese Film Company NDF Sets Up Unit Here'. *Business Times*, 21 September. LexisNexis™ Academic. p. 2.

Teh, Hooi Ling. 1993. 'NDF Inc Setting Up S$20 Million Fund for Film Projects'. *Business Times*, 27 September. LexisNexis™ Academic.

Toh, Hai Leong. 2001. 'Still Room to Grow, but Volatile—The Singapore Film Industry'. http://www.filmsasia.net/gpage104.html.

Toh, Han Shih. 1996. 'Films in Search of Funding'. *Straits Times*, 7 December. LexisNexis™ Academic. p. 1.

Tsui, Clarence. 2006. 'Screen Test'. *South China Morning Post*, 18 June. Review section. p. 4.

Uhde, Jan and Yvonne Ng Uhde. 2000. *Latent Images: Film in Singapore*. Oxford: Oxford University Press.

Walsh, Bryan. 2002. 'Neo is the One'. *Time Asia Magazine*, 8 April. http://www.time.com/time/asia/magazine/article/0,13673,501020408-221199,00.html.

Wee, Agnes. 1996. 'Singapore Firm in Hollywood Film Tie-up'. *Straits Times*, 22 April. LexisNexis™ Academic. p. 1.

Wong, Kim Hoh. 2004. 'New Film Makes Fun of Singapore Censors: Now the Wait is on to See if Sideswipe at Censors will be Censored'. *Straits Times*, 7 March. Posted *AsiaMedia: Media News Daily*. http://www.asiamedia.ucla.edu/article.asp?parentid=8687.

8. TAIWAN

James Udden

Of all the small national cinemas represented in this volume, Taiwan seems almost out of place. Population-wise it is by far the largest at 23 million, at least 50 per cent higher than the population of Burkina Faso, which comes in at a distant second. More importantly, in this case one has to qualify the terms 'nation' or 'national' with quotation marks. Taiwan may function, act and in many ways even thrive like a small 'nation' should, but most countries in the world do not recognise the island as an independent nation out of geopolitical obsequiousness towards its neighbouring behemoth, the People's Republic of China (PRC). (Still officially called the 'Republic of China', Taiwan from 1949 to the present day has been considered a renegade province by the PRC.) While undoubtedly the largest and most inextricable shadow cast over Taiwan itself, the PRC is not the most important shadow in the case of Taiwanese cinema. Nor is Hong Kong, no matter how long the film industry there thrived in Taiwan at the expense of Taiwanese-made films; nor is it even Hollywood despite how much it dominates Taiwanese screens today. No, the core shadow shaping Taiwan's cinematic predicament is cast by its own government, whether old or new. Decades of government policy eventually produced a cinema now almost entirely predicated on art and culture at the expense of any industry whatsoever.

How its cinema came to this has been a perennial question in Taiwan for the last two and a half decades. People in Taiwan see a fully-fledged commercial film industry as viable; the island provides ideal conditions for filmmaking with spectacular mountains, bountiful forests, beautiful coastlines, and even large plains on the western side of the island; and Taiwan has other East Asian models to draw from: Japan, Hong Kong and now South Korea have all proven that a local/regional commercial film industry can be sustained even in the face of world domination by Hollywood. Indeed, Taiwan has the economic where-withal as it is one of the most successful economies in the world, with Taiwanese business, after first fully developing the island, now pouring close to US$50 billion into the economy of mainland China. When it comes to cinema, however, private Taiwanese money historically has gone mostly to Hong Kong, and very little, relatively speaking, has been invested at home. Cinema is the one industry that missed out on Taiwan's 'Economic Miracle'. To understand this, we have to go back to 1949.

'If Hong Kong Can, Why Can't We?' The Rise and Fall of the Local Film Industry

The example of Hong Kong cinema's commercial success, often at the expense of Taiwan's film industry, seems especially to goad Taiwanese scholars and commentators. Yet given the respective history of the two film industries, this outcome should not be that surprising. Take, for example, the mass cinematic diaspora of 1949 when the Communists took over China. At that time Taiwan held few prospects for long-term stability. Even the KMT (the Nationalists, the Kuomintang, who lost the mainland to Mao and the Communists) saw the island as merely a temporary base from which they were one day to retake the mainland. Thus, only 5 per cent of the Shanghai film community moved to Taiwan in 1949, a mere fraction compared to the number who migrated to Hong Kong. Furthermore, those who did relocate to Taiwan were mostly in the Agricultural Education Film Company, a government-run studio that mainly engaged in documentary and propaganda work. They brought along a certain amount of equipment and technical personnel, but almost no creative talent (Li 1997: 106; Lu 1998: 35–7).

These conditions persisted for quite some time after 1949. For years the Taiwanese film industry seemed more like an itinerant roadshow in search of a permanent home as government oversight hampered the development of a more established and upscale film industry. The KMT government directly supervised every private film company and film organisation in Taiwan. Any head of a public organisation pertaining to cinema was invariably a member of the party. The movie industry was declared a 'special' industry, and like other 'special' sectors of the economy, the film business was squeezed for all it could yield. No country would let taxes on films exceed 30 per cent, yet in Taiwan entertainment taxes ran up to 60 per cent. Stamp taxes on film tickets were eleven times higher than those in any other industry. More importantly, customs duty on imported film equipment – all counted as 'luxury items' – exceeded that of other industries by over 50 per cent (Huang 2001: 35–6). This latter policy was to have a profound effect on the industry in the long run, most of all because it forced producers in Taiwan to cut corners with film stock, leaving only the smallest margin of error and resulting in often awkward and stilted films. Hong Kong, by comparison, suffered few constraints from its own government and this allowed a commercial cinema to thrive there early on. The KMT in Taiwan even exacerbated this situation by offering Hong Kong film producers special favours and protections aimed at currying political support (Lu 1998: 48–52).

One policy allowed Hong Kong producers to bring film stock into Taiwan duty-free. At first, this policy yielded not more Mandarin-language films made in Taiwan, but instead the first major wave of films in the Taiwanese dialect. Thanks to the duty-free imports, local producers in Taiwan could now get film stock from Hong Kong sources, even if not always legally. Suddenly twenty-one films were made in Taiwanese in 1956, and five times that many the next year. During the period 1955–59, a total of 178 Taiwanese-language films were made in Taiwan, more than three times the number made in Mandarin (Lu 1998: 79). One should not construe this as the beginning of a bona fide private industry, however. In fact, the object was not regular and sustainable studio production so much as short-term speculation and exploitation by fly-by-night operators. The numbers may be somewhat impressive, but the films for the most part were not. One of the best-known directors of these Taiwanese-language films was Xin Chi, who has over ninety films in the local dialect to his credit. According to Xin, the determining factors were the high cost of film stock and lack of time:

> The film we used for Taiwanese-language movies in those days was gen-
> erally imported, or bought on the black market. One movie required 800
> shots on average. With the high cost of film, we couldn't afford to waste
> it. Also, we were making so many movies – around 100 a year – that the
> time spent filming each was very short, about two or three days per movie.
> (Wu 2001: 87–8)

With film stock being such a precious commodity, producers used as little as possible and dumped the rest on the black market. The actual creation of films was just as often of secondary concern (Lu 1998: 80).

These Taiwanese-dialect films became a training ground for industry talent such as Li Xing (Li Hsing), who became the godfather of Taiwanese film directors from the mid-1960s onward. Nevertheless, these low-budget production practices would find echoes in the more upscale Mandarin-language production that eventually developed on the island. In particular, the need to use film stock sparingly led to overly standardised production practices such as averaging 800 shots per film. The director of the first Taiwanese-dialect film in 1956, He Jiming, even used the leader from every reel for empty transitional shots in the finished film, in the end consuming only 9500 feet of total stock with almost no outtakes (Lin 2003: 93). Over twenty years later, Hou Hsiao-hsien, working as an apprentice in the industry, would see in the Mandarin-language films similar practices such as never shooting a master shot of a scene. One director, he says, got the shooting ratio in the early 1980s to under 1.8 to 1 (Hou 2001). These persistent practices, coupled with extremely short production schedules, remained the hallmarks of the bulk of film production in Taiwan up to the 1980s.

No government policy had a more lasting impact than one that started in 1956. Hong Kong was exempted from the existing quota system, and its Mandarin-language films were classified as *guopian*. This category, which literally means 'national films', was applied to any Mandarin-language film coming from either Hong Kong or Taiwan, essentially classifying the British colony's films as a part of domestic production and giving them unlimited access to the Taiwanese market. This policy consolidated Hong Kong's domination of the Taiwanese market (Lu 1998: 76; Liang 1998: 135). This favouritism shown by the KMT government made Taiwan fair game, not only for exploitation, but eventually for obliteration by Hong Kong in the 1980s and the early 1990s. By 1993, 44 per cent of all films shown in Taiwan were from Hong Kong as opposed to only 6 per cent from Taiwan. The box-office for Hong Kong films in Taiwan was seven times that of locally made films (Huang 2003: 160–1). In short, the commercial industry in Taiwan was ill-equipped to keep pace with the continued rise of the Hong Kong film industry. Hong Kong, by contrast, benefited tremendously, not only from government policies in Taiwan itself, but also from both Taiwanese investment and the Taiwanese market, which became the single most important overseas market for the film industry in the British colony all the way up the mid-1990s, allowing it to go more upscale (Liang 1997: 152–63).

What complicates this picture is the 1960s and 1970s, when Taiwan as a 'national' cinema seemed to emerge in spite of the difficult conditions created by government policy. Until the 1960s, the Nationalist government saw cinema as nothing more than a propagandist tool of the state. Chiang Kai-shek and company were determined not to repeat the mistakes made in 1930s Shanghai when leftist influence was allowed to thrive in the film industry. Starting in 1963, however, the government now seemed to recognise that some sort of commercial cinema was worth having, a tacit admission on its part that Taiwan had become something more than a temporary base. Still, it had to be a commercial cinema that served their political interests, or at least did not violate them. In that year, a party functionary, Gong Hong (Kung Hung), was chosen as the new head of the CMPC, the main party-run studio in Taiwan. Gong's surprisingly visionary tenure lasted nine and a half years, during which time he upgraded the studio's management structures, production facilities and theatrical chains. As a result of these changes, the CMPC became one of the leaders in the Taiwanese industry. In 1963, Gong also saw a Mandarin-language film, *Our Neighbour* (*Jietou xiangwei*), directed by Li Xing, and decided to hire Li to direct a new type of Mandarin-language film he would label as 'Healthy Realism'. The films in this trend were not numerically significant, but the three most significant works – *Oyster Girl* (*Ke nu*, 1964), *Beautiful Duckling* (*Yangya renjia*, 1965) and *The Road* (*Lu*, 1967) – found box-office success on a scale no previous government-made film had achieved (Lu 1998: 113–14). More significant is that these films were focused on life in Taiwan itself (usually in a rural, agricultural setting), albeit in a fashion that reminds one of Soviet Socialist Realism, an indication of how they still served the propaganda needs of the state.

Despite all of these positive steps taken by the CMPC in Taiwan, the Hong Kong film industry was just as much responsible, if not more so, for the emergence of a more permanent commercial industry in Taiwan. In 1963, *Love Eterne* (*Liang Shanbo yu Zhu Yingtai*) was released by the Shaw Brothers studio. A Mandarin-language opera film of a type known as *huangmeidtiao* [Yellow Plum Opera], this production achieved monumental success at the time in Taiwan and has retained a cult status ever since. *Love Eterne* played for a record 186 days in Taipei and took in more than NT$8 million at the box-office, beating all existing records and giving Taipei the reputation of 'a crazy man's city' in Hong Kong (Chiao 1993: 16–18). *Love Eterne's* economic impact on Taiwan was long-lasting. It highlighted the importance of the Taiwanese market for Hong Kong. It also led many theatres in Taiwan to break their contracts with American companies and begin showing Mandarin-language films instead (Li 1997: 117). Furthermore, it jump-started a more upscale private film industry when the director of the film, Li Hanxiang, suddenly moved to Taiwan, bringing with him big plans and a throng of technical talent. With the backing of Taiwanese and Hong Kong sources, Li formed the Grand Motion Picture Company [*Guo Lian*], which upped the production standards of the Taiwanese private film industry as a whole. Soon King Hu, who is arguably the single most important Chinese-language filmmaker of his generation, was also in dispute with bosses in Hong Kong. He was enticed by Union Pictures [*Lian Bang*], a Taiwanese distributor, to make his films in Taiwan. Both *Dragon Gate Inn* (*Longmen kezhan*, 1967) and *Touch of Zen* (*Xianu*, 1970) took full advantage of the geographical diversity Taiwan provided, and arguably form the pinnacle of King Hu's entire career.

With the CMPC, Grand and Union leading the way, the number of indigenously made Mandarin-language films in Taiwan increased by twenty times over the decade of the 1960s. In 1960, only five Mandarin films were made in Taiwan. In 1964, there were twenty-two. By 1969, there were eighty-nine. (This was also the first year that the number of Mandarin films surpassed their cheaply made counterparts in the Taiwanese dialect.) By 1971, the number of Taiwanese-made Mandarin films had exceeded a hundred.

However, as impressive as these numbers seemed at the time, the negative effects of initial governmental policies towards cinema continued to have an impact. For one thing, the Taiwanese industry was well-meshed with the Hong Kong industry; finances, talent pools and political connections were all so intertwined that it is often hard to make a distinction between a truly Hong Kong film and a truly Taiwanese film during the 1960s and 1970s, especially since all of them were classified as *guopian*. Even to this day Taiwan and Hong Kong do not see eye to eye on this issue. Every history of Taiwanese cinema in Taiwan will mention the made-in-Taiwan classics of this era – *The Winter* (*Dongnuan*, 1967, Li Hanxiang), *Touch of Zen* (*Xianu*, 1970, King Hu) and *Four Moods* (*Xinuaile*, 1970, Li Hanxiang, King Hu, Li Xing and Bai Jingrui) – and speak of them as Taiwanese films. At the same time, however, Stephen Teo's history of Hong Kong cinema discusses all three films as if they were Hong Kong productions, which is the common view there (Teo 1997). *Touch of Zen*, given its special technical award at Cannes in 1975, is particularly contentious.

In retrospect, there were already signs in the 1970s of how the two industries would eventually diverge. Hong Kong made its mark with comedies and action film, mostly swordplay [*wuxia pian*] and kung fu. Taiwan made its mark elsewhere. Lu Feiyi has broken down by genre all of the feature films produced in Taiwan from 1949 to 1994. Of the 3500 titles listed, over one-third fall under the broad category of *wen yi*. Thus, *wen yi* films overshadow the number of comedies (a 'mere' 490), crime films (450 titles) and even swordplay films (368 total). (Only fifty-three films made in Taiwan have been classified as kung fu films (Lu 1998: appendix 12).) The generic term *wen yi* seems to have a broad application in Taiwan. The predominance of this category, however, does say much about standardised filmmaking in Taiwan since *wen yi* films were much cheaper to produce on average than action-oriented pictures (Lu 1998: 137, 139).

Central to the Taiwanese commercial industry was a sub-category of *wen yi* films that were known as simply 'Qiong Yao films', named after the author of the romance novels on which most of these were based. By 1983, a total of forty-nine films were based on Qiong Yao novels, and there were several clones as well (Li 1997: 150–3). Easily exportable to markets such as Singapore or Malaysia, these films are considered by many today as grotesquely escapist romantic fantasies. Brigitte Lin, a major star in Qiong Yao films before she 'defected' to Hong Kong in the 1980s, bluntly said that these films were powerful precisely because they served as necessary illusions in a time when life was hard (Lu 1998: 134). As the predominant strain of film production in Taiwan in the 1970s, they revealed an uncomfortable truth. Even in the best of times, Taiwan was in a sense the poorer cousin of the Hong Kong film industry which continued to receive better treatment overall from the avuncular KMT government.

Yet given the peculiar geopolitical conundrum faced by the Nationalist government in Taiwan, it is not surprising that its film policies from 1949 onwards were more often political than economic in nature. Eventually, however, political considerations resulted in economic duress. Starting with the loss of its seat at the United Nations in 1972, the ROC (the 'Republic of China', as Taiwan is still officially known) faced one diplomatic crisis after another, not to mention a brief economic crisis due to the oil shocks of 1973. A rash of films served either to vent the government's frustration, or to shore up its tattered image. A new head of the CMPC, Mei Changling, had steered the party-run studio on to a path of expensive film projects (Huang 1994: 176–7). Most striking was a wave of virulent anti-Japanese films that came out after Japan broke ties with the ROC in 1972, a trend best epitomised by *Victory* (*Meihua*), directed by Liu Jiachang. This film became number one at the box-office in 1975 and won Best Picture at the Golden Horse Awards (Huang 1994: 169). Later films were clearly responses to the loss of US recognition in 1979. The most notoriously expensive was *The Battle for the Republic of China* (*Xinhai shuangshi*, 1981, Ding Shanxi). This film featured hyperbolic heroism, a large number of extras, some kung-fu, and a fire at the climax that rivals the burning of Atlanta in *Gone with the Wind*. Nearly everyone saw this film in Taiwan, yet almost no one paid to see it, as free screenings were offered all over the island. As a result, even the most stable entity in the Taiwanese film industry, the CMPC, was now on the verge of bankruptcy due to policies based on political expediency and economic shortsightedness.

Statistical trends from this era would seem to indicate there was no cause for alarm, but numbers do not tell the whole story. Zhang Yingjin reports that between 1978 and 1981 the annual movie attendance rose by roughly 50 per cent, before it dropped off sharply throughout the 1980s (Zhang 2004: 241). At the same time the number of films produced in Taiwan rose to 144 in 1982 (Lu 1998: appendix 11a). Still there was already much cause for alarm. For starters, Taiwanese films were already losing their overseas markets in Malaysia and Singapore. Other pressures emerged as well. During the second half of 1980, for example, Tsui Hark, Ann Hui and others from the Hong Kong New Wave began to trounce locally made films at Taiwan's own film awards, the Golden Horse (Xiao 1990: 93). At the same time, after the long interregnum of the Cultural Revolution, the PRC was once again making films such as Xie Jin's *The Legend of Tianyuan Mountain* (1981), and showing them abroad. In July of 1980, the *Min Sheng Daily* in Taiwan expressed concern that films from the PRC were now being distributed in the same overseas markets that Taiwan was already starting to lose (*Min Sheng Daily* 1980).

Thus, it was during this time that many finally began to recognise that something was amiss. This realisation led to some profound changes for Taiwanese cinema which have lasted until this day. Nevertheless, the actual nature of these changes was not anticipated at the time. The government, and the party-run CMPC in suit, tried to devise a plan to save the floundering film industry. In this they would utterly fail. Yet what they attained instead was a new cultural beacon in cinematic form, creating what would become its most effective form of diplomacy when official channels dried up. This put Taiwan on the international cinematic map, even while its cinema was disappearing from its own screens.

The New Cinema and the Rise of Taiwanese Film Culture

As early as the 1960s, Taiwanese literature had already revealed an underlying cultural fermentation despite the oppressive political atmosphere, something most evident in the heated debate between the 'Modernists' and the 'Nativists' over whether literature should be more Westernised/modernised, or more 'native' in form (Chang 1993). On the margins of this intellectual ferment were some film journals that echoed these debates, which in retrospect showed early evidence of the potential for a film culture forming in Taiwan. In the 1960s, the journal *Theatre* [*Zhuchang*] focused on international film trends using criteria that reveal a Modernist bent. Starting in December of 1971, *Influence* [*Yingxiang*] expressed hope for artistic films that would 'grow in the local soil,' giving this journal more of a 'Nativist' flavour. To some extent these journals paved the way for the New Cinema in Taiwan, as *Cahiers du cinéma* had done for the French New Wave, except in this case the writers did not become directors later on.

Yet nothing would have come of this were it not for changes in the system itself when Taiwanese cinema would find its own version of Jacques Flaud, director of the Centre National de la Cinématographie (CNC) in France in the 1950s. James Soong was the head of the Government Information Office (GIO), which was in charge of overseeing cinema through both policy implementation and censorship. Soong recognised right away that the problem was both government officiousness and the structure of the film industry itself. He published his views in a famous open letter to the industry in June of 1981. According to Soong, the government had now loosened control in order to give producers more creative space, but the industry had not taken advantage of this. Instead, there was the usual shortsightedness that looked for quick returns at the expense of long-term investment. More importantly, the letter clearly declared that, if film was to be of artistic and cultural significance, it needed to be able to perform not just domestically, but also on the international stage (Soong 1981: 2–3). Meanwhile, the current head of the CMPC, Ming Ji, was running a studio on the verge of bankruptcy due to the production of over-priced propaganda pictures by his predecessor, already mentioned. While Ming took his cues from Soong's reformist intimations, for practical economic reasons he decided to implement a new 'low budget/low risk policy' (Xiao 1990: 99–100). Two young writers within the CMPC, Xiao Ye and Wu Nianzhen (who would eventually become leading figures in the New Cinema movement), convinced Ming Ji to allow young directors to direct for the first time. The result was the portmanteau film, *In Our Times*, a film about growing up in Taiwan helmed by four new young directors, including Edward Yang.

Released in August of 1982, *In Our Times* is often considered to mark the official birth of the Taiwanese New Cinema. This movement marked the key transition from cinema as a largely commercial enterprise to more of a cultural endeavour, one that would be a beacon of dramatic changes in Taiwanese society as a whole. Over the next five years several young directors would put out new films that displayed a restraint, a new sort of realism, and a level of artistry that Taiwanese cinema had rarely pursued before. Both the CMPC and private companies began supporting these young directors making this new sort of cinema. Hou Hsiao-hsien would become the most famous of these directors after he joined the next major portmanteau work, *The Sandwich Man*, in 1983. He followed this with noted features such as *The Boys from Fengkuei* (1984), *Summer at Grandpa's* (1984), *A Time to Live, A Time to Die* (1985) and *Dust in the Wind* (1986). Edward Yang achieved nearly equal fame with his urban trilogy of *That Day, at the Beach* (1983), *Taipei Story* (1985) and *The Terrorizers* (1986). Chen Kunhou would direct *Growing Up* (1983), the unexpected box-office success of which convinced several private producers that this New Cinema was the way to go. Soon Zhang Yi, Zeng Zhuangxiang, Ke Yizheng and Li Youning made one or two more works identified as part of the movement, yet none of them achieved long-term success; others, such as Wan Ren and Wang Tong, also made films as part of this movement, and have made several more since. Adding to the prestige of the New Cinema was the presence of several literary figures such as Huang Chunmin and Zhu Tianwen, along with Wu Nienzhen and Xiao Ye, as mentioned above. Equally important was the backing from prominent young critics such as Lin Shiqi, Peggy Chiao and Edmond Wong.

Despite all this support, and despite initial box-office success with *In Our Times*, *The Sandwich Man* and *Growing Up*, most of these films floundered in the local market. As a result of having failed in its original goal of saving the domestic commercial film industry, the movement is usually said to have ended in early 1987. Yet the New Cinema launched Taiwanese films into the international festival realm, giving them a presence that has continued to this day. Failures at home, these films were successes abroad, even though at first they were submitted to film festivals by the government more as an afterthought than as a clear-cut strategy. More importantly, for the first time Taiwanese cinema was recognised as distinctly Taiwanese, in part because many of these films used the Taiwanese dialect which had been absent from Taiwanese screens for many years.

This change was part of a larger shift in Taiwan as a whole during the 1980s, of trends that only accelerated in the 1990s. For Taiwan, the 1980s were much like the 1960s were elsewhere. Much of this new-found openness was the result of liberalisation from within by Chiang Kai-shek's son, Chiang Ching-kuo, who unlike his father recognised Taiwan as his true home. Through massive development projects in the 1970s and the inclusion of numerous Taiwanese into the KMT, Chiang opened doors to indigenisation that would never be closed again. When an opposition party often advocating Taiwanese independence (long grounds for sedition) was formed in 1986, and Chiang Ching-kuo lifted martial law in 1987, there was no turning back from the eventual democratisation that defines the island today. Moreover, Chiang's hand-picked successor after his death in 1988 was Lee Denghui, a Taiwanese-born president who pushed for Taiwanese independence from within the KMT. (Lee was ousted from the KMT in 2001 for openly siding with the current president, Chen Shui-bian, who comes from the opposition Democratic Progressive Party or DPP.)

Even in the early 1980s, the culture at large was already reflecting these changes in numerous ways, and the New Cinema was one clear indication of this. But it was in 1989, after the New Cinema was officially over, that the single most important film – indeed the single most important cultural event ever in Taiwan – appeared: Hou Hsiao-hsien's *City of Sadness*. This film managed to win the Golden Lion at the Venice Film Festival that year, an event that sent shock waves throughout the entire Chinese-language film community, even in mainland China. Never before had a top prize at a major festival been won by a Chinese-language film, making this the equivalent of when *Rashomon* won this same award back in 1951. But it was an even bigger event in Taiwan for another reason, since martial law there had been lifted only recently. This film dealt with an incident back in 1947 where the Chinese KMT government had slaughtered thousands of Taiwanese, an incident that was officially hushed up for forty years. That this film broached the subject and the government allowed it to be shown, uncut, was tantamount to an official acknowledgement of the incident. And it opened the floodgates to a more Taiwanese, as opposed to a Chinese, identity on the island in the 1990s. This film was also a vindication of the Taiwanese New Cinema. Hou Hsiao-hsien and Edward Yang were already quite well known in both Europe and Japan, having received numerous awards at lesser film festivals. Yet since they had not saved the domestic film industry as the New Cinema was intended to do, many found it convenient to blame these young directors rather than face the real problems in the film industry. *City of Sadness* was the ultimate revenge. It made over $US 2 million dollars in Taipei alone (Ye 1990: 141); some estimates say that over ten million people – roughly half the island's population – saw this film in the theatres in its first run (Current Biography 1999: 34). This is remarkable given how difficult and challenging the film is, but it shows the importance of this 1947 incident to the entire Taiwan question today, most of all whether the island should ultimately reunify with China or become independent.

Given its stupendous box-office success, some almost felt it was a revival of the film industry itself. Sober heads, however, knew that it would be a one-off success resulting strictly from being the first film to bring the 228 Incident to the screen. The industry as a whole remained essentially unchanged (Wong 1990: 4). One other thing did emerge in 1989, however: the Assistance and Guidance Grant for cinema. This grant system has formed the near-totality of Taiwanese film policy to the present day. Every year since 1989, a dozen films or fewer will receive varying amounts of money, usually barely enough to produce a low-budget film. Granted, this subsidy system has paid some political dividends; it has subsidised films that have gone on to win awards at major film festivals. It also helped jump-start the careers of both Ang Lee and Tsai Ming-liang with their debut films, *Pushing Hands* (1992) and *Rebels of a Neon God* (1992) respectively. The problem is that there continues to be almost no local investment in local films outside of this government subsidy system. Most importantly, the grant system does nothing to alter the sorry state of local distribution and exhibition, which were taken over by Hollywood in the course of the 1990s. Most of these subsidised films make hardly anything at the local box-office, as there are almost no screens set aside for them. During the first ten years the grant system was in operation, seventy-six films received government funds, and yet only three of them managed to make this grant money back at the local box-office. Roughly half of the films receiving these funds over the years have never been released, or even completed in some cases (Yang 1998: 4).

As a result, the Assistance and Guidance Grant has been a contentious issue in the local press every year. Many argue that this grant system provides neither assistance nor guidance. Some detractors (ignoring the fact that the problems began long before this system was in place) charge that the grants themselves are responsible for the sorry state of the industry itself. Others counter by saying that this film subsidy should not be seen as a way to save a film industry to begin with, a task that will require much more than what is being offered; instead they argue that these grants should only subsidise a handful of art films that can serve as cultural diplomats on the world stage. One director, He Ping, queried whether, with such small sums of money, one should use a glass of water to help a man dying of thirst or to put out a burning house (Zhou 1998: 26)? But filmmakers continue to clamour for these grants and the money is spread pretty thinly. Peggy Chiao, a renowned producer and film critic, says that the grant system is like 'distributing a bowl of rice to a group of starving beggars, which is not enough to sustain any of them' (Zhung 2001: 20).

Meanwhile, the level and viability of domestic film production have declined alarmingly. In 1990, locally made films made up only 16 per cent of all the films shown in Taiwan in that year, and pulled in just under 6 per cent of the total box-office. By 1999, a mere 3 per cent of all films distributed in Taiwan were Taiwanese in origin, and these collectively pulled in a dismally low box-office share of less than one-half of 1 percent! (Huang 2003: 160–61). Culture aside, as an industrial entity Taiwanese cinema had practically ceased to exist as the new millennium dawned.

TAIWANESE CINEMA IN THE NEW MILLENNIUM

Yet at the same time Taiwanese cinema had apparently accomplished a great deal in the 1990s. Towards the end of 1999, for example, a survey was conducted of film-related institutions all over the world, including the British Film Institute (BFI), Museum of Modern Art (MOMA), film festivals such as Cannes, and nearly every film archive in existence. Each was asked to name the top ten films from the 1990s, and the top ten performing countries in terms of cinema. It did not come as too much of a surprise that number one was France or that number two was the United States, but remarkably third place was a virtual tie between Taiwan and Iran. Moreover, a top twenty-five list based on the results of this survey revealed no less than four titles from Taiwan – one by Edward Yang, *A Brighter Summer Day*, and three others directed by Hou Hsiao-hsien, including *Flowers of Shanghai*, which came in sixth overall (Chiao 2000: 123). Meanwhile, *Crouching Tiger, Hidden Dragon* (directed by Lee) not only became the first Taiwanese film to win best foreign picture at the Oscars, it also set a record at the US box-office for a foreign-language film.

Yet all of these recent events only highlight the continuing split between Taiwanese cinema as an industrial enterprise and as a purely cultural endeavour. *Flowers of Shanghai* may have played in Paris for two months in 1998, but it barely cracked Taipei's top ten list for Chinese-language films. Worse yet, Chinese-language films overall comprise a mere 3 per cent of the total box-office in the capital city, and most of this small percentage still goes to films from Hong Kong. Edward Yang may have won the Best Director award for *Yi Yi* at Cannes in 2000, but he still has not even bothered to release the film at home. *Crouching Tiger, Hidden Dragon* seems the exception, as it did much better in the Taiwanese market than any recent films by Hou, Tsai or Yang, all of whom have tended to make art cinema fare better suited for an international festival market. However, this only confirms how thoroughly dominated Taiwan is by Hollywood today, just as it was once dominated by Hong Kong. Aside from the director, Ang Lee, and a few lesser crew members, there is little, if anything, Taiwanese about this particular film. The crew and talent were mostly from Hong Kong; the money, marketing and the distribution might were mostly from Hollywood. Local distributors at one time played a key role in allowing Hollywood to take over the Taiwanese market, but even they are now being edged out. In the year 2000, the box-office for foreign-language films, most coming from Hollywood, was fourteen times that of Chinese-language films. Hollywood distributed only 27 per cent of the total number of foreign films shown, yet they captured three-quarters of the total box-office in Taiwan (Wang 2001: 110–20). Worse still, more than half of the local box-office in Chinese-language films comes from *Crouching Tiger, Hidden Dragon*, and yet even this was directly distributed by Columbia/Tristar in Taiwan. Indeed, it shows not only how thoroughly Hollywood dominates the screens, but also the extent to which it has wiped out local distributors with whom it was once in league, to the point of now distributing Chinese-language films (Li 2002: 28–38). By 2004, in fact, Hollywood distributors were earning close to 90 per cent of the total box-office in Taiwan on their own, with no help from local distributors, since the government had eliminated the few remaining restrictions on their doing business in Taiwan (Wang 2004: 79–80). Even more alarming are the recent inroads made into exhibition by Hollywood. In 1998, the state-of-the-art Warner Village opened in eastern Taipei, at the time the single largest movie complex in all of Asia. Within half a year it was accounting for one-third of the total box-office for the entire city (Wang 1999: 63). It only gets worse; today there are Warner Villages all over the island, taking over exhibition in each locale. In short, Taiwan is now arguably the most Hollywood-dominated market in all of Asia.

While Taiwanese cinema seems to be on the verge of becoming a mere cultural artefact, the response of the Taiwanese government seems particularly puzzling, since its policies have made it possible for Hollywood to dominate as thoroughly as it does, in much the way that Hong Kong once did. In March of 2000, a dramatic regime change occurred with the presidential election, and many in the film world hoped changes were afoot. Yet the new government's film policy simply continued that of the old one; as before, the solution has been to toss some money at the problem, and mostly small change at that. One incident in particular illustrates how the Taiwanese government thinks everything can be solved by money alone, and with much less than what is actually required. Upon the international success of Zhang Yimou's *Hero* in 2003, the Prime Minister in Taiwan met with Ang Lee and asked him to make the Taiwanese equivalent to *Hero*: in this case a bio-pic about the Ming general, Koxinga, who is often considered the father of Taiwan. He offered Lee an unprecedented sum of NT$100 million, or a little over US$3 million. Ang Lee's response was that to produce something similar to *Hero* would require four times that amount, or well over US$10 million. The Prime Minister was shocked. Such a proposed budget for this one film, in fact, would have exceeded the entire amount of money put into the grant system over the last decade and a half (Tang 2003: 15). Needless to say, the project never got off the ground. Yet this plan by the current administration is revealing, for it shows how little members of the government are willing to face up to the actual economies of scale that are involved in filmmaking, or the amount of institutional support that is necessary.

More importantly, however, the government is either unable or unwilling to acknowledge how much protection cinema requires compared to other industries. Many have looked at the recent success of South Korea, which has not only protected its domestic market, but has also created a system of large-scale investment and market savvy that has appealed to audiences throughout Asia. The government in Taiwan, however, does not have the will to do any of this. This is not simply due to neglect; it is in fact a calculated, do-nothing policy based on Taiwan's peculiar geopolitical situation. Critics within Taiwan have said over and over again that the government should shelter its own media industries under the protective umbrella of the 'Cultural Exception'. Yet the government, including the new regime, has paid no attention to this argument. In 2001, Taiwan was officially admitted to the World Trade Organization (WTO) – a major diplomatic coup for a country with such uncertain international status. While a nation can join the WTO and still claim a cultural exception for cinema – and most members do that to some extent, France most significantly of all – Taiwan's only viable policy is to rely on its economic clout, and this was indeed the only reason it was even considered for admittance to the WTO. It is now clear that the government made the film industry a sacrificial lamb in order to curry the favour of the Americans during the negotiations. In order to honour these tacit agreements, the Taiwanese government soon lifted all restrictions on the number of prints per film in Taiwan (Feng 2001: 8–9). This only further aided Hollywood and its multiplexes, something that became evident when Hollywood firms inundated Taiwan with an unprecedented number of prints for *Lord of the Rings*, and then proceeded to undersell every local theatre, selling seats at prices with which the latter could not compete (Tu 2002: 30).

In short, what distinguishes Taiwan as a small national cinema is not limitations of size, population or economic clout; instead it is the direct result of government policies dating back to 1949 when the island became the last stand of the KMT. Ever since then, governments in Taiwan have had exactly the sort of cinema they deserve. Old or 'new', the government in Taiwan has never respected cinema as either an art form or even as a commercial industry. Instead they see it as a tool of the state: either for propaganda purposes or as an endless source of tax revenue. The only active way the government supports filmmaking today is the controversial grant system, yet as we have seen, this does nothing to change the structure of the market. It might seem as though the government was very film-savvy in allowing the New Cinema to thrive, but in reality this was merely a form of cultural diplomacy, much needed when most avenues of normal diplomacy had dried up by the 1980s. Even in the heyday of the Taiwanese film industry, the government nourished the industry with one hand, yet strangled it with the other, and Hong Kong reaped the benefits. That Taiwan has had such cinematic achievements with world-renowned directors is a small miracle, considering the situation, but most of these men rely on expert crew members who received their training in the commercial film industry that once existed. Today there is no real training ground for the next generation of talent. If anything is going to change, and if Taiwan is ever going to follow the path of Korea, Taiwan's government will first of all have to decide that a film industry is actually worth having at all. Sadly enough, there is little indication that this is likely to happen.

WORKS CITED

Chang, Sung-sheng Yvonne. 1993. *Modernism and the Nativist Resistance: Contemporary Chinese Fiction from Taiwan.* Durham, NC: Duke University Press.

Chiao, Peggy. 1993. *Five Years that Changed History: A Study of Kuo-lien Studio* [*Gabian lishide wunian: guolian dianying yanju*]. Taipei: Wan Xang.

Chiao, Peggy. 2000. 'When Will Taiwan Catch Up to Taiwanese Cinema?' *Tian Xia*, 1 January. p. 123.

Feng Jiansan. 2001. 'Absurdities, Surprises and Hope: Notes and Reflections on the Changes in Film Laws'. *Film Appreciation* [*Dianying Xinxiang*], Vol. 109, Fall. p. 89.

Hou Hsiao-hsien. 2001. Interview with the author, 20 June, Sinomovie Company Office, Taipei, Taiwan.

1999. 'Hou Hsiao-hsien'. *Current Biography*, Vol. 60, No. 7, July. p. 34.

Huang Ren. 1994. *Film and Government Propaganda* [*Dianying yu zhengzhi xuanchuan*]. Taipei: Wan Xiang.

Huang Ren. 2001. *The Film Era of Union* [*Lianbang dianying shidai*]. Taipei: National Film Archives.

Huang Shikai. 2003. 'A Study on the Concentration Ratio of Taiwan's Film Market in the 1990s [Jiushiniandai Taiwan dianying yingyan shichang fenxi: chanye jizhong-dude guandian]'. *Communication and Management Research* [*Chuanbo yu guanli yanjiu*], Vol. 2, No. 2. pp. 160–1.

1990. *Journal of the Beijing Film Academy* [*Beijing dianying xueyuan xuebao*], Vol. 13, Issue 2.

Li Tianzo. 1997. *Taiwanese Cinema, Society and History* [*Taiwan dianying, shehui yu lishi*]. Taipei: Ya Tai.

Li Yamei. 2002. '*Crouching Tiger, Hidden Dragon* and Misperceptions about International Co-productions'. *2002 Cinema in the Republic of China Yearbook* [*Zhunghua minguo jiushiyinian dianying nianjian, 2002*]. Taipei: National Film Archives. pp. 28–38.

Liang Hai-chiang. 1997. 'Hong Kong Cinema's "Taiwan Factor"'. In Law Kar (ed.) *Hong Kong Cinema Retrospective: Fifty Years of Electric Shadows*. Hong Kong: Urban Council of Hong Kong. pp. 152–63.

Liang Liang. 1998. *Studies on the Three Chinese Cinemas* [*Lun liangan sandi dianying*]. Taipei: Mao Lin.

Lin Zangting. 2003. *Cinematography in Taiwan 1945–1970: History and Technical Development* [*Taiwan dianying shying jishu fazhan gaishu*]. Taipei: Cultural Development Office.

Liu Chenghan. 1992. *Dianying fubpi xingji*. Taipei: Yuan Liu.

Lu Feiyi. 1998. *Taiwanese Cinema: Politics, Economics, Aesthetics (1949–1994)* [*Taiwan dianying: zhengzhi,jingji, meixue*]. Taipei: Yuanliu.

Soong, James. 1981. 'A Letter from James Soong'. *True Beauty Movie Magazine* [*Zhenshanmei dianying zazhi*], July. pp. 2–3.

Tang Zaiyang. 2003. 'Saving *Guopian* by Providing a Golden Goose'. *United Evening News* [*Lianhe wanbao*], 20 December. p. 15.

Teo, Stephen. 1997. *Hong Kong Cinema: The Extra Dimensions*. London: British Film Institute.

Tu Xiangwen. 2002. '*Lord of the Rings* Incites a War between Local and Foreign Theaters'. *Liberty Times* [*Ziyou shibao*], 17 January. p. 30.

United Daily News. 2002. 15 March. p. 27.

Wang Chinghua. 1999. 'General Situation for the Distribution of Chinese-language and Foreign Films in 1998'. In *1999 Cinema in the Republic of China Yearbook* [*Zhunghua minguo dianying nianjian, 1999*]. Taipei: National Film Archives. p. 63.

Wang Chinghua. 2001. 'General Situation for the Distribution of Chinese-language and Foreign Films in 2000'. In *2001 Cinema in the Republic of China Yearbook* [*Zhunghua minguo jiushinian dianying nianjian, 2001*]. Taipei: National Film Archives. pp. 110–20.

Wang Chinghua. 2004. 'A Summary of Film Market in 2003'. In *2004 Cinema in the Republic of China Yearbook* [*Zhunghua minguo jiushisannian dianying nianjian, 2004*]. Taipei: National Film Archives. pp. 79–80.

Wong, Edmond. 1990. 'A Look at the Future of Taiwanese Films from the Perspective of *City of Sadness*'. In *1990 Cinema in the Republic of China Yearbook* [*Zhunghua minguo dianying nianjian, 1990*]. Taipei: National Film Archives.

Wu Ling-chu (Sharon Wu). 2001. 'Director Hsin Chi and the Golden Age of Taiwanese Cinema'. *Sinorama*, February, pp. 87–8.

Xiao Ye. 1990. *The Beginning of a Movement* [*Yige yundundte kaishi*]. Taipei: Shi Bao.

Yang Yiping. 1998. 'The Interconnections between the Assistance and Guidance Grant and *Guopian*'. *Dacheng Bao*, 16 September. p. 4.

Ye Hua. 1990. 'General Situation for 1989 Distribution of *Guopian*'. In *1990 Cinema in the Republic of China Yearbook* [*Zhunghua minguo dianying nianjian, 1990*]. Taipei: National Film Archives.

Zhang Yingjin. 2004. *Chinese National Cinema*. New York: Routledge.

Zhou Wenyou. 1998. 'The Creative Film League's Argument to the GIO'. *United Daily News* [*Lianhe Bao*]. 21 July. p. 26.

Zhung Mingfei. 2001. 'Differences of Opinion on Loosening of Requirements for Assistance and Guidance Grants'. *Liberty Times* [*Ziyou shibao*], 25 September. p. 20.

9. NEW ZEALAND

Duncan Petrie

In his spoof documentary, *Forgotten Silver*, Peter Jackson uncovers the story of a lost New Zealand film pioneer called Colin McKenzie whose astonishing achievements – unacknowledged by film history – included the manufacture of a motion picture camera in 1900 at the age of 13, followed by a revolutionary sound recording system in 1908, a colour film process in 1911, and the production of a lost three-hour epic feature based on the tale of Salome and John the Baptist and shot on a huge set constructed in the New Zealand bush. *Forgotten Silver* caused a minor sensation when it was broadcast on 11 November 1995, the year of the official centenary of cinema. Many New Zealanders were all too ready to believe in this discovery of a new 'national hero', whose achievements against the odds so embodied the resilience, ingenuity and modesty that defined the national character. And when the film was subsequently revealed as a spoof, the animosity towards Jackson from some quarters was vitriolic, implying a sense of betrayal (Roscoe and Hight 1996).[1] The irony here, of course, lies in the stark discrepancy between the (fictitious) achievements of Colin McKenzie and the reality of New Zealand's marginal place in cinema history, a country that produced a mere seven theatrical features between 1940 and 1976. With *Forgotten Silver* Jackson and co-director Costa Botes create a sophisticated fantasy that simultaneously depends on the peripheral status of New Zealand while mobilising a potent myth of innate Kiwi virtue and talent. But a further ironic twist is provided by the fact that the filmmaker responsible for this counter-historical narrative, whose own unkempt demeanour and down-to-earth personality marked him out as a stereotypical New Zealander, would within a decade guarantee his country's place in cinema history.[2]

The predicament of small or peripheral cinemas in an era of globalisation would seem to be increasingly precarious, given the profoundly unequal exchange characterising the international moving image market, a market in which the dominant player, Hollywood, has doubled its share over the last fifteen years. Yet against the odds, particular small national, sub-national and diasporic cinemas have survived and even, on occasion, appeared to flourish. The reasons for this are inextricably bound up with the same complex processes of economic, political and cultural change driving globalisation. While the dominance of the most powerful players in the market place has been consolidated, new opportunities have been created for the circulation of alternative kinds of cinema through specialist distribution networks including DVD and cable/satellite television channels. But the advent of what Toby Miller et al. label the 'New International Division of Cultural Labour' (Miller et al. 2001; 2005) has also radically altered the way in which governments provide support for local filmmakers. The most instructive element of *The Lord of the Rings* saga in this regard is not so much that a Hollywood studio was prepared to back Peter Jackson to make the trilogy entirely in New Zealand, but rather that the New Zealand government was prepared to provide tax incentives to New Line Cinema amounting to some NZ$217 million, or roughly one-third of the trilogy's total production budget.[3] While historically state intervention in film production had been a protective response to Hollywood domination, the new global economy has created the situation in which governments can actively assist transnational corporations while simultaneously serving the national interest. This is not entirely a sleight of hand in that the international success of Peter Jackson has accrued tangible benefits to New Zealand cinema in various ways: through enhancing the production industry's infrastructure and facilities; encouraging the government to increase its commitment to film production; and inspiring a wider awareness of the value, cultural and economic, of the moving image to a small and peripheral nation. Whatever the wider concerns, Jackson has helped to keep New Zealand on the radar, engendering a sense of possibility and confidence in local filmmaking.

A distinct and identifiable New Zealand cinema is a relatively recent phenomenon. The creation of the New Zealand Film Commission (NZFC) in 1978 provided the means by which a small but sustainable level of film production, of around 4–6 features a year, could be guaranteed. But while output has remained steady (if necessarily limited) since then, the critical profile of New Zealand films has fluctuated between all too brief moments of international recognition and visibility and more extended periods of relative obscurity. Early signs of promise were provided by the work of filmmakers such as Roger Donaldson – *Sleeping Dogs* (1977), *Smash Palace* (1981); Geoff Murphy – *Goodbye Pork Pie* (1980),

Utu (1983), *The Quiet Earth* (1985); and Vincent Ward – *Vigil* (1984), the first New Zealand film screened in competition at Cannes. This was followed by a more high-profile boom in the early 1990s led by critical successes like *The Piano* (Jane Campion, 1993), *Once Were Warriors* (Lee Tamahori, 1994) and *Heavenly Creatures* (Peter Jackson, 1994). More instructive, however, was the speed at which these moments rapidly evaporated into thin air. In large part this is due to the size and limitations of the New Zealand production sector; sustaining momentum in such a hand-to-mouth industry has always been difficult. It is significant that all of the filmmakers noted above, with the single exception of Jackson, were quickly lured by more lucrative opportunities overseas, creating a talent vacuum in the process that subsequently took time to fill.

But since the release of *The Fellowship of the Ring* in 2001, New Zealand cinema has experienced its third moment in the spotlight and this time the upturn may be potentially more substantial, encouraged in part by some of the changes brought about by globalisation. While accessible art-house films like *The Piano* and *Heavenly Creatures* had been able to take advantage of international sources of funding and distribution, New Zealand cinema in the new millennium appears to be characterised by a broader range of productions. These range from high-profile Hollywood-financed epics like *The Lord of the Rings*, *King Kong* and *The Chronicles of Narnia*, through more modest and culturally specific co-productions like *Whale Rider*, *In My Father's Den* and *The World's Fastest Indian*, to low-budget films bankrolled by the Film Commission like *Rain* and *Eagle Vs. Shark*. Moreover, the last six years have also seen a significant increase in levels of public support for local filmmakers in New Zealand, part of a larger package of policy measures that constitute a direct response by the New Zealand government, state funding agencies and the film industry at large to new challenges and opportunities. This enthusiasm for culture on the part of the state has helped to underpin the increased diversity of film production, ensuring that some kind of national agenda endures within the transnational conjunction that characterises globalisation.

A Nation in Transition

With a population of just over 4.1 million and located 1,400 miles from Australia, its nearest neighbour, New Zealand is a small and remote nation literally 'on the edge' of the world. Crucially it is also a settler society whose dominant culture and identity can only be grasped in relation to a process of historical development which, historian James Belich argues, is marked by three distinct periods. The first of these is the process of colonisation and settlement which began in the early nineteenth century and rapidly displaced the indigenous Maori who had migrated from Polynesia some time around the first millennium. This was followed by a period from the 1880s to the 1960s that consolidated New Zealand's identity as an independent Dominion that continued to rely heavily on close cultural and economic ties to the mother country and conceived of itself as a kind of 'Better Britain'. Finally, we have the more recent and on-going transformation towards the forging of a distinctive and separate New Zealand national identity, described by Belich in terms of a process of 'decolonisation' (Belich 2001). The decisive moment was the UK's decision to join the European Economic Community in 1973, which at a stroke undermined 50 per cent of the New Zealand export economy, forcing a fundamental re-orientation towards the rest of the world. This was followed by a second major shock in 1984 in the form of the newly elected Labour government's programme of wholesale and rapid economic deregulation and privatisation, radical policies which would rapidly transform New Zealand from one of the world's most state-centralised, interventionist and egalitarian liberal democracies into one of the most market-dependent. As elsewhere, neoliberalism brought with it increased entrepreneurial activity, social mobility and consumer choice, but also greater economic insecurity, higher unemployment and a widening gap between rich and poor.

The period of decolonisation entailed more than a distancing of mainstream New Zealand from Britain and the forging of a new kind of Kiwi cultural nationalism. The 1970s also saw the beginning of increased political activity on the part of the indigenous Maori in response to long-standing grievances over the appropriation of their tribal lands and fisheries, the marginalisation of their culture and their virtual exclusion from the major arenas of power and decision-making.[4] The Maori struggle was to be assisted by the same Labour administration whose policies had served to exacerbate pre-existing patterns of socio-economic inequality and structural disadvantage. In 1985 the government considerably enhanced the powers of the Waitangi Tribunal, established ten years earlier to hear Maori grievances and make recommendations to Parliament, by extending its remit to consider retrospective historical claims in relation to land and fishing rights, invoking a direct confrontation with the legacy of European settlement in the process. The Tribunal took its name and mission from the 1840 Treaty of Waitangi between the Crown and the Maori tribes that established British sovereignty over New Zealand but also guaranteed the indigenous people possession of their lands and fisheries and enshrined their legal rights and privileges as British subjects. Systematically ignored during the period of colonisation, the treaty has been resurrected as a constitutional instrument in the renegotiation of relations between Maori and Pakeha New Zealanders (the latter being of European descent), providing the basis for a new sense of partnership or biculturalism in which the rights and needs of the *tangata whenua* (translated as 'people of the land') have come to be explicitly acknowledged in public policy and discourse. Maori political advance was also accompanied by a cultural renaissance, including the revival of the Maori language, Te Reo, which by the 1970s was considered to be on the brink of extinction. The media have played a key part in this revival with the beginning of Maori language radio in 1988, followed more recently by the establishment of a Maori television channel in 2004 which has served to give Te Reo and other aspects of Maori cultural identity a presence in the wider society that is something more than symbolic.

While the Maori renaissance and Pakeha response helped to engender an ideology of biculturalism in Aotearoa/New Zealand, the transformations of the last twenty years have also created the conditions for a more multicultural society. Encouraged by the economic liberalisation of New Zealand, new migrants began to arrive in greater numbers from the Pacific Islands and from East and South Asia, complementing the more established immigration flows from Britain and Continental Europe. While in 1986 81 per cent of the New Zealand population was of European descent and 12.5 per cent Maori, the 2001 census revealed that Pakeha had declined to 67 per cent, with an additional 4 per cent comprising European immigrants, and Maori had grown to 15 per cent, and Pacific Islanders and Asians comprised 7 per cent each. In Auckland, the largest urban area with almost one-third of the national population, the percentage of the Pacific Island and Asian groups rises to 12.5 per cent each, affirming the cosmopolitan culture of the country's only metropolis. This cumulative transformation, brought about by decolonisation, the Maori renaissance and increased immigration, has not only created a markedly different kind of social formation in New Zealand, it has also provided a catalyst for reinvigorating forms of cultural expression, including the emergence and development of a distinct and vibrant national cinema.

The Emergence of a Small National Cinema

At one point in their insightful analysis of the characteristics and operation of the New International Division of Cultural Labour, Toby Miller et al. briefly acknowledge a rather different consequence of globalisation: namely, the pressure on the part of nation states to re-forge a sense of national subjectivity or belonging among increasingly heterogeneous and diverse populations. While such a project of identity-building is often associated with the cultivation of a narrow nationalism or cultural homogenisation – with cinema being co-opted as a powerful ideological tool – the moving image can also be a potent mechanism for a more creative and critical engagement with the complexity of specific social formations. In the case of New Zealand, the creation of a national cinema required the intervention of the state through the establishment of the New Zealand Film Commission in 1978. This came about after a long process of political lobbying which began in 1970, with advocates highlighting both the cultural and the economic benefits that a national cinema would entail. [5] An additional incentive was provided by recent developments across the Tasman Sea which had seen the emergence of a dynamic and highly visible new Australian cinema under-pinned by government funding initiatives. However, in the New Zealand case, the most constant refrain in the public discourse was the contribution that film could make to a sense of national identity. The timing was fortuitous as this was at precisely the moment when New Zealand's sense of itself had been thrown into a state of flux by the onset of decolonisation, as described above.[6] While the dis-course of national identity tended to translate into a demand for local stories and images to counter the dominance of imported films from the United States and Britain, what is interesting and significant is the substance of the images and stories characterising the initial batch of Film Commission-funded projects that appeared in the late 1970s. Taking their lead from Roger Donaldson's indepen-dently financed feature, *Sleeping Dogs* (1977), which concerns one man's strug-gle for survival in a New Zealand that has been taken over by a repressive totalitarian regime, these films collectively present an overtly critical image of New Zealand society. Their focus is on issues such as the stultifying conformity of suburban life – *Angel Mine* (David Blythe, 1978), *Middle Age Spread* (John Reid, 1978); small-town hypocrisy – *Skin Deep* (Geoff Steven, 1978); racism – *Sons for the Return Home* (Paul Maunder, 1979); police corruption – *Beyond Reasonable Doubt* (John Laing, 1980); and psychic frailty – *Smash Palace* (Roger Donaldson, 1981), *Bad Blood* (Mike Newell, 1982).

This collective articulation would appear to correspond with Susan Hayward's assertion that:

> The paradox of a national cinema becomes clear in that . . . it will always – in its forming – go against the underlying principles of nation-alism and be at cross purposes with the originating idea of the *nation* as a unified identity. (Hayward 2000: 95)

Hayward's argument is motivated by the key role so often played by those on the margins of a national culture in the creation of dynamic and innovative cin-ematic responses to that culture, and this holds true in the New Zealand case in that the fledgling independent production sector was dominated by members of the 1970s counter-culture including hippies, leftists and other kinds of overt non-conformists. Their creative endeavour also countered the unremittingly positive representations produced by the National Film Unit, established in 1941 to make promotional documentaries for government departments and industry and consequently another emblem of the 'Better Britain' ideology. In contrast, the feature films enabled by the New Zealand Film Commission pro-vided precisely the kind of dynamic and critical engagement with the society and culture – elements of a wider 'national conversation' in a period of radical transformation – that only a truly 'national' cinema could achieve.

KEY POLICY ISSUES

In addition to nurturing a fledgling national cinema, the New Zealand Film Commission was also charged with developing a viable local film industry. From the outset this mission to strike a balance between culture and economics involved a consideration of the relationship between the local and the global. While the rhetoric of cultural expression could be used as a justification for local film production, the high costs involved in film production necessitated a larger audience which could only be addressed by enlarging the international market for New Zealand films. Perhaps unsurprisingly, the Commission's record in this regard has been rather patchy given the near impossibility of maintaining a high international profile with a small number of films, most of which lack recognisable stars and are made on tiny budgets by relatively inexperienced filmmakers. However, instructive developments have occurred under the leadership of the present Chief Executive, Ruth Harley, that in part reflect a changing international landscape. A seasoned and savvy cultural bureaucrat, Harley had previously headed New Zealand On Air, the organisation set up in 1989 to guarantee the survival of local television production and public radio within an otherwise free-market broadcasting environment. On joining the Commission in 1997, Harley assumed control of an institution that had conspicuously lost its way after the short-lived boom of the early 1990s. Consequently she set about developing a strategy informed by the ways in which screen production had changed that would also provide a platform to re-energise local filmmaking in a meaningful and sustainable way.

Harley's top priority was to forge a more productive relationship with the exhibition and distribution community, both domestically and internationally, a strategy underlined by the subsequent appointment of an experienced local exhibitor, Barrie Everard, as Commission Chairman. This enhanced focus on the market – 'the audience is where the rubber meets the road',[7] as Harley puts it – echoes the identification by former head of British Film Institute (BFI) production, Colin MacCabe, of 'the complicated dialectic between author and audience which is fundamental to all art but the very currency of film making' (MacCabe 1999: 16). It is also a recognition of the way in which public funding agencies, in a world increasingly driven by the ideology of the market, have been subject to more stringent levels of monitoring and accountability to ensure 'value for money'. Whatever the beliefs and motivations of those in charge of funding bodies like the New Zealand Film Commission, they are now compelled to pay more than lip service to the economics of culture. However, delivering the goods, in terms of improving the share of the domestic market for New Zealand films, let alone building an international audience through increased sales and marketing, has proven a very tough nut to crack. In recent years the highest share of the domestic box-office gained by New Zealand films was 5 per cent in 2005, compared to a paltry 1.1 per cent and 4.3 per cent in 2004 and 2003 respectively. Moreover, the 2003 and 2005 figures are bolstered by the performance of *Whale Rider* and *The World's Fastest Indian* – currently at numbers three and one in the table of top-earning New Zealand films in the domestic market, which account for 94 per cent and 98.5 per cent of the total local revenue for New Zealand films in their respective years of release. As far as the international market is concerned, emphasis has been placed recently on the Commission's sales agency in order to foster a more effective understanding of the potential value of New Zealand films in various territories.

Harley's second priority was to expand the resources available to local filmmakers, particularly established directors aspiring to larger-budgeted projects with the potential to reach a wider audience. Most New Zealand features are made on budgets of NZ$4 million or less and the Commission does not publicise the value of individual investments on the grounds that the low cost of local films can harm their sales prospects. Such budgets also preclude the kinds of element that assist the marketing process, such as stars or special effects. This led to the establishment of a new NZ$22 million Film Fund in 2000 to facilitate a more ambitious scale of production that could also attract investment from international sources (a precondition of the Fund) while retaining a distinctively New Zealand cultural focus. Projects that have benefited from the Film Fund to date include *Whale Rider* (Niki Caro, 2003), *Perfect Strangers* (Gaylene Preston, 2004), *The World's Fastest Indian* (Roger Donaldson, 2005), *River Queen* (Vincent Ward, 2006) and *Perfect Creature* (Glen Standring, 2006). The Film Fund also created the conditions for realising Harley's third priority, which was to reconnect with the New Zealand diaspora by making it possible for successful filmmakers who had relocated overseas to come back home. This strategy has paid dividends, with high-profile directors Vincent Ward and Roger Donaldson making their first New Zealand films since the 1980s. While the slate of projects supported by the Fund constitute a valuable addition to New Zealand cinema culture, it is perhaps significant that none of these films – with the exception of *Whale Rider* – has enjoyed significant international box-office success.

Harley's strategy to make the Film Commission more effective has been assisted by the Labour-led Government of Prime Minister Helen Clark, who since coming to power in 1999, has also assumed personal responsibility for her administration's Culture and Arts portfolio. In addition to being a staunch advocate of the cultural value of state investment in film, regularly emphasising the centrality of film and other cultural forms to the project of nation-building, Clark has also increased the levels of public support for film production. Between 2001 and 2005 public investment in film production and development through the NZFC, the Film Fund, Creative New Zealand and New Zealand On Air stands at more than NZ$78.5 million. At current exchange rates this is the equivalent of £26 million or 39 million Euros, an average of just over £5 million (7.8 million Euros) per annum. While this allows a favourable comparison with the £3 million distributed by the Scottish Screen Lottery Fund, it compares less well to the 9.2 million Euros and the 9.7 million Euros invested in local production and development by the Irish Film Board in 2003 and 2004, let alone the staggering 17.8 million and 17.9 million Euros of state funding provided in Denmark in the same two years. Moreover, producers in small European countries such as Demark and Ireland have greater recourse to regional and co-production finance than their counterparts in New Zealand.

Despite the new emphasis on the market and more effective business strategies, the New Zealand Film Commission continues to be informed by a cultural (or even cultural nationalist) imperative, backing filmmaking talent driven by the desire to 'tell their own stories'. But at the same time the increasing emphasis on economics has also influenced the New Zealand government in its dealings with the film industry. This can be seen in relation to the emergence of a 'creative industries agenda', which has also gained prominence in Australia and the UK and is characterised by a more overtly market-driven conception of the economic value of cultural activity. In terms of the relationship between the local and global, this agenda has also involved a vigorous and explicit marketing of a 'national brand', yoking the creative industries to tourism in the process. And given its overt dependency on external economic forces, it is no surprise that New Zealand has danced enthusiastically to this tune. While aspects of the Film Commission's strategy under Ruth Harley sit fairly comfortably alongside this agenda, the promotion of a business imperative has also generated certain tensions, perhaps most notably a desire articulated by some producers for greater public investment in screen production businesses rather than culture in order to grow the sector in New Zealand. Given the levels of state funding already committed to film, it is likely that any new investment of this kind would be at the expense of the levels of support currently channelled through the Commission.

The department driving the creative industries agenda is the Ministry for Economic Development (MED), whose perceptions and activities are more directly informed by the New International Division of Cultural Labour. For example, the department provides core funding for Film New Zealand, the national film locations office, which promotes the country internationally as a film-friendly production base to offshore producers. It is also responsible for the large budget production grant scheme, launched in 2004 to provide an automatic subsidy of 12.5 per cent of production spend in New Zealand where that spend is $15 million or over. Given the budgetary level of most New Zealand productions, the primary beneficiaries of this scheme are international films like Peter Jackson's *King Kong*, financed by Universal, and the Disney production *The Chronicles of Narnia: The Lion, the Witch and the Wardrobe* – which received grants of $48.6 million and $18 million respectively. The scale of such awards immediately throws the $22 million Film Fund – and the comparative relationship between economic and cultural imperatives in the determination of state support for filmmaking in New Zealand – into a rather different light. In 2003 the Ministry of Economic Development convened a Screen Industry Task Force charged with making recommendations for growing the New Zealand production sector, primarily by taking advantage of globalisation. Their subsequent report included recommended changes to recoupment arrangements and intellectual property rights to the greater benefit of producers, while the Minister for Economic Development, Jim Anderton, stated unambiguously in his foreword that the mechanism of cultural subsidies of the kind which the film industry in New Zealand had been reliant on 'inevitably limits growth' – clearly implying that the priority for state investment in the sector should be revised in favour of a more business-oriented approach than the essentially cultural remit of the Film Commission. The tension that emerges here is a concern in that it creates a potential fault line that could prove detrimental to a small nation where collaboration and the pooling of resources are essential for survival. Moreover, any significant shift in public support away from the Commission towards a more commercial agenda will not only cede control to overseas investors and markets (which realistically is the only way in which the local screen production sector can grow); it will also undermine any truly national cinema in New Zealand.

Making Sense of New Zealand Cinema

But what kind of national cinema has been developed in New Zealand as a consequence of the interplay of the kind of political, cultural and economic forces I have touched upon? The array of state interventions echoes similar policy developments in Ireland in the early 1990s, which Martin McLoone has insightfully analysed in terms of the consequences these measures have had for Irish cinema, locating this in the context of Ireland's post-colonial dilemma between a nationalist or internationalist way forward, or as he more pithily puts it, 'between a self-defeating essentialism or a self-abusing capitulation' (McLoone 2006: 90). As in New Zealand, the Irish interventions were designed to nurture distinct levels of filmmaking activity aimed at different markets and audiences – from large-budget Hollywood productions taking advantage of tax breaks, through medium-budget co-productions combining Irish funding and international investment, to more overtly indigenous low-budget filmmaking. McLoone relates this configuration to the tripartite model that emerged out of the 'Third Cinema question': with First Cinema signifying the commercial mainstream of Hollywood and its imitators; Second Cinema, bourgeois auteur or art cinema; and Third Cinema, a more overtly oppositional cinema informed by anti-imperialist struggle and a commitment to alternative production practices. McLoone maps this model on to the different levels of Irish film production, demonstrating some interesting correspondences while also addressing the vexed question of what constitutes an Irish film by recourse to a critical judgement on how particular works engage with and articulate the complexities of the national formation. In this regard McLoone's analysis is informed by Paul Willemen's assertion that 'the issue of National Cinema is . . . primarily a question of address rather than a matter of the film-maker's citizenship or the production finance's country of origin (Willemen 2006: 36).

A similar analysis can be productively applied to the kind of New Zealand cinema nurtured by government film policies and key institutions. First Cinema is clearly constituted by the recent big international productions serviced by Film New Zealand and now encouraged by the large budget grant scheme. These include Hollywood runaways like *The Last Samurai*, *The Chronicles of Narnia: The Lion, the Witch and the Wardrobe*, *The Lord of the Rings* and *King Kong*. The films directed by Peter Jackson tend to be regarded as somehow maintaining a meaningful connection to the local but it is notable that his earlier low-budget work such as *Braindead* and *Heavenly Creatures* did engage in a direct and critical way with the local culture while simultaneously being accessible to an international audience. By the time we get to Middle Earth or Skull Island this specificity had been considerably diluted in the service of securing a mass international audience. The category of Second Cinema has been central to the identity of New Zealand cinema since the late 1970s, which encouraged the development of distinctive writer-directors ranging from genre-oriented filmmakers like Roger Donaldson, Geoff Murphy and Jackson, to exponents of art cinema such as Vincent Ward, Jane Campion and Niki Caro. This tendency has been boosted by the existence of the Film Fund and the encouragement of high-profile projects that have attracted international co-production finance such as *Whale Rider*, *In My Father's Den*, *Perfect Creature*, *The World's Fastest Indian* and *River Queen*. But again, as in the Irish case, the slippage between the distinct categories in this kind of schema is revealed, with some of these productions being informed by aspects of First Cinema, most notably the vampire film, *Perfect Creature*, while others such as *Whale Rider* and *River Queen*, which in very different ways address the Maori presence in New Zealand, contain elements that can be related to a Third Cinema perspective.

The lower-budget domain of local production comprises films that are either majority-funded or fully financed by the Commission, supported by other sources such as the micro-budget Screen Innovation Fund or in some cases funded by private sources. While most of these also fit into the Second Cinema category, including innovative lo-fi productions such as Florian Habich's *Woodenhead* (2004), this domain also includes examples that can be more readily regarded as Third Cinema, namely works by Maori filmmakers that provide an internal perspective on indigenous culture, tradition and experience, entailing a political critique of the history and legacy of colonialism. This includes Barry Barclay's three features, *Ngati* (1987), *Te Rua* (1991) and *The Feathers of Peace* (2000), Merata Mita's *Mauri* (1988) and, in a rather different vein, Lee Tamahori's *Once Were Warriors*. Whether or not the category of 'Third Cinema' is appropriate in this context is a subject of debate, with Barclay advocating a new category of 'Fourth Cinema' as an expression of indigenous cultures, arguing that 'First, Second and Third Cinemas are all cinemas of the modern Nation State – from the indigenous place of standing they are all invader cinemas' (Barclay 2003: 10).[8] While the mobilisation of this schema is motivated by an attempt to define different kinds of New Zealand cinema, it is also notable that all of the categories – First, Second and Third/Fourth Cinema – all have a global dimension, be it the high exposure and mass distribution of the Hollywood machine, the film festivals and more specialised circulation of art cinema, or the equally distinctive international networks, seasons or exhibitions dedicated to Third, indigenous or diasporic cinemas.

In addition to the application of this framework as a means of grasping the complex specificity of New Zealand cinema while simultaneously acknowledging the necessary global dimensions of that cinema, there are also certain overarching and recurring themes and issues that provide additional insight. The most resonant of these remains Sam Neill and Judy Rymer's controversial identification of 'A Cinema of Unease' in their 1995 documentary made as part of the BFI Centenary of Cinema series. Neill and Rymer invoke a rather dysfunctional national culture marked by social conformity, Puritanism, fear, insanity and violence, which has in turn generated a cinema offering a dark and troubled reflection with a central trope being the destructive force of the landscape itself. This perspective draws on a discourse of Pakeha cultural nationalism that emerged in the inter-war period as an oppositional element within the 'Better Britain' culture of re-colonisation and which clearly resonated with the generation of filmmakers who struggled in the 1970s to establish a cinema in New Zealand. While critics of the 'Cinema of Unease' have condemned its inability to engage with the more diverse range of representations that have emerged from the 1990s onwards, there remains a brooding presence in the national cinematic imaginary that can be related not to a critique of colonial subservience but to the acknowledgement, whether conscious or otherwise, of the prior displacement of the indigenous people of Aotearoa. This is invoked by Martin Blythe in a compelling analysis of the responses by Pakeha filmmakers to the Maori cultural and political revival. Blythe identifies a range of narrative and thematic strategies that collectively convey a deep sense of settler anxiety generated by reconfigured questions of identity, belonging and legitimacy (Blythe 1994). And while his study ends in the late 1980s, the analysis is equally applicable to the key works of the 1990s, including *An Angel at My Table, The Piano, Crush* and *Heavenly Creatures*, and more recent productions such as *Rain, Perfect Strangers* and *In My Father's Den* in which motifs of fear, isolation, psychic frailty, violence and the disintegration of families continue to abound. In stark contrast, the films made by, or with the creative participation of, Maori from *Ngati* to *Whale Rider* tend to offer a more comfortable or harmonious set of images bearing on questions of belonging, community and tradition and the relationship between people and their environment. Even *Once Were Warriors* counters the violence and dysfunction of Jake Heke and poor urban Maori with an appeal to the values of tradition, of *whanau* (family) and the Marae.

But there are also some important exceptions to the 'cinema of unease' emanating from within Pakeha film culture. Geoff Murphy's iconic 1980 road movie, *Goodbye Pork Pie*, is an evocation of a very different kind of relationship to place in which the two directionless heroes travel the entire length of New Zealand in a stolen yellow mini on the flimsiest of premises. But in the process the film defines a particular sense of (male) Kiwi identity based on laconic mateship, irreverence for authority and a daredevil approach to adventure. Equally definitive is Roger Donaldson's recent production, *The World's Fastest Indian*, which immortalises New Zealand legend Burt Munroe, who at the age of 67 set a new world speed record at Bonneville Flats, Utah, on his 40-year-old Indian Scout Motorcycle, a machine that he had modified in his own idiosyncratic and resourceful way. *The World's Fastest Indian* inverts almost all the elements of Donaldson's 1981 classic evocation of 'the cinema of unease', *Smash Palace*. Both films are about obsessive loners who have a preoccupation with speed, but where Al Shaw turns in on himself and becomes increasingly aggressive and alienated from family and friends, culminating in him kidnapping his daughter, Burt Monroe embodies a 'salt of the earth' humanity that wins over everyone he encounters in his journey from Invercargill to Utah. Moreover, Monroe's remarkable achievements against all the odds constitute another version of the Colin McKenzie myth. Yet in the final analysis, this myth is also deeply grounded in the Pakeha settler experience, constituting the flip side of the 'Cinema of Unease' in its utopian embrace of common humanity as an alternative strategy of dealing with the trauma of the past.

In this regard, the feel-good simplicity of *The World's Fastest Indian* could not be more at odds with *River Queen*, Vincent Ward's uneven but lyrical meditation on the land wars of the 1860s. While Donaldson's film is arguably founded on nostalgia for a less complicated moment before New Zealanders were forced to confront the consequences of colonisation, Ward confronts the legacy of history head-on in his tale of the search of an Irish settler for her son who had been kidnapped by his Maori grandfather some years previously. This quest, which culminates in the reconstitution of a hybrid or bicultural nuclear family, is set against the backdrop of conflict between colonial troops and the Maori tribes along the mighty Whanganui River. Drawing on specifically European contemplations of colonial contact from Joseph Conrad's novel *Heart of Darkness* to Werner Herzog's feature *Aguirre, the Wrath of God*, Ward's ambition to create a challenging and epic vision of this definitive period of conflict, which continues to haunt the relationship between Pakeha and Maori, represents a very different kind of attempt to engage with local and international audiences. Tellingly, it was Donaldson's film that had an impact in New Zealand, with box-office earnings topping NZ$7 million, a record for a domestic film, compared to a mere NZ$1 million for *River Queen*.[9]

Conclusion: Into an Uncertain Future

The transformation of New Zealand society through the interlinked forces of decolonisation and globalisation has energised the national culture, while rendering any meaningful conception of a national identity outside the domain of shared citizenship rights very tentative at best. What is more interesting are the variety of ways in which the local and the global, the specific and the universal are being reconfigured, experienced and expressed by different kinds of New Zealanders, be they Pakeha, Maori, Polynesian or Asian. The changing face of New Zealand society is encouraging a more diverse local film culture as witnessed by the recent release of *No. 2* (Toa Fraser, 2006) and *Sione's Wedding* (Chris Graham, 2006), two films dealing with the Pacific Island presence in Auckland. The last two years have also seen a number of short films and at least two low-budget digital features being made by young New Zealand Asian filmmakers. Meanwhile a promising new Maori talent has emerged in Taika Waititi, whose short film *Two Cars, One Night* was nominated for an Oscar in 2005 and whose debut feature, *Eagle Vs Shark*, has been bought by Miramax.

But while certain effects of globalisation have been positive, there are also grounds for caution. As noted above, the desire on the part of some to grow the local production sector is potentially at odds with the maintenance of an engaged and engaging national cinema, generating instead the production of either imitative low-budget genre films or reductive images of brand New Zealand. The contrast between *Smash Palace* and *The World's Fastest Indian* is one manifestation of this desire for greater universal appeal. In a similar vein (although without the presence of an 'A' list star) is *Whale Rider*, which markedly ignores any acknowledgement of wider grievances or tensions, distancing it from the more overtly politicised Maori films made by Barry Barclay and Merata Mita. The desire for greater international appeal risks the proliferation of exotic sentimentality (*Whale Rider*), utopian myth (*The World's Fastest Indian*), anodyne images of a new MTV-inspired cosmopolitan urban culture (*Sione's Wedding*), de-localised genre films (*Heaven, Perfect Creature*) or third-rate imitations of Hollywood or Asian popular genres (most micro-budget digital features). The terrain of co-productions has also thrown up its own problems, from the intense pressure placed on Brad McGann by British investors to make *In My Father's Den* more commercially appealing (success-fully resisted) to 20th Century Fox's temporary shelving of *Perfect Creature*, a film that generated impressive sales at Cannes in 2005 but which more than a year on has yet to be released in any territory.

Yet at the same time New Zealand filmmakers are forced to swim with the tide of globalisation and to confront the realities of raising finance for projects. But the problem will increasingly be one of resisting the alternate traps of cre-ating anodyne national stereotypes, the cinematic equivalent of sheepskins, replica Maori carvings and other products pushed at the tourist market; or sub-standard generic fare, a kind of Hollywood on the cheap. In his analysis of Australian national cinema, Tom O'Regan mobilises the concept of antipodal-ity, which he suggests moves in two directions: on the one hand generating a cinema that directly acknowledges interdependence and external influence (however unequal cultural exchange may be) while at the same time avowing and even valorising personal integrity and local agency (O'Regan 1996: 106–10). Rather than simply imitating Hollywood, European art cinema or Hong Kong action cinema, the antipodal filmmaker must negotiate these influ-ential cultural forms in order to engage fully and productively with local speci-ficity. Such an understanding remains cognisant of international influences and the complexity of cultural expression while avoiding any kind of sterile binary of them/us, outside/inside, international/national. This kind of approach has arguably informed some of the most globally successful New Zealand films, including *Once Were Warriors* and *Braindead*, both of which were low-budget and indisputably local productions.

Despite the boost provided by *The Lord of the Rings* and *Whale Rider*, the international market place remains a difficult challenge for New Zealand film-makers. On an institutional level, the New Zealand Film Commission has helped to enrich film culture with a broader range of production while also enabling the production of some films of substance, but many of these films have struggled to find a domestic audience, let alone internationally. Yet it is worth reminding ourselves that high rates of market failure are common in all modes of film production, including Hollywood with all its commercial power, suggesting that overt commercialism does not in itself guarantee success. Consequently, embracing a more market-oriented approach may not deliver a better or more sustainable New Zealand film industry. And it is instructive to remember that the overt commercialisation of television and the press in New Zealand has driven down quality at the expense of ensuring high levels of profitability, much of which flows offshore. While being cognisant of the market place and of economic realities, New Zealand cinema needs to retain its integrity and self-determination and to continue to strike a balance between economics and culture. Some expansion at the more commercial end of the production industry may be beneficial, provided this is not at the expense of support for locally engaged projects. In this regard the role of government also remains essential, but even here there is a sense of uncertainty as a change of administration may very well result in major funding cuts or a re-emphasis on business initiatives. There is certainly no figure in the opposition National Party who appears to share Helen Clark's enthusiasm for the arts. But in the end, the viability of a truly national cinema in New Zealand is not only a question of dependence. There may, in the final analysis, also be a certain virtue in remaining small.

NOTES

1. In addition to a sense of betrayal of trust between the audience and the national broadcaster, TVNZ, Roscoe and Hight note a strand of anti-intellectualism; as one letter writer to the *Listener* put it, 'I can't express my disappointment at having lost a genius and gained another "clever" film maker.'
2. In addition to generating almost US$3 billion at the international box-office, *The Lord of the Rings* trilogy won seventeen Oscars, including eleven awards for *The Return of the King,* which equalled the record held by *Ben Hur* (1959) and *Titanic* (1997).
3. The details of the tax break to *The Lord of the Rings* are confirmed by John Braddock in 'Behind the Making of *The Lord of the Rings*', posted on *World Socialist Web Site,* http://wsws.org/articles/2002/mar2002/lor2-m21.shtml.
4. In common with other dispossessed first peoples around the world, Maori tend to be structurally disadvantaged in terms of economics, health and education and more likely to be involved in crime as both perpetrators and victims compared to their Pakeha neighbours; these statistics suggest that for Maori any meaningful process of decolonisation has yet to begin and this underpins the title of Ranginui Walker's book, *Ka Whawhai Tonu Matou/Struggle Without End* (Auckland: Penguin, 1990, 2004), the most authoritative history of Aotearoa/New Zealand from a Maori perspective.
5. A comprehensive analysis of this process is contained in Pointon 2005.
6. For a detailed discussion of this process see Gregory A. Waller, 1996, 'The New Zealand Film Commission: Promoting an Industry, Forging a National Identity', *Historical Journal of Film, Radio and Television,* Vol. 16, No. 2, p. 248.
7. Ruth Harley, 2005, interview with the author, Auckland, 8 December.
8. These films can also lay claim to the status of a Deleuzian minor cinema with their 'deterritorialisation of language, connection of the individual to a political immediacy, and collective assemblage of enunciation'. See Deleuze and Guattari 1986, p. 18.
9. Significantly, neither film has been successful in any major territories outside New Zealand.

WORKS CITED

Barclay, Barry. 2003. 'Celebrating Fourth Cinema'. *Illusions*, No. 35, Winter. pp. 7–11.
Belich, James. 2001. *Paradise Reforged: A History of the New Zealanders from the 1880s to the year 2000.* Auckland: Penguin.
Blythe, Martin. 1994. *Naming the Other: Images of Maori in New Zealand Film and Television.* Metuchen, NJ: Scarecrow.

Deleuze, Gilles, and Felix Guattari. 1986. *Kafka: Towards a Minor Literature*. Minneapolis, MN: University of Minnesota Press.

Hayward, Susan. 2000. 'Framing National Cinemas'. In Mette Hjort and Scott MacKenzie (eds), *Cinema and Nation*. London: Routledge. pp. 88–102.

MacCabe, Colin. 1999. *The Eloquence of the Vulgar: Language, Cinema and the Politics of Culture*. London: British Film Institute.

McLoone, Martin. 2006. 'National Cinema in Ireland'. In Valentina Vitali and Paul Willemen (eds), *Theorising National Cinema*. London: British Film Institute. pp. 88–99.

Miller, Toby, and Nitin Govil, John McMurria, Richard Maxwell, Ting Wang. 2005. *Global Hollywood 2*. London: British Film Institute.

O'Regan, Tom. 1996. *Australian National Cinema*. London: Routledge.

Pointon, Suzy. 2005. *The Independents: The Creation of a New Zealand Film Industry*. PhD thesis, University of Auckland, Chapter 8.

Roscoe, Jane, and Craig Hight. 1996. 'Silver Magic', *Illusions*, No. 25, Winter. pp. 14–19.

Walker, Ranginui. 1990/2004. *Ka Whawhai Tonu Matou/Struggle Without End*. Auckland: Penguin.

Waller, Gregory. 1996. 'The New Zealand Film Commission: Promoting an Industry, Forging a National Identity'. *Historical Journal of Film, Radio and Television*, Vol. 16, No. 2. pp. 243–62.

Willemen, Paul. 2006. 'The National Revisited'. In Valentina Vitali and Paul Willemen (eds), *Theorising National Cinema*. London: British Film Institute. pp. 29–43.

PART THREE

THE AMERICAS AND AFRICA

10. CUBA

Ana M. López

A 'Small' Nation?

By any standard marker, Cuba is a 'small' nation. Its national territory occupies only 110,860 sq km, its population is slightly less than 11.5 million, and it has a small economic patrimony.[1] Yet, by other standards, it can also be considered a major nation. In the context of the Caribbean region, Cuba is not only the largest and most populous island; it is also, in many ways, the richest. Because of its strategic location, Cuba has always been the epicentre of the Caribbean – it was always a central node of transatlantic trade and, since the 1959 Revolution, has been perceived as the heart of the movement of non-aligned nations. Therefore Cuba has not suffered from what Mette Hjort calls 'the pathos of small nationhood': 'a cluster of debilitating and troubling insecurities prompted by a demeaning stance on the part of more powerful players in the game of culture, by indifference and the sense of invisibility that it entails' (Hjort 2005: 30). Instead, it has been the source of extraordinarily rich and powerful expressions in all areas of cultural production, from music, literature and the fine arts, to cinema. Cuban 'nationness' (*cubanía*) has always been intensely felt, a source of pride, and if anything, Cuba has even greater claims to exceptionalism than most other nations. Its trajectory has never followed standard patterns and its nationalism has been conceived of as unique.

After 1952, when Fulgencio Batista's coup d'état undermined Cuba's democratic aspirations and eroded its self-image, Cuban nationalism was in crisis and national identity became the central issue contested in the cultural domain.

La patria (homeland) and *el pueblo* (the people) became the key signifiers in the search for national redemption (Pérez 1999). In 1953, Jorge Mañach argued that Cubans had become 'a disoriented people . . . without direction and therefore without history' and critiqued the popular saying that the island was like a cork that would never sink by pointing out that that also meant that it was 'fluffy and lightweight, floating without a course on the waters of History' (Mañach 1953: 9). Cubans were keen on transcendence, as Juan Antonio García Borrero has argued in his perceptive *La edad de la herejía*, and the cinema, although not yet a visible national player in the cultural realm, was set soon to become one (García Borrero 2002a: 62–3).

In 1959, Fidel Castro and the 26th of July Movement chased Batista into exile and took over the government with widespread popular support. Since then, and especially throughout the 1960s, Cuba was the laboratory for a thorough and unique social and political experiment: the development of an egalitarian socialist society in an underdeveloped Caribbean island in the face of the active opposition of its nearest powerful neighbour, the US. The vicissitudes of this process are too complex to outline in detail here; suffice it to say that the Revolution was, in part, sustained by the belief that, although the present required individual and collective sacrifices, the future outcome – socialist utopia – justified the effort and was attainable. Those who could not abide by the consequences of this paradigm left the island and sought exile elsewhere (primarily in the US), and the diaspora that began in 1959 continues to have dramatic consequences for Cuban cultural production and, concomitantly, how we conceive of Cuban nationalism.

Redefining the nation, the Revolution teleologically established its own myth of origins in Cuba's revolutionary past – from independence leader/poet, José Martí, and the rebels of the 1930s to the insurgent leaders of the 1950s – and mapped 'the people' (*el pueblo*) and the class struggle at the centre of the national imaginary. *El pueblo* thus became the rationale and motor for social action; the besieged nation had to remain unified around its core values in order to attain a socialist utopia in the future. Underscoring the primacy of the collective good, the Revolution thus promulgated its egalitarian principles as massive collective enterprises. Examples include the literacy campaign that in a few months essentially erased illiteracy from the island, health-care initiatives that trained cadres of doctors and brought services to even the most remote locations, an investment in media – radio, television, cinema, print – to disseminate information widely to the increasingly savvy population produced by guaranteed access to education, and a focus on building infrastructures in the formerly underdeveloped countryside. The Revolution also adopted a *tabula rasa* imaginary and unilaterally declared the equality of all Cuban citizens by officially eliminating racism and discrimination by decree. In the new order all Cuban citizens were ostensibly empowered by the Revolution as equals regardless of race, gender, age and so on. In this context, the individual's principal social responsibility was to strive for the collective good, synthetically encapsulated as 'the Revolution'.

The seams of this uneasy social compact began to erode in the late 1980s, when the demise of the Soviet Union and the disappearance of the Soviet aid and Eastern bloc trading partners, upon which Cuba was economically dependent, plunged the nation into the deepest economic crisis it has ever faced. In the space of a few years, Cuba lost from one-third to one-half of its income. Officially dubbed the 'Special Period in a Time of Peace', the early 1990s were thus characterised by untold daily difficulties for most Cubans (for example, blackouts that lasted longer than the periods with electricity, the disappearance of public transport, and terrible food shortages) and a series of governmental measures designed to re-invent the Cuban economy.

Although many – especially on the northern side of the Florida Straits – believed that Cuba could not survive the Special Period, it did, but at a cost. In order to stave off the worst of the crisis, the government was reluctantly forced to introduce a limited number of 'capitalist' economic measures that problematised social relations. These included the authorisation of some kinds of private enterprise, the elimination of some inefficiencies in the work force which generated unemployment, the courting of foreign investments, the legalisation of the dollar, the authorisation of foreign remittances, and the growing reliance on tourism. Where once social inequalities were barely visible, by the mid-1990s they were glaring and it was unquestionable that those with access to dollars – whether in the form of family remittances, private enterprises or the tourist sector – were markedly better off. The crumbling of the revolutionary social contract had a profound effect, seemingly making it possible for new constructions of individual (and possibly collective) subjectivities to emerge, no longer exclusively aligned with the collective *pueblo*, yet also not wholly in another orbit.

A Not-so-small National Cinema

Cuban cinema precedes 1959, yet it is only with the Revolution that the national cinema emerged at the forefront of cultural production. The Cuban Film Institute, ICAIC (Instituto Cubano de Arte e Industria Cinematográficos), was created via one of the first cultural acts of the new Revolutionary government. Defined as 'the most powerful and suggestive medium of artistic expression and the most direct and extensive vehicle for education and the popularisation of ideas', the cinema was called upon to participate actively in the ideological realm of the revolutionary process. ICAIC was set up as an independent agency, governed by an appointed director and by a three-member advisory board that, until the mid-1970s, was responsible for all activities.

ICAIC was the first organisation of its kind in Latin America: a government agency directly financed through the state, entrusted with all aspects of the national cinema and run primarily by filmmakers rather than government bureaucrats. Alfredo Guevara, who had been an active participant in the revolutionary struggles, was appointed its first director and held the post until 1983.

Between 1959 and the late 1980s, ICAIC demonstrated its vitality and viability through the production of thousands of documentaries and newsreels, as well as of some of the most significant feature films of Latin America, including Tomás Gutiérrez Alea's *Memories of Underdevelopment* and Humberto Solás's *Lucia*, both from 1968. It established a solid base for production (with reasonable studio facilities and equipment) as well as an extensive distribution and exhibition network.[2] Above all, ICAIC set out to build a national audience for Cuban cinema.

The institute also weathered difficult political crises in this period, managing to remain an independent entity while sustaining its commitment to the goals and spirit of the Revolution. An early battle in 1961 – only weeks after the October Missile Crisis – over the exhibition of a non-ICAIC film, *P.M.* (sponsored by a newspaper literary supplement and directed by Orlando Jiménez Leal and Sabá Cabrera Infante), was victoriously debated and led to the proclamation by Fidel Castro of the principal leitmotiv of Cuban Revolutionary culture: 'Within the Revolution everything; against it, nothing.' What is striking about this pronouncement is how it is phrased: it does not state 'for' the revolution everything, but rather 'within' it, leaving open a wide range of positions that could be accommodated. As Alfredo Guevara commented, almost forty years later:

> In the framework of the revolution there could be, there were, other ideological and religious conceptions; what is inconceivable, however, and I hope can be understood, is that outside it there could not be any counterrevolution. Which is why, within it, all was possible, and against it, nothing would be. And isn't. (Guevara 1998: 44)

In other words, for those within the revolution this meant the maximum liberty, but for those against it, the strictest censorship entailed. Obviously, this would become a slippery slope for many individuals and institutions to traverse. But ICAIC was one organisation that seemed to have accomplished it for several decades, maintaining hegemony over national film production and cinematic nationhood in alignment with the overall nation-building project of the Revolution.

Throughout the 1960s and 1970s, in line with Cuba's political and ideological solidarity with the revolutionary efforts in other Latin American countries, ICAIC also became an important promoter and part of the nascent pan-continental

New Latin American Cinema movement. As Cuba was one of the few Latin American countries to remain politically stable throughout these turbulent decades, ICAIC also became the central reference point for the movement, especially for filmmakers forced into exile by dictatorships. Cuba's central role was confirmed by the inauguration of the Festival Internacional del Nuevo Cine Latinoamericano in Havana in 1979, at a historical conjuncture in which the New Latin American Cinema movement project was fully accepted but had in fact stopped being viable.[3]

However, two subsequent crises indicated that the relationship between the ICAIC, national identity and the Revolutionary state had become less comfortable. In 1981–2, Humberto Solás's free adaptation of the Cuban foundational novel, *Cecilia Valdes*, generated a widespread controversy over how ICAIC was managed and its 'fit' with the Revolution and, by extension, the nation. Produced in co-production with Spain (a novelty at the time), the film had enjoyed a considerably larger budget and had taken longer to finish than most ICAIC productions. Allegedly, ICAIC had invested most of its resources in its production, which rankled many who were extremely displeased, even perturbed, by the film's re-reading of the literary classic. Solás had undertaken an iconoclastic re-rendering of the tropes and themes of the novel – the genesis of the Cuban mestizo nation in the encounter between the beautiful mulata and a Spanish aristocrat, sprinkled with healthy doses of *santería* – that problematised its sacrosanct status as the Cuban foundational novel. In the debates following the film's release, party critics attacked *Cecilia* not just for its alleged excesses but for its 'freedom' with the national literary patrimony and railed against both the film and ICAIC. To put an end to the controversy, ICAIC was re-organised internally and Alfredo Guevara was replaced by the no less senior filmmaker, Julio García Espinosa, who created three production groups to democratise decision-making (and budgetary decisions) and to foster the development of a new generation of filmmakers. These groups were headed by senior filmmakers with distinct creative personalities: the dialectical Gutiérrez Alea, the operatic Solás and the more commercial Manuel Pérez. They created important spaces for debates during the creation and production phases, producing a visibly evolving aesthetics of complexity that seemed to culminate in the late 1980s with films like Orlando Rojas's *Papeles secundarios* (*Supporting Roles*, 1989).

However, this productive trajectory was interrupted in 1991, when Daniel Díaz Torres's satiric comedy, *Alicia en el pueblo de las maravillas* (*Alice in Wonder Town*), generated yet another crisis for ICAIC. The Alicia of the film's title is a young theatre teacher who is assigned to work in the town of Maravillas de Novera, an odd place in which the most unexpected situations are accepted as normal and which is populated by an odd mix of unrestrained animals and former government bureaucrats recently fired from their jobs.

Alicia premiered at the Berlin Film Festival and received favourable reports, but subsequently the Cuban press began to publish corrosive political critiques, accusing the film of falsifying Cuban reality and arguing that it was an inappropriate film for that particular moment in Cuba's history. Alfredo Guevara argued, when he was called back to Cuba from his Parisian diplomatic post to address the situation, that the fact that the film could generate multiple readings was not the problem, but rather 'that it is politically ambiguous in a country set on edge by feeling fenced-in' (Guevara 1998: 491). The *Alicia* débâcle almost led to the disappearance of ICAIC as an independent entity; indeed, a proposal to fold it into the activities of the Cuban Radio and Television Institute was openly discussed. But once again the institute and its filmmakers organised themselves and managed to stave off disaster. After several months of discussion, Julio García Espinosa resigned as director, with Alfredo Guevara returning to helm the institute for a second time. In aesthetic terms, however, the *Alicia* incident left its mark on Cuban cinema of the 1990s. As García Borrero argues, without abandoning an interest in contemporary reality, mid- to late 1990s films tended to create symbolic or parallel universes through which to produce their critiques (García Borrero 2002a: 183).

The crisis over *Alicia* was only one of the many difficulties ICAIC faced during the Special Period. Whereas it once enjoyed a budget that allowed it to produce as many as a dozen feature films per year in addition to many more documentaries, the economic changes of the 1990s included the elimination of state subsidies to ICAIC, forcing severe cutbacks in production. The weekly newsreel that had been produced since 1959 ended and documentary production disappeared almost completely. Since then ICAIC has been almost completely dependent on co-production deals – primarily with European producers – to sustain feature film production. Typically, the co-producer provides hard currency and one or two actors and/or production staff, and ICAIC provides the talent (script, director, actors) technical labour and infrastructural, support for filming in Cuba. This situation has led to a marked decrease in the number of films ICAIC can produce each year, as well as to a visible shift in the kinds of scripts that find financing opportunities. Only forty films or so were produced in the 1990s and most had foreign financing of some kind, with the result that many featured foreigners in the cast, non-Cuban settings, a certain reliance on stereotypes to connote *cubanía* (sexy mulatas, exuberant musicality and so on). Furthermore, what had been a very collaborative and dialogic environment for film production became atomised and individualistic, with filmmakers struggling to secure their own financing or leaving the island (temporarily or permanently) to seek production opportunities elsewhere. Above all, the Special Period fractured the nationalist project that had prevailed for three decades, creating what critic Ambrosio Fornet has called the feeling of being in a 'fortress under siege' ('en una plaza sitiada'), bombarded by change, uncertain about the future and disillusioned with the past (Fornet 2002: 27).

Other Cuban Cinemas?[4]

In its heyday the ICAIC actively promoted itself as the epicentre of the national cinema in order to present a monolithic front to the world, especially to Latin America, and to highlight an alleged perfect equivalence between state, nation and cinema. Given its goals, this was not an unproductive strategy, but it resulted in a historiographical distortion that excluded and suppressed other voices from the pantheon of the national cinema. At its most Machiavellian, the institute's own records of 'Cuban' films did not include ICAIC-produced films by directors who had left the country.[5] Also relatively unknown were the many film projects that for multiple reasons were not produced after scripts had been completed, or were shelved after production and never released, or were released only for very short runs years after the fact.

Less motivated by politics and more by institutional hubris, ICAIC's records of Cuban cinema also did not include films produced outside of its domain. Yet as early as the 1960s other official state organisms such as the Fuerzas Armadas Revolucionarias (FAR, Revolutionary Armed Forces) and the Instituto Cubano de Radio y Televisión (ICRT, Cuban Radio and Television Institute) were producing films. And while since 1978 ICAIC has officially organised the amateur movement throughout the island via the Movimiento de Cine Aficionado de Cuba (Cuban Amateur Cinema Movement) and the national web of cine clubs, the works produced by these filmmakers have also not been included in the national canon.

During the 1980s amateur production increased prodigiously, enabled by the growing availability of video technology in the latter part of the decade. New groups sprouted up throughout the island, linked to *casas de cultura* (regional culture centres) or, after 1986, to the newly created youth cultural association, Asociación Hermanos Saíz. In 1980, the first Encuentro de Cine Aficionado (Meeting of Amateur Cinema) took place in Havana, bringing to light a new generation of filmmakers, among them Jorge Luis Sánchez and Tomás Piard.[6] Rather than position this cinema as an alternative to an 'official' cinema, it is important to consider it a direct outgrowth and part of the national cinematic scene. As Piard argued in 1980:

> The amateur film movement . . . is a consequence of the very same national cinema and of a need for self expression at popular levels. It has been manipulated, even internationally, as a parallel cinema, but this is not what I believe it is. It is a Cuban art form, reflecting all of our problematics. (Piard, cited in García Borrero 2001: 21)

Throughout the 1980s and 1990s, alternative sites for filmmaking multiplied, especially after the inauguration of the Escuela Internacional de Cine y Televisión (EICTV) in December 1986 and, later, the creation of a programme in audio-visual production at the Instituto Superior de Arte (ISA) in 1988.

The work of EICTV is particularly interesting to consider. Located in the outskirts of Havana, in San Antonio de los Baños, EICTV was created as an outgrowth of the New Latin American Cinema movement. Central to that movement had been a Comité de Cineastas de América Latina (Committee of Latin American Filmmakers), which worked to establish pan-continental strategies and collaborations. In 1985, the Comité decided to establish a Latin American cinema foundation (Fundación del Cine Latinoamericano, FCLA) with the lofty goal of 'achieving the integration of Latin American cinema' (García Márquez 1986). At its first meeting, the executive council of the foundation set out as its first goal the creation of a film and television school for the developing world. With the enthusiastic support of the Cuban government (which provided the facilities for both the foundation and the school), the school was inaugurated a year later, with Gabriel García Márquez as its president and Argentine filmmaker Fernando Birri (a pioneer of the New Latin American Cinema) as director. The goal of the school is to contribute to the development of the audio-visual potential of the developing world, anchored in the belief that

> another cinema is possible because the visibility of our nations is necessary. A country without images is a country that does not exist. All that we do, all that we want to do, is to have the right to be the protagonists of our own image. (García Espinosa 2006)

Given the amazing mix of talent, EICTV quickly became a laboratory for aesthetic innovation and experimentation. Since 1986, the school has enrolled thousands of students (60–90 annually) from more than sixty nations and has boasted an international faculty of professional filmmakers. It has also produced thousands of films, videos and, more recently, digital fictional and documentary shorts and mid-length works. Its graduates have gone on to win more than a hundred awards in national and international festivals (EICTV 2006).

In a way, the entire creative output of EICTV could be considered part of the Cuban national cinema corpus, were it not for the accepted truism that the nationality of the filmmaker is more significant than the location in which the film was conceived and produced. That all student films are shot in Cuba and also often tell Cuban stories and prominently feature well-known Cuban actors adds to the complexity of the conundrum. Be that as it may and without contesting the orthodoxies of film historiography, a significant number of Cubans have also studied at the school and constitute a new generation of filmmakers

who have brought to the national cinema a spirit of adventure and experiment-
ation that ICAIC's old guard was unable to sustain in the 1990s, most notably
Juan Carlos Cremata, Arturo Sotto, Jorge Molina and, most recently, Miguel
Coyula.

The Special Period and Beyond

As cultural critics within and outside the island have amply debated, the collapse of the socialist project during the Special Period generated a new complex
cultural field for *cubanía*. The cohesive national imaginary created since the
1960s became, almost overnight, a memory. As José Quiroga eloquently argues
in his recent *Cuban Palimpsests*:

> It was the revolutionary past itself – the recent past, not the distant past
> of the nineteenth century – that gave the nation its sense of identity, and
> created a sense of cohesive nationalism. At one level one could say that as
> a result of the 'Special Period in Times of Peace,' the present folded upon
> itself. It was not engaged in memory, but in memorialization, while at the
> same time it produced the sense that things that had not been said before
> were now being said. (Quiroga 2005: 4)

With the disappearance of the Cold War and of Cuba's almost mythical status
as the only revolutionary nation in the Americas, the island seemed to have been
'replotted on a North–South divide between permanent affluence and permanent, if latent, warfare' (Dopico 2002). And, almost to the same degree that
political discourses of nation remained authoritarian, cultural production
exploded in expressivity. It was as if what could not really be debated in the
public sphere became the obsession of cultural workers and artists.

The cinema was slow to recover from the blows of the first years of the
Special Period. Most of the films produced by ICIAC between 1990 and 1994
had been in gestation since the late 1980s and clearly reflected a certain pre-
Special Period ethos of experimentation and exploration. Productions like
María Antonia (Sergio Giral, 1990), *Adorables mentiras* (*Adorable Lies*,
Gerardo Chijona, 1991) and the much-heralded *Fresa y chocolate* (*Strawberry
and Chocolate*, Tomás Gutiérrez Alea, 1993) eschewed complacency for a salu-
tatory transgressive spirit, tackling themes (respectively, the legacy of racism
and machismo, the contradictions and difficulties of daily life, and homosexuality) that had not been prominent in ICIAC cinema. But, after *Fresa*, ICAIC
stalled to the degree that it produced no feature films at all in 1996. For critic
García Borrero, the Special Period is marked by the absence of a plural poetics
and by the gradual emergence of singular, individualistic voices. Among them,
the most significant has been Fernando Pérez: 'the 90s belonged to Fernando

Pérez,' argues Borrero unequivocally (2002a: 185). Certainly, Pérez's *Madagascar* (1994) set the tone for the decade by producing a poetic symbolic universe rooted in daily contemporary reality within which to explore the almost existential crisis of being Cuban in the 1990s.[7]

Officially, Cuba produced only twenty-six fictional feature films between 1995 and 2005, all of them collaborations between ICAIC and foreign producers. By comparison, in the previous ten years, ICAIC self-produced forty-five fictional features and was involved in only one co-production (Tomás Gutiérrez Alea's *Cartas del parque* [*Letters from the Park*] in 1988). Given ICAIC's reliance on foreign backers, it is not surprising that the vast majority of these films suffer from the worst consequences of co-productions. Examples include two films set in the famous Tropicana nightclub: *Kleines Tropikana* (*Little Tropicana*, Daniel Díaz Torres, 1997) and *Un paraíso bajo las estrellas* (*A Paradise under the Stars*, Gerardo Chijona, 1999). Not since the 1940s and 1950s had *cubanía* been so unproblematically and salaciously linked to the cabaret experience. Even Tomás Gutiérrez Alea's film, *Guantanamera* (co-directed with Juan Carlos Cremata and co-produced with Spain and Germany, 1995) suffers from an over-reliance on stereotypical characters, facile plot twists and nationalistic clichés, not the least of which is the song which gives the film its title.

However, there have also been some less negative developments in Cuban cinema since 1995. As if taking their cue from *Madagascar*, the most interesting films of this decade (even those that are flawed, like *Guantanamera*) could be described as allegories of national disconnectedness. With no recourse to utopian dreams, they reflect a national social fabric that is in tatters: a nation with frayed edges and exhausted to the core. Rather than national plenitude and self-sufficiency, we see an attempt to rethink *cubanía* as marked by isolation, insularity and ambivalence. The most common trope of this disconnected nation is the journey, not as a satisfying trip with a beginning, middle and end, but as a problematic, endless wandering that raises more questions than it can answer (Díaz 2000; Chanan 2004: 487–95). Often, it is not even that the characters actually undertake journeys, but that they desperately long to do so (or think they do), as in *Madagascar*, *La ola* (*The Wave*, Enrique Alvarez, 1995) and Arturo Sotto's *Amor vertical* (*Vertical Love*, 1997).

Of course, in the Cuban context travelling is also invariably associated with the losses and displacements of the exile experience. With a couple of exceptions, Cuban cinema had never addressed the drama of exile and had essentially ignored that other, painful and estranged side of the nation[8] (López 1996; García Borrero 2006). However, since the mid-1990s and especially after 2000, the diasporic experience has become a constant, appearing in most films either as the main thematic/dramatic axis or as a significant background issue. In *Nada +* (*Nothing More*, Juan Carlos Cremata, 2001), for example, the main character Carla is a bored young postal clerk who dreams of leaving to join her parents in Miami. To pass the time, she amuses herself by rewriting some of the sadder letters that come her way in order to make the lives of those who receive them more palatable. After an inspector discovers her subversion, the film veers into farce – including Keystone Kops-like chases – while Carla falls in love with a handsome postman who comes to her rescue. Unexpectedly she learns that she has won the visa lottery to the US (*el bombo*)[9] and then must choose to stay with the man she loves and help solve people's problems or to leave to lead a better live elsewhere.

Humberto Solás's *Miel para Oshún* (*Honey for Oshún*, 2001) is also centred on the exile experience, here of returning to the island in the context of a family melodrama. Roberto, the protagonist, is a middle-aged college professor who has been in the US with his father since the age of seven. Upon his father's death, he discovers that he had been taken out of the country illegally and that his mother is still alive in Cuba; the film subsequently chronicles Roberto's re-encounter with the island and his repressed Cuban identity while following his search for his mother that takes him on a crazy road trip from Havana to the small town of Gíbara on the far eastern tip of the island. The film's subtext is simple, but for Cuban cinema, remarkable; exile tears apart those who leave and those who are left behind, but in the end even those who have left remain Cuban too. Roberto's inevitable climactic encounter with his mother may be predictable (although casting Adelá Legrá, the actress who played Lucía in the third segment of *Lucía* thirty-three years earlier, as the mother is powerful), but viewing the contradictions and problems of daily life through Roberto's fresh eyes and an insistent hand-held camera does produce an interesting, almost documentary distanciation.

Fernando Pérez's *La vida es silbar* (*Life is to Whistle*, 1998) is a far more complex and experimental film that borders on the surreal while remaining an allegory of national de-centeredness. The film follows three young orphaned characters – Mariana, Julita and Elpidio – who are looking for each other (but do not know it) and have in common a profound yearning for a happiness that eludes them. They are the metaphorical stand-ins for a generation that has been spiritually and psychologically 'orphaned' by the loss of all previous social constructions of citizenship. A mysterious narrator, Bebé, who is ubiquitous, keeps the stories of the three orphans together until their inevitable meeting, and serves to provide an almost spiritual substratum: 'I am alone, Havana is also alone' is a leitmotiv of her narration, invoking an overall context of loss and abandonment. Other minor characters also mark the development of the story with pointed remarks, such as the bicycle taxi driver who looks carefully at a snail and exclaims 'Snails are almost perfect because they are the only ones who can live abroad without feeling nostalgia for home.' The three orphans come together serendipitously on the feast day of St Barbara (4 December) at the

Plaza de la Revolución (the iconic square where Castro used to speak to the masses for hours at a time and where the Pope held mass during his visit to Cuba) during a heavy, cleansing rainstorm. The ending is cryptic and melancholic, yet inspiring. Bebé sits alone on the Malecón, looking at the sea, as we hear the classic song 'La vida es rosa' (Life is a Rose) whistled on the soundtrack. According to critic Rufo Caballero, with this film Fernando Pérez 'was finally able to come out of the tunnel of uncertainty into a landscape that is sad but not devoid of beauty' (Caballero 1998) – and, I would add, hope for a future that will come regardless of whether we see its shape or not.

Pérez's next film, the documentary *Suite Habana* (2003), elaborates a very congruent project to that of *La vida es silbar*. *Suite*'s project is deceptively simple: a portrait of Havana produced by tracking the life of a dozen or so ordinary Habaneros in a single day.[10] They range in age from ten to seventy-nine: Amanda, a retiree who survives selling peanuts wrapped in paper cones; Juan Carlos, a young doctor who wants to be an actor and moonlights as a clown; Jorge Luis, a middle-aged man in love with a Cuban American who decides to emigrate; Francisco, a widowed architect who takes care of his Down syndrome son, Francisquito; Julio, a humble shoemaker who likes to party; Ernesto, a young dancer who does construction work on the side to fix his house; and Ivan, a hospital worker who leads a second life as a transvestite. Rather than rely on the power of the testimony, the portrait produced by the daily routines of this cast of characters becomes a complex city symphony of interwoven sounds and images. Without any dialogue or voice-over narration and accompanied only by ambient sounds (traffic, construction work, kitchen utensils, a woman's voice calling her child in the street, or the waves crashing on the Malecón) and songs by Cuban composers Silvio Rodríguez, Sindo Garay and Gonzalo Roig (among others), the power of the film rests on its complex montage, narratively linking the small (or large) dramas lived by the characters, and produces a powerful collective, symbolic protagonist: 'the city, the island, the archipelago' (Santos Moray 2003). Once again, Pérez avoids the facile identification of the public sphere with the nation's social project and instead focuses on the fissures produced in the private sphere, where individuals are hard pressed to think much further than their daily needs. In an astute analysis, Cuban critic Dean Luis Reyes argued that the film presents a universe of alienation unique to socialism, which makes it impossible for individuals to take actions about their own contexts (Reyes 2004). Yet the film ends with each 'character's' dream (except for Amanda, who says that she no longer has dreams), presented as perhaps an antidote to their alienation. For Pérez as a filmmaker, hope is embedded in the possibility of producing a sense of nation 'that integrates and gives a foundation to those who have been forgotten and demonstrates a wider consensus that welcomes all dreams' (Reyes 2004).

Prior to the great impetus generated by the release of *Suite Habana* in 2003, the establishment of the Muestra Nacional de Nuevos Realizadores (National Young Filmmakers Festival) in 2001 had begun to give visibility to a new generation of filmmakers with different aspirations. The Muestra, celebrating its fifth anniversary in 2006, is sponsored by ICAIC in recognition of the need to take into account filmmakers working outside the institute. As described by ICAIC president, Omar González:[11]

> We are working to improve the cinema, it is therefore important to listen and to structure a renovation, looking towards the future. ICAIC has always played an integrative role and it must continue to have an important role in the audiovisual realm. This is a festival produced in harmony with the various generations and with filmmakers from other institutions who have tenaciously pursued their work. (González 2001)

Sponsoring this festival was a keen move on ICAIC's part, since it dispersed the fear of generational battles for scarce resources, and while the institute could not offer participants extensive funding possibilities, it could promise limited funding and the opportunity to have work seen more widely. Indeed, the Muestra has opened up the cinematic/audio-visual sphere significantly and served as a platform for a number of filmmakers who have already begun to deliver on the promise of renovation and who have very different approaches to the national in Cuban cinema, among them Humberto Padrón, Miguel Coyula, Juan Carlos Cremata, Esteban Insausti, Pavel Giroud, Hoari Chong, Aaron Vega, Luis Leonel León, Tamara Morales and Arturo Infante.

Padrón, a graduate of ISA, is an interesting example. His thesis video, *Video de familia* (*Family Video*, 2002), merited a special award at the 2002 Muestra and revealed a fresh new voice. Shot with a VHS camcorder in five uninterrupted ten-minute takes, the premise of the piece is simple. A family gathers to film a video letter to send to an elder son who has migrated to the US, but in the hustle and bustle of the filming, the sister discloses that the absent brother is gay, provoking a horrified repudiation from the father, an old-fashioned communist. Through its home video *mise en scène* and extraordinary acting (including veteran actress, Veronica Lynn, as the mother), *Video de familia* draws the spectator deep into the interior of a family psychodrama that stands in for the social drama of the nation itself. *Video* actively questions a panoply of issues central to contemporary Cuban identity: authoritarianism, difference, respect for others, and the profound disconnect between official discourses and everyday social existence.

Another important stimulus for alternative cinematic spaces was the creation in 2003 of the Cine Pobre (poor or no-budget cinema) festival by veteran filmmaker Humberto Solás. Solás had spent a decade without filming and was only able to pull off *Miel para Oshún* in 2001 by shooting on digital video (for a total final budget of $300,000, a paltry sum by international standards, but sizeable in Cuba).[12] The experience inspired him to create a venue to foster low/no-budget work, and while attending *Miel*'s premiere in Gíbara, where the final scenes of the film take place, Solás decided to locate it there. That *Miel* received much international attention was fortuitous, as he was able to use his several festival/lecture tours to promote the festival and obtain international sponsors. The first festival in 2003 was accompanied by the *Manifiesto del cine pobre* (No-budget cinema manifesto), in which Solás defined *cine pobre* as:

> (N)ot lacking in ideas or artistic quality, but a cinema made under restricted economic conditions in underdeveloped nations or regions. It implies that we take advantage of the same technological revolution that impels globalization and the chasm between rich and poor nations, but in the opposite direction. (Solás 2003)

He also succinctly argued that low/no-budget filmmaking that maximises the potential of new technologies is the only way to contest an encroaching cinematic globalisation that 'sacrifices diversity and the legitimacy of other national and cultural identities' (Solás 2003). Interestingly, all the awards are intended to expand the makers' technological capabilities, depending on individual needs (a 35mm blow-up, computers/cameras, editing studio time and even a full scholarship to EICTV). The festival has been quite successful, attracting a large national contingent as well as international participants. Above all, it has stimulated much discussion about how to produce (and distribute) with limited resources aided by new technologies. That Solás's latest fiction feature, *Barrio Cuba* (2005), began its life with almost no budget and went on to win the top award at the Havana Film Festival has further consolidated the potential legitimacy and viability of this approach.

In this context, it is not surprising that ICAIC has recognised the need not only to acknowledge new voices, but actually to create new, less institutionalised spaces for them. Rewriting decades-old policy, ICAIC is now not only willing to co-sponsor digital projects, but also to review films produced independently for national exhibition. Furthermore, it has also, at least on one occasion, given filmmakers absolute independence (no prior script approval) in a project that it sponsored, albeit with an extremely low budget: *Tres veces dos* (*Three Times Two*, 2005), a compilation of three half-hour or so shorts directed by young filmmakers Pavel Giroud, Lester Hamlet and Esteban Insausti. Emerging as a demand of the young filmmakers who participated in the second Muestra in 2003, ICAIC assigned the three two mentors (Senel Paz, noted writer and scriptwriter of *Fresa y chocolate*, among others, and Fernando Pérez to help with the production), but waived its requisite review by the administrative council. The result is a set of sometimes uneven, but audacious films that have galvanised the Cuban critical world and have been used to cement the need for new voices and visions.

A POROUS NATIONAL CINEMA

At the present moment the boundaries of Cuban cinema are difficult to discern. ICAIC is no longer self-contained and has recognised the need to be inclusive if it is to continue to function as gate-keeper for the national cinema. New technologies for production and distribution have made it impossible to exercise the kind of control it once had. For example, most of the editing of the three films in *Tres veces dos* was done by the filmmakers themselves on their home computers. At the same time, the Cuban economy has rebounded; the ban on the US dollar in 2004 and the creation of a new convertible currency in effect proclaimed the end of the Special Period. Further economic reforms in 2005 – such as wage and pension increases – and the emergence of new political and economic partners like Hugo Chávez in Venezuela and Evo Morales in Bolivia have put Cuba in the vanguard once again.

Independent filmmaking, inconceivable twenty years ago, is now the norm. Although some might still aspire to be part of 'the industry', as they half-jokingly refer to ICAIC production, they seem content to express themselves in other ways, using whatever technology they have at their disposal.[13] Others have consciously decided to pursue their projects without collaborating with ICAIC. Pavel Giroud, for example, after completing *La edad de la peseta* (*The Silly Age*) for ICAIC in 2006, was denied script approval for his next film (entitled *Omertá/Code of Silence*) and so is pursuing the production independently (González Lemes 2006). Juan Carlos Cremata, on the other hand, did not even approach ICAIC for his low-budget feature, *Viva Cuba* (2005). Instead he formed a small collective (jokingly called *El Ingenio* – the sugar mill – not only as an homage to sugar but because in Spanish the word also means ingenuity, of which they needed much). Cremata also collaborated with the Casa Productora de Telenovelas de la Televisión Cubana (a unit within the Cuban TV institute that produces dramatic serials) in addition to receiving financial and technical support from a French producer (QUAD productions). Soon after the 35mm blow-up was completed in France, *Viva Cuba* was shown at Cannes and awarded the Grand Prix Ecrans Juniors, the first Cannes award for Cuban cinema. Subsequently, ICAIC welcomed the film to national screens, where it played to packed houses for weeks.[14]

Humberto Padrón has been even more radically independent. For his feature, *Frutas en el café* (*Fruits in the Coffee*, 2005), he completely bypassed ICAIC as well as any outside backers; with a very modest budget, volunteer work by crew and actors, and a tight eighteen-day shooting schedule, Padrón was able to self-finance the production in mini-DVD (he later obtained post-production support in Spain). *Frutas* has an inventive narrative with a central MacGuffin, a painting that the spectator never sees, but which links the stories of three different sets of characters, each facing a similar dilemma: whether to succumb to sexual corruption in exchange for something they want, be it pleasure, money or an object.

This independent spirit has created a more porous Cuban cinema featuring new kinds of collaboration between local filmmakers and international collaborators. An even more overtly porous example of Cuban cinema is the work of Miguel Coyula, another independent filmmaker who is now working outside the island. A 2001 graduate of EICTV, Coyula made a name for himself with inventive shorts and a satirical musical comedy (*El tenedor plástico* [*The Plastic Fork*], 2001), which won awards at the Muestras. He obtained a scholarship to study at the Actors Studio in New York and, while there, filmed the feature fiction *Red Cockroaches* (2003). Produced for a total budget of $2000, shot entirely in New York in the English language, and featuring a surreal, futuristic and passionate story that has nothing to do with Cuba, *Red Cockroaches* is the oddest example of 'Cuban' cinema.[15] But it is perhaps the work that best exemplifies the challenges and possibilities of 'cinema' in a global world. In 2006 Coyula was completing *Memorias del desarrollo* (*Memories of Development*), a sequel to Cuba's most famous film (*Memorias del subdesarrollo*) in collaboration with Edmundo Desnoes (author of the two novels). The film was shot in New York, Havana, Paris and Venice and follows the lead character, Sergio, into exile and old age.[16]

Further complicating the scenario, this new 'Cuban cinema' has been thoroughly inserted into multiple zones of consumption and interpretation. Some films are shown on traditional big screens, but other works reach Cuban audiences primarily through pirated copies or unofficial video/DVD stores. Internationally, the internet has proven to be a generative distribution medium. For example, Eduardo del Llano's *Monte Rouge* (2004), an independently produced short that satirises the state police, became an instant internet hit adopted by the exile community.[17] Meanwhile, Cuban films regularly appear on youtube and Google video. Miguel Coyula has made several of his shorts available on youtube (*Buena Onda/Nice Going* and *Bailar sobre agujas/Dancing on Needles*). Furthermore, while some Cuban films have been legally released on DVD in the US, many others are available through 'grey' market distributors who obtain pirated copies from Cuba and reprint them, typically with different cover art, often proclaiming that the film was 'banned' or censored' in Cuba in order to attract the exile market.

The Cuban diaspora – in its many layers – has also contributed to the current porosity of the national cinema. Of course, the 'historical' exiles – those who left in the early days of the Revolution – have already created their own niche in the US, but currently, leaving the island is no longer necessarily equivalent to exile. Miguel Coyula, for example, considers himself a Cuban filmmaker who is 'currently living in New York', but he travels back and forth with ease. Similarly Humberto Padrón spends most of his time in Spain. The children of the historical exiles, who either left young or were born in the US, are also returning to Cuba with cameras. Juan Carlos Zaldívar's *90 Miles* (2001), for example, recounts his journey into exile via the Mariel boat lift as a 13-year-old as well as his re-encounter with his Cuban family in 1998. The film went on to win the best documentary award at the Havana Film Festival a year later.

Consequently, it is now impossible to conceive of the force field of 'Cuban cinema' as delimited by the frontiers of the nation. The 'national' remains in it, but its sphere of creation and influence exceeds both the limits of 'Cuba' as an island and the limits of 'cinema' as a medium.

NOTES

1. Other markers of 'smallness' that are relevant in a European context become more complicated in the American continent, where every nation, large or small, had to fight for independence from a colonial power. As the US, itself a former colony, asserted its 'manifest destiny' across the region in the twentieth century, it became the nexus of an imperial attitude vis-à-vis the continent that has indelibly marked national identity throughout the region. For film and nation in the Americas, US hegemony redirected the colonial heritage.
2. All pre-Revolutionary film production, distribution and exhibition facilities were nationalised in the early 1960s and placed under the stewardship of ICAIC.
3. In fact, in my *Third and Imperfect: The New Latin American Cinema* (manuscript in progress for the University of Minnesota Press) I argue that 1979 and the opening of the festival mark the end of the New Latin American Cinema as a movement, since it had splintered into national cinemas (as in Brazil) or exilic practices (as in Chile). Yet it is also true that in its heyday in the 1960s, the New Latin American Cinema already exhibited many of the complex relations among the local, the national and the transnational that have been identified as characteristic of 'global' cinemas today.
4. Juan Antonio García Borrero (2001, 2002b) has dubbed these 'other' Cuban cinemas a 'submerged' Cuban cinema.
5. The *Filmografía del cine cubano, 1959–1981*, produced by ICAIC in 1982, does not include short or feature-length films made within ICAIC by directors Fausto Canel, Nestor Almendros, Eduardo Manet or Robert Fandiño in the 1960s, before leaving the country permanently.
6. Piard is an exception to the 'young' rule, given that he is older than most of these other filmmakers and had been working in amateur circles since the 1960s (*Crónica del día agonizante/Chronicle of an Agonizing Day*, 1966).
7. *Madagascar* was to have been the first part of a trilogy called *Pronóstico del tiempo* (*Weather Prognosis*). The other two films were Rolando Díaz's *Melodrama* and Daniel Díaz Torres's *Quiéreme y veras* (*Love Me and You'll See*). The trilogy as such never came to be and the films were released independently, as they were completed. These were the last films of the 1990s to be completely funded by ICAIC and, as such, their production took much longer than predicted due to financing and practical problems. Previously ICAIC had imported all its film and development

chemicals from the Soviet Union. Without them, negatives had to be sent to Venezuela for processing, which made it impossible to review dailies and forced the directors to 'shoot blind'.

8. Jesús Díaz's *Lejanía* (*Distance*, 1985) and one of the five short films that make up *Mujer transparente* (*Transparent Woman*, 1995) are the only previous ICAIC films to have explicitly addressed the exiled or the diasporic part of the Cuban nation.

9. The US grants Cuban citizens wishing to emigrate 20,000 visas per year through an allegedly blind lottery system known as *el bombo*.

10. The film was originally commissioned as part of a documentary series about cities for European television. When the TV deal fell through, the project gained the support of a Spanish producer (Wanda Vision) and ICAIC, and was reconceived as a feature. See Santos Moray (2004: 64).

11. Alfredo Guevara resigned from ICAIC's presidency in 2000 to assume the directorship of the film festival. Omar González, who is ICAIC's first non-filmmaker president, has held the job since then.

12. For Humberto Solás, who had always been considered a luxurious filmmaker because his projects tended to command huge (by Cuban standards) budgets and droves of technical support personnel, this is an amazing transformation.

13. A wonderful example is the sixty-minute documentary, *Fractal* (2006), produced by three secondary school students – Marcos A. Díaz Sosa, Kayra Gómez Barrios and Marcel Hechevarría Pérez – using a digital camera with only enough memory for ten minutes of shooting. It took them five months to shoot the film in a marginal neighbourhood of Havana, where they asked the residents their opinions on contemporary polemical issues. The film won several awards at the 2006 Muestra.

14. *Viva Cuba* tells the story of two pre-adolescent children who are best friends and who run away so as not to be separated when the mother of the girl announces that they are leaving for the US. Their journey takes them across the island until they reach a lighthouse where, literally, the island ends. Fabulously acted, the film is both charming and magical; it is also the first non-animated Cuban feature film explicitly designed for children (and their parents too). It had tremendous box-office success throughout the nation and also received a number of international awards.

15. See www.redcockroachesmovie.com for further details.

16. For a brief excerpt of the novel and the script (in Spanish) see http://www.miradas.eictv.co.cu/index.php?option=com_content&task=view&id=36&Itemid=75&lang=es.

17. A Google search discloses multiple sites where it is posted and a plethora of blogs discussing it. This is one of the best postings: http://www.cubaverdad.net/monte_rouge.htm.

Works Cited

Caballero, Rufo. 1998. 'La vida es silbar al otro lado del túnel'. *Boletín Festival*, No. 12. Havana: Festival Internacional del Nuevo Cine Latinoamericano.

Chanan, Michael. 2004. *Cuban Cinema*. Minneapolis, MN: University of Minnesota Press.

De la Fuente, Alejandro. 2001. *A Nation for All: Race, Inequality and Politics in Twentieth-Century Cuba*. Chapel Hill, NC: University of North Carolina Press.

Díaz, Desiree. 2000. 'El síndrome de Ulises. El viaje en el cine cubano de los noventa'. *La Gaceta de Cuba*, No. 6. pp. 37–40.

Dopico, Ana María. 2002. 'Picturing Havana: History, Vision, and the Scramble for Cuba'. *Nepantla*, Vol. 3, No. 3. pp. 451–93.

EFE. 2004. 'La cubana *Tres veces dos* abre el Festival de Cine de Huelva'. *El Mundo*, 14 November. http://www.elmundo.es/elmundo/2004/11/14/cultura/1100439637.html.

EICTV. 2006. http://www.eictv.orghome.jsp.

Fornet, Ambrosio. 2002. *La coartada perpetua*. Mexico: Siglo Veintiuno.

García Borrero, Juan Antonio. 2001. *Guía crítica del cine cubano de ficción*. Havana: Editorial Arte y Literatura.

García Borrero, Juan Antonio. 2002a. *La edad de la herejía*. Santiago de Cuba: Editorial Oriente.

García Borrero, Juan Antonio. 2002b. *Rehenes de la sombra: Ensayos sobre el cine cubano que no se ve*. Huesca: Festival de Cine de Huesca.

García Borrero, Juan Antonio. 2006. 'Sobre el discurso audiovisual de la diáspora'. *La Gaceta de Cuba*, July. http://www.lajiribilla.cu/2006/n269_07/269_07.html.

García Espinosa, Julio. 2006. 'El porqué de otro cine es posible'. http://www.eictv. org/otro_cine/index.jsp.

García Márquez, Gabriel. 1986. 'Una idea indestructible'. In EICTV, *Anuario 1987*. San Antonio de los Baños: EICTV.

González, Omar. 2001. For *Granma*, cited by Tony Piñera. 'Inaugurada muestra nacional del audiovisual joven'. http://sn.cubacine.cu/muestrajoven/muestra1.htm.

González Lemes, Ivet. 2006. 'Alma Mater: Siempre en festival de cine'. *Alma Mater*, 16 December. p. 6. http://www.almamater.cu/cultura/pag06/festival.htm.

Guevara, Alfredo. 1998. *Revolución es lucidez*. Havana: ICAIC.

Hjort, Mette. 2005. *Small Nation, Global Cinema: The New Danish Cinema*. Minneapolis, MN: University of Minnesota Press.

López, Ana M. 1996. 'Greater Cuba'. In Chon A. Noriega and Ana M. López (eds), *The Ethnic Eye: Latino Media Arts*. Minneapolis, MN: University of Minnesota Press. pp. 38–58.

Mañach, Jorge. 1953. 'Palabras preliminarias'. In Gustavo Pittaluga, *Diálogos sobre el destino*. Havana: Isla.

Pérez, Jr, Luis A. 1999. *On Becoming Cuban: Identity, Nationality and Culture*. Chapel Hill, NC: University of North Carolina Press.

Quiroga, José. 2005. *Cuban Palimpsests*. Minneapolis, MN: University of Minessotta Press.

Reyes, Dean Luis. 2004. *Varado en utopía*. Pinar del Río: Cauce. Cited by Dean Luis Reyes. 2004. 'Architectura del postdocumental'. *Miradas*. http://www.miradas. eictv.co.cu/index.php?option=com_content&task=view&id=189&Itemid=50&lang=es.

Rojas, Rafael. 1998. *Isla sin fin: Contribución a la crítica del nacionalismo cubano*. Miami: Universal.

Santos Moray, Mercedes. 2003. 'Suite Habana, una obra maestra del cine cubano'. In Enrique Ubieta Gómez (ed.), *El valor de las pequeñas cosas*. Havana: La Cinemateca de Cuba. http://www.cubacine.cu/suitehabana/asuite3.html.

Santos Moray, Mercedes. 2004. *La vida es un silbo: Fernando Pérez*. Habana: ICAIC.

Solás, Humberto. 2003. 'Manifiesto del cine pobre'. http://www.festivalcinepobre.org/index.html

Whitehead, Lawrence. 2003. 'On Cuban Political Exceptionalism'. Oxford: Nuffield College Politics Working Papers. http://www.nuff.ox.ac.uk/Politics/papers/2003/On%20Cuban%20Political%20Exceptionalism.pdf.

11. BURKINA FASO

Eva Jørholt

As complex as it may be in general, the concept of national cinema is even more complicated when applied to film-producing countries in Africa. Most theories of nationhood and nationalism need rethinking in relation to the African continent, where territorial borders and the very concept of nation-states were inherited from the colonial powers. What is more, theories of national cinema need some re-adjustment if applied to film production on a continent where regional, pan-African and international ties tend to be as important as strictly national ones, and sometimes even more important.

From the birth of sub-Saharan African filmmaking in the 1960s, cinema in Africa has been wedged between the national, the transnational and the international. In the newly independent states, filmmaking was seen as a tool for building individual nation-states, but at the same time, African filmmakers aligned themselves with the anti-colonial pan-African discourse of the era and conceived of their work within the framework of an overall African solidarity. However, due to political censorship and general economic hardship in their home countries, the filmmakers soon looked for funding outside Africa, primarily in Europe, which added a strong international dimension to film production on the continent. This international dimension is also evident when it comes to the consumption of African films. As a result of the absence of a working distribution infrastructure in Africa, the main audience for these films is to be found at international film festivals and amongst art cinema aficionados in the (rather few) countries where they are imported for ordinary theatrical release. In addition, most of the filmmakers have been trained in Europe, and Europeans are usually prominent in their film crews, not least in the crucial functions of cinematographer and editor.

According to the Ghanaian-born British filmmaker John Akomfrah, most African filmmakers consequently nourish a particular double consciousness:

> The local and the international have to be in the frame at all times. You need to secure a certain degree of international recognition, but you cannot function without the local either, and therein lies a paradox. Francophone African film-makers who have lived in Paris for thirty years are still regarded as African film-makers, even as African film-makers from very specific countries . . . but they know that the language of nationality does not make sense if divorced from the all-embracing pan-African discourse. This is what actually helps the national dialogue to cohere. (Akomfrah 2006: 287)

In this essay, I shall focus on one particular African country, Burkina Faso in Francophone West Africa. In many respects, Burkina Faso is no exception to the general picture, but at the same time, it holds a very particular position in African cinema. Often referred to as Africa's Hollywood – a somewhat mis-leading term considering the enormous difference in culture and financial means – Burkina Faso, ranked by the UN as the third poorest country in the world (2005), is considered a kind of role model for sub-Saharan African cinema. Not only does its capital, Ouagadougou, host the bi-annual pan-African film festival, FESPACO (Festival Panafricain du Cinéma et de la Télévision de Ouagadougou), the largest and most important film festival on the African continent, it is also the home of various pan-African film institutions like the filmmakers' association, FEPACI (Fédération Panafricaine des Cinéastes), and the African Cinematheque.

But while Burkina Faso is thus a pioneer on the pan-African film scene, it is also one of very few African states to have an active national film policy, and film ranks highly in the nation's cultural self-image. Although the annual pro-duction volume is modest – an average of five feature films per year in the decade from 1988 to 1999 (UNESCO 2001) – it outranks not only neighbour-ing states like Mali and the Ivory Coast, but also, and perhaps more surpris-ingly, even Morocco, Algeria and Tunisia (ibid.). And Burkina Faso can boast of several internationally recognised directors – Idrissa Ouedraogo, Gaston Kaboré, Pierre Yameogo, Dany Kouyaté and Fanta Régina Nacro, to name the best known – whose films have garnered awards at some of the world's most prestigious film festivals.

In order to give the reader a more precise idea of the ambivalences and para-doxes encountered when examining the concept of national cinema in relation to Burkina Faso, I shall start by giving a brief presentation of the country, its history and population, as well as its film policy and cinematic institutions from independence in 1960 until today.

CINEMA AS A TOOL FOR NATION-BUILDING

Landlocked in the dry Sahel region just south of the Sahara desert, Burkina Faso holds close to 14 million inhabitants who belong to sixty-four different ethnic groups, each with their own language. A little more than half of the population are Mossi, who speak Mooré, but Fulfuldé-speaking Peul, and Bobo, who speak Dioula, also form important ethnic groups. The majority of the population understands either Mooré, Dioula or Fulfuldé, but the official language is French. It is estimated that about half of the Burkinabè are Muslims and 10 per cent are Christians (mainly Roman Catholics), whereas 40 per cent – actually, the percentage is probably much higher – adhere to traditional religions.

This striking ethnic, linguistic and religious heterogeneity is, of course, a result of Europe's colonial partitioning of the African continent. But like so many other African states, Burkina Faso – or Upper Volta, as it was then called – preserved 'the ethnicity-defying frontiers that had been arbitrarily drawn up by the colonialists' (Gellner 1983: 83) when it gained its independence from France. Establishing a homogeneous and peaceful nation, in which all ethnic, linguistic, cultural and religious groups within the state borders would feel as one community, became a prime objective for the newly independent state. Because of the linguistic diversity and widespread illiteracy, print media were of little use to this nation-building project, whereas film – and television – were considered crucial instruments for creating a national sense of belonging.

Only three years after independence, Upper Volta launched national television, albeit on a small scale and with only a few locally produced programmes. In 1969, it established the FESPACO film festival, and the following year, the government confronted the French monopoly on film distribution and exhibition in the former colonies by nationalising all the country's (at the time six) film theatres. A state-controlled company, SONAVOCI (Société Nationale Voltaïque du Cinéma), took charge of the cinemas and introduced a special tax on their income, 10 per cent of which was allocated to a special fund for the development of cinema in the country (Bachy 1983).

As Upper Volta had no trained film workers of its own, the films produced in the early post-independence years were made by Frenchmen. Most of them continued the colonial tradition for educational content, only now cinema was put in the service of the state. Many films focused on topics like literacy, health care, agriculture and so on, but the state also commissioned films to celebrate independence and the unity of the new nation – as, for instance, *A Minuit, l'indépendance* [*At Midnight, Independence*] (1960), *Espoir d'une nation* (1961) [*The Hope of a Nation*] and *Fière Volta de nos aïeux* [*Proud Volta of Our Forefathers*] (1961) (Bachy 1983).

In 1972, the film fund was able to finance the production of the first (16mm) feature film by a local director, *Le Sang des parias* [*The Blood of the Pariahs*]

(Djim Mamadou Kola), which contributed to the national homogenising project by addressing the issue of castes. Four years later, the fund even enabled the government to establish a film school, INAFEC (Institut Africain d'Education Cinématographique), at the time the only film school on the African continent, and, in 1977, a national film directorate which encouraged national film production. In 1982, its director, Gaston Kaboré, could present Upper Volta's, and his own, first 35mm feature film, *Wend Kuuni* [*Gift of God*]. Inspired by the famous Sundiata legend and set in a distant pre-colonial past, *Wend Kuuni* both mirrors the pan-African agenda that characterised early African cinema and marks the beginning of national film production.

When the young army captain, Thomas Sankara, seized power in a military coup in August 1983, the nation-building project entered a new and decidedly more vigorous phase. Although pan-African solidarity was high on the new government's agenda, the Sankara regime also sought to render the country as economically independent as possible through a policy of self-sufficiency and nationalisation. And in August 1984, in celebration of the first year of the revolution, the regime replaced the French name Upper Volta (Haute Volta) with Burkina Faso. Burkina Faso, which translates into 'the nation of the free and the proud', is composed of the Mooré word 'burkina' for 'free and proud people' and the Dioula word 'faso' meaning 'father's house'. In order also to satisfy the Peul, the suffix '-bè', meaning 'those originating from' in Fulfuldé, was used to designate the country's inhabitants, the Burkinabè (Hien 2003). The new name was thus carefully designed to mould the most important ethnic groups into a national unity and, at the same time, boost national pride.

Many of the films produced from 1983 until the Sankara regime was overthrown in 1987 aligned with and supported the government's intensified nation-building project by taking up issues like self-supply and independence from international aid. Prominent in the films of the era were also a number of other key revolutionary objectives – the improvement of women's conditions (including a ban on female circumcision and a condemnation of polygamy) and freedom of the press.

Blaise Compaoré, who succeeded Sankara as president in 1987, has also been supportive of cinema, for, as Teresa Hoefert de Turégano rightly points out, the reputation that Burkina Faso has gained as the most important film nation in sub-Saharan Africa 'benefits the country both economically and through prestige, serving as a diplomatic platform, and it is unlikely that any president would want to damage this positive reputation that extends well beyond sub-Saharan Africa' (Hoefert de Turégano 2004: 72).

Since the 1990s, however, all of Francophone West Africa has been subjected to de-nationalisation and what are typically referred to as 'structural adjustments' imposed by international institutions like the International

Monetary Fund (IMF) and the World Bank, in conjunction with France. The 1994 devaluation by 100 per cent of the regional West African currency, the Franc CFA, dealt a devastating blow to all national economies in the region and was a blatant demonstration of the limited powers of the West African nation-states (Diawara 1998).

These so-called structural adjustments have had serious consequences for the already underfinanced Burkinabè film sector. While an admission price of between 0.30 and 1.50 Euro was already prohibitive for the majority of the population, even fewer Burkinabè went to the cinema after the ticket prices suddenly doubled as a result of the devaluation. Cinema attendance has, therefore, been on a continuous decline since the mid-1990s, whereas, on the other hand, the incitement to fraud at the ticket offices has been rapidly increasing. For both these reasons, the national exhibition company, SONACIB (Société Nationale d'Exploitation Cinématographique du Burkina), the Burkinabè successor to the old SONAVOCI, saw its debts multiply disastrously while the national film theatres fell into decay. Due to fraud and lack of control, there are no reliable statistics for the actual cinema attendance in Burkina Faso, but it is estimated that it dropped from somewhere between 3.5 and 5 million admissions in 1992 to 1.5–2 million admissions in 2002 (UNESCO 2006).

In the mid-1990s, the decline in SONACIB's box-office receipts made the company unable to finance the special fund that had been established in 1970. Whereas the state had produced or co-produced eighteen films for theatrical release in the period 1982–9 and fourteen between 1990 and 1994, the number dropped to six from 1995 to 1999, and three between 2000 and 2004 (UNESCO 2006). State support for film production is now, for the most part, reduced to lending equipment to filmmakers either through the national film directorate, which was restructured and rebaptised DCN (Direction de la Cinématographie Nationale) in 1991, or through the public television channel TNB (Télévision Nationale du Burkina Faso). In addition, the films may receive some support from various public institutions interested in specific topics like, for instance, health or education, but in the overall budget of a film, these contributions usually amount to little more than peanuts.

SONACIB was privatised in 2004, but unlike in neighbouring African countries where film theatres have been turned into supermarkets, new age religious temples, casinos and so on, the government sought to ensure that the cinemas would continue to be used for the exhibition of films by handing the company over to the association of African directors and producers, ARPA (Association des Auteurs, Réalisateurs et Producteurs Africains), under the leadership of Idrissa Ouedraogo.

Due to financial difficulties, the film school, INAFEC, was closed down in 1986, but recently Burkina Faso has launched no less than two new film training facilities: a private school, IMAGINE, led by Gaston Kaboré, in 2004 and the state-funded IRIS (Institut Régional de l'Image et du Son) in 2005. Both schools are open to students of all nationalities, not solely Burkinabè.

Despite economic hardship and structural adjustments imposed from the outside, Burkina Faso's national commitment to cinema is still unparalleled in Africa. Whether the films bearing the label Burkinabè can also be conceived of as a national cinema, is, however, less certain, at least from a theoretical point of view. This is the question that will be addressed in the following pages.

A Cinema By and For Whom?

When you sleep on someone's mattress, if that person takes away the mattress, you end up on the floor. (Traditional Burkinabè proverb, quoted by Idrissa Ouedraogo in Ukadike 2002: 157)

If we take Andrew Higson's four approaches to national cinema (Higson 1989) as our starting point, the difficulties related to speaking of Burkina Faso's cinematic output in national terms soon stand out. Not only does Burkina Faso lack the financial means to sustain a domestic film production on its own, in addition, the films produced are rarely shown in the country itself. From the sole point of view of Higson's economic and exhibition-led approaches, it is, therefore, doubtful whether the films usually referred to as Burkinabè can be characterised as a national cinema.

Since 1972, only thirteen feature films, long and short, have been produced entirely on the basis of local funding. Like their colleagues in the other former French colonies, the Burkinabè filmmakers have usually found the money for their films in France, primarily through the so-called Ministry of Cooperation – which was dissolved in 1999 and subsumed under the Ministry of Foreign Affairs – and the French film institute, CNC (Centre National de la Cinématographie). In the last decades, the European Union and various European television channels – not least the Franco-German culture channel ARTE and the British Channel Four – have also been important funding sources for African, including Burkinabè, cinema.

A detailed account of the French funding conditions has been offered by Teresa Hoefert de Turégano (2004). Suffice it to say that one of the constraints imposed by the Ministry of Cooperation was that the films must take place in Africa. Some directors, though not all, maintain that the ministry favoured village films and thus contributed to promoting exoticism and the sustaining of an image of Africa as backward and undeveloped. When applying for funding from the French CNC, the directors are faced with other constraints: only French films or international co-productions under specific intergovernmental agreements can be subsidised by the CNC; the production company must be French – that is, controlled by French citizens; and until 1991, when Burkina

Faso and France signed a co-production agreement which allowed the use of local languages, the film's language had to be French.

While other international institutions have less restrictive subsidising policies, they are also less important financial partners for Burkinabè cinema. But the specific constraints practised by the French funding institutions have had several consequences for the films produced by filmmakers from Burkina Faso. Not only do most of the filmmakers live in self-chosen exile in Paris, where they have their own, legally French production companies, some of them have also adopted French citizenship in order to be eligible for production aid from the CNC.

Another consequence of the dependency on primarily French funding institutions is the adoption of the French tradition for auteurist art cinema – which can rarely boast of high box-office ratings. While this is certainly not the sole nor the main reason for the absence of a commercial popular cinema in Francophone West Africa, it must be considered at least part of the explanation. Another reason for the predominance of art cinema in West Africa is, of course, that unlike countries such as India, Hong Kong and Korea, the countries of Francophone West Africa have not had the financial means to establish commercial film industries of their own.

While it is thus debatable whether the films generally referred to as Burkinabè can qualify as a national cinema from an economic point of view, Higson's consumption-based approach only serves to muddle definitions further, for the fact is that these films do not have any national audience to speak of. The market is not important enough to sustain a national distribution circuit, and the attempts at establishing pan-African or regional distribution circuits have failed, primarily due to a lack of funding in addition to political incompatibilities between the countries concerned. And outside the larger cities, in the rural areas where 85 per cent of the Burkinabè population lives, there are simply no cinemas. So, those of the Burkinabè who can afford to pay the price of a ticket feed on a steady diet of cheap American, French, Hindi and Hong Kong films distributed by primarily French, Lebanese and American companies, whereas Burkinabè films – and African films in general – are quasi-absent from the national screens. African films are, as the Burkinabè critic Emmanuel Sama has put it, 'strangers in their own countries' (Sama 1996).

To Rod Stoneman, former Commissioning Editor at Channel Four, the fact that the production of African (including Burkinabè) cinema depends so heavily on foreign funding, combined with its quasi-unavailability to local audiences, adds up to 'a cinema which is not based on productive interaction with its own social context', a cinema which he characterises as 'displaced, adrift' (Stoneman 1994). While the films usually subsumed under the label Burkinabè cinema certainly do challenge most definitions of national cinema – for to what extent is it possible to speak of a national cinema if the majority of the films are neither locally produced nor seen by local audiences? – I would argue that they do not preclude such a designation. If we look to common linguistic practices, to Burkina Faso's cultural self-image, and to the way the films are marketed at international film festivals and referred to in general works on African cinema, there is no doubt that these films constitute a national Burkinabè cinema.

Now, this common-sense understanding is, of course, not a solid basis for a theoretical discussion of national cinema; on the other hand, it also seems wrong to disqualify common sense just because the particular production and consumption conditions in Burkina Faso (and other African countries) do not harmonise with two of the most fundamental theoretical approaches to national cinema. Maybe the economic and consumption-based approaches – as defined by Higson and others – are not always as important as they would seem to be, at least not when discussed outside a European context. If applied universally, some countries – those lacking the means to sustain national film production and distribution – would, by definition, simply never be able to lay claim to having national cinemas.

Higson's criticism-led approach will have to be discarded as well, for the simple reason that Burkinabè film criticism (with a few notable exceptions) is still at its humble beginnings. Of his four approaches to national cinema, only Higson's so-called text-based approach, however imprecise it may be, is potentially useful in discussions aimed at identifying the specificities of national cinemas in countries like Burkina Faso. Yet, this approach is hardly sufficient as it stands and requires further specification to be relevant to the case at hand.

When investigating the concept of national cinema in an African setting, we may need to allow for other parameters than, say, the ones defined by Higson. One such parameter might be what Stoneman refers to as the interaction between the films and their social context, for contrary to Stoneman and despite economic hardship and foreign influence, I consider, in this case, Burkinabè cinema to be deeply rooted in the country's political, social and cultural reality.

However slippery a concept 'social interaction' may be, it is of the utmost importance to most Burkinabè filmmakers, who consider themselves modern-day *griots*: that is, their community's spokespersons and social commentators. Moreover, in so far as the films are available in Burkina Faso, the local audience seems to delight in the mere familiarity of the settings, actors, language, everyday problems and so on. At least, that is the impression one gets when, during the FESPACO, the inhabitants of Ouagadougou dress up and defy long hours of waiting in order to see local Burkinabè films, upon which they comment vividly during projection.

I would, therefore, suggest that with regard to the issue of national cinema, the Burkinabè films should be assessed primarily on two levels, both of which concern interaction with a social and cultural context. One level concerns their function as critical commentaries on life in the nation of Burkina Faso; the other has to do with their projection of immediately recognisable images of the local spectators' everyday surroundings in a way that constitutes a kind of 'banal aboutness' (Hjort 2000). The two levels overlap but should be distinguished for analytic purposes.

SOCIAL COMMENT AND 'BANAL ABOUTNESS'

While West African filmmakers have never been much influenced by any Third Cinema theories or manifestos, in the 1960s and 1970s they did co-sign various pan-African declarations that called for African alternatives to the internationally predominant cultural models. These alternatives were first and foremost to be found in oral tradition: in oral narrative structures and, not least, in the function of the *griot* which was readily adopted by the filmmakers.

Even today, when the return-to-the-sources discourse is no longer on top of the cultural agenda, most filmmakers in Francophone West Africa think of themselves as carrying on the communicative function of the traditional *griot*. Within oral tradition, the *griot* was the king's bard, flattering the ruler and spreading his word, but the *griots* were also historians as well as social commentators. In this respect, they were considered the community's conscience and memory, living storehouses of information and true 'masters of discourse'.

The way in which the Burkinabè filmmakers have carried on this *griot* tradition has varied with the political climate in the country, from a primarily bardic function in the early years over a combination of bard, historian and social critic to a primarily critical function. It is impossible to set precise dates for these shifts, but although the different phases are hardly directly linked to the varying political regimes, it is probably not quite wrong either to say that the first shift occurred around the time when Thomas Sankara seized power in 1983, and the second when Blaise Compaoré succeeded him in the presidential palace in 1987.

Early film production in post-independent Upper Volta was, as already mentioned, in direct service of the state, and the filmmakers, therefore, can be said to have functioned primarily as bards. During the Sankara regime, they performed a combination of the bardic and critical aspects of the traditional *griot* functions by siding with the revolutionary project while simultaneously addressing social problems in the country.

Examples of films from the Sankara period are *Yam daabo* [*The Choice*] (Idrissa Ouedraogo, 1987), which takes up the issue of self-supply through the story of a poor peasant family that refuses passively to receive international aid and sets out to find a less barren piece of ground to cultivate; and through its story of a young woman who is forced to marry a repulsive rich man, with tragic consequences, *Histoire d'Orokia* [*The Story of Orokia*] (Jacques Oppenheim and Jacob Sou, 1987) aligns with the government's efforts to improve women's conditions. The same goes for *Dunia* [*Le Monde/The World*] (Pierre Yameogo, 1987), about a small girl who must choose between traditional village life with her family and an education in the big city. Many of the themes discussed were, of course, not specifically Burkinabè, but the films supported official policy by pointing to the very problems that the government sought to solve through its national political programme.

Since the late 1980s, the ties to the government in place, or the bardic aspect, as it were, have been toned down to the point of virtually disappearing. The films produced in the last two decades form a very heterogeneous group, but following the *griot*'s traditional function as social commentator, most of them have in common the fact that they critically explore political, social and cultural issues that touch upon everyday life in the country. I would argue that in this sense – that is, from a strictly functional point of view – the group of films is, in fact, rather homogeneous.

A typical contemporary theme addressed by the films is corruption. Although a bright young man, the protagonist of *Laafi* [*All is well*] (Pierre Yameogo, 1991) is not eligible to study medicine, simply because his family is poor and without connections to those in power. The corruption inherent in the educational system leads to a severe brain drain that is announced in the film as the theme of a local television programme. Due to its critical content, the programme is never aired, however – just as a critical live programme on urbanisation is cut off by order of the president himself in Gaston Kaboré's *Zan Boko* (1988). Pierre Yameogo also focuses on corruption in, for instance, *Silmandé-Tourbillon* (1998), where national rice contracts are given to those who can offer the most persuasive bribes to the minister in charge.

Another prominent contemporary theme is the question of modern education versus traditional knowledge. This topic is most explicitly discussed in *Keïta – L'Héritage du griot* [*Keïta – voice of the Griot*] (Dany Kouyaté, 1994), in which a traditional *griot* sets out to tell a boy the origin of his name, Keïta, which goes back to the thirteenth century and the legendary founder of the Malian empire: Sundiata Keïta. Soon the boy is so absorbed in the *griot*'s stories that he neglects his schoolwork. While the *griot* maintains that learning about one's roots is more important than geography, mathematics and foreign languages, the boy's schoolteacher argues that modern education will prepare the boy for a life and a career in the modern world. A similar theme is touched upon in both Yameogo's *Dunia* and in *Rabi* (Gaston Kaboré, 1992).

In general, children hold an important place in Burkinabè films, primarily because they are seen as the bearers of the future. Partly for the same reason, women (who 'give birth to the future') are also featured prominently, but many films also critically address the almost inhuman conditions to which many women are subjected. Numerous women, especially in the rural areas, have little or no access to education and have very few legal and economic rights, if any at all. They are still not allowed to choose their own husbands; they must accept polygamy, which is an exclusively male privilege; widows are forced to marry a male relative of their late husband; they have no property of their own, and although female circumcision is illegal in Burkina Faso, a large number of women are still subjected to these mutilating practices. From various angles, the issue of women's conditions is taken up in, for instance, Gaston Kaboré's *Wend Kuuni*, Pierre Yameogo's *Dunia* and Idrissa Ouedraogo's documentary *Obi* (1992), as well as in his modern-day gender fable *Le Monde à l'endroit* (2000), and, not least, in the female director Fanta Régina Nacro's short and medium-length films, *Puk Nini – Ouvre les yeux* [*Puk Nini – Open Your Eyes*] (1995), *Le Truc de Konaté* [*Konaté's Thing*] (1998) and *Bintou* (2001).

The frictions between traditional customs and urban modernity are the focus of many films. The topic comes in a variety of disguises – traditional knowledge versus modern education, as already mentioned, and, more frequently, rural tranquillity and serenity versus crime and corruption in the cities – as seen, for instance, in *Haramuya* (Drissa Touré, 1995) about the criminal underworld in Ouagadougou, Pierre Yameogo's *Wendemi – L'Enfant du bon dieu* [*Wendemi – Child of the Good God*] (1993) and *Silmandé-Tourbillon*, both of which highlight prostitution as the fate of many young girls in the city, as well as in Idrissa Ouedraogo's *Yam Daabo*, in which the child of a peasant family is killed in a traffic accident in the big city, and the same director's *Samba Traoré* (1992), about a 'prodigal son' who returns to the village after having committed armed robbery in the capital. It is worth noting, however, that usually the films do not set up tradition and modernity as two irreconcilable poles of an abstract dichotomy. Rather, the subject is depicted as a lived reality in a country whose urban centres form an integral part of global modernity, whereas the vast rural areas still largely adhere to tradition. But to most Burkinabè, the two dimensions co-exist peacefully in their daily lives.

Interestingly, the subject of inter-ethnic diversity among native Burkinabè is rarely touched upon in the films. Reflecting the high proportion of Mossi in the population at large, the majority of the directors are Mossi, and Mooré is the language most frequently spoken in the films. When other ethnic groups appear in predominantly Mossi films, however, they are never depicted as enemies, rivals or adversaries. If anything, we are offered a glimpse of a different but equally valuable and dignified culture. And while linguistic barriers may be addressed, this is always done in a factual way that does not ridicule or downgrade 'the Others'. Examples of this can be seen in *Wend Kuuni* and, especially, in *Buud Yam* (Gaston Kaboré, 1997), which recounts the initiatory journey of a young man in search of his roots. In addition, Mossi actors, who are obviously more abundant than those from other ethnic groups, may appear in films about other ethnic communities. This is the case in *Sia – Le Rêve du python* [*Sia – The Dream of the Python*] (Dany Kouyaté, 2001) and *Tasuma (Le Feu)*

[*Tasuma (The Fire)*] (Kollo Daniel Sanou, 2003), which are spoken in Dioula and could, perhaps, be called Bobo films. Yet, ethnicity is never emphasised. Indeed, there is considerable evidence to suggest that it is not in fact a major concern in Burkinabè films.

The only exception to this rule of ethnic unison is Fanta Régina Nacro's audacious feature film debut, *La Nuit de la vérité* [*The Night of Truth*] (2004). In an undefined African country, the leaders of two rival ethnic groups meet for a reconciliation dinner to end the civil war that they have been waging for years. But 'the night of truth' ends in a disaster that may, perhaps, clear the way for a new beginning. It is worth noting that the film's plot is not specifically linked to Burkina Faso, so the fighting ethnic groups are not Mossi and, for instance, Bobo or Peul but freely invented ethnicities called Bonandé and Nayaks. Inspired by the genocides in both former Yugoslavia and Rwanda, the film is a general comment on civil wars and ethnic cleansing, but however transnational its message, and despite the fact that Burkina Faso has not experienced any wars of this kind, the film also contains several specifically Burkinabè traits that did not escape the domestic audience's attention. The leader of the rebels bears a remarkable physical ressemblance to Thomas Sankara, and the Sankara regime's revolutionary slogan is painted on a wall outside the presidential palace.

One might perhaps have expected the French to play the part of the ethnic 'Other' in Burkinabè cinema, but this is rarely the case – due, perhaps, to the massive French funding of the films. The category of 'Other' is instead primarily bestowed upon Lebanese immigrants – as seen, for instance, in *Haramuya*, *Wendemi – L'Enfant du bon dieu*, *Silmandé-Tourbillon* and *Tasuma*. By and large, the Lebanese are depicted as unscrupulous business people profiting from other people's misery. Although they are to some extent placed on the outskirts of the national community, they are (at least in *Silmandé-Tourbillon* and *Tasuma*) also portrayed as an integral part of an already ethnically diverse community. And *Silmandé-Tourbillon* even seeks to explain their presence in the country in terms of their being refugees from political tensions in their home country.

At a time when an increasing number of Africans are migrating to Europe in the hope of finding work to sustain themselves and their families in Africa, the issue of exile is becoming more prominent in West African films. Till now, however, it has only inspired two Burkinabè films, Idrissa Ouedraogo's *Le Cri du cœur* [*The Heart's Cry*] (1994), about a Malian family in Paris, and *Moi et mon blanc* [*Me and my White Man*] (Pierre Yameogo, 2003). The latter examines the 'otherness' issue from both sides, albeit in a humorous manner. After having suffered all the most common European clichés about Africans while studying in Paris, a young Burkinabè returns to his home country with a French friend, only to be met with all the most common African clichés about Europeans.

Compared to neighbouring countries like Mali and Senegal, the cinema of Burkina Faso offers few historical films, the majority of which play in a pre-colonial past, prior to the arrival of the Europeans. Examples include Gaston Kaboré's *Wend Kuuni* and its 'sequel', *Buud Yam*, as well as Dany Kouyaté's *Keïta – L'Héritage du griot* and *Sia – Le Rêve du python*. Following oral tradition, in which the *griots* were never interested in the past for the sake of the past alone but always saw it as a reservoir of potential answers to contemporary problems, these historical films are usually comments on present-day issues. *Wend Kuuni*, for example, takes up the issue of gender roles, focusing on the plight of both men and women in arranged marriages, as well as on the traditional law that forces widows to marry one of their husband's male relatives – both practices that have changed little since the pre-colonial past in which the film plays, at least in the rural areas. In *Sia – Le Rêve du python* the action also takes place in a distant past, but the film is above all an allegory about all authorities who suppress the truth. In fact, the film's ending, in which the female protagonist is seen wandering about the streets of present-day Ouagadougou crying out the truth like a madwoman, was reportedly (Kouyaté 2002) interpreted by Burkinabè spectators as a reference to the assassination in 1998 of the critical journalist, Norbert Zongo. At the time, the murder case (which is still under investigation) brought about mass demonstrations because people suspected the President's brother to have been directly involved in the murder. The Norbert Zongo affair is, by the way, directly referred to in Pierre Yameogo's *Moi et mon blanc*.

With the possible exception of the so-called village films – especially Idrissa Ouedraogo's *Yaaba* [*Grandmother*] (1989), *Tilai* [*The Law*] (1990) and *Samba Traoré* (1992) – which have been accused of resorting to an abstract 'universalist realism' (Akomfrah 2006: 284–5), the majority of the films are firmly rooted in West African reality. Although most of the issues pertain to the entire region of Francophone West Africa rather than being specific to Burkina Faso, they are certainly highly relevant to most Burkinabè spectators.

The films' function as social commentaries is one reason why it makes sense to speak of a national cinema, but it is not sufficient. What must also be taken into consideration is the films' 'banal' reflections of life in the specific nation of Burkina Faso – the 'banal aboutness' factor. As already mentioned, the fact that the domestic films play in surroundings that are immediately recognisable to the local audience as their own, is of tremendous importance to Burkinabè spectators, and the same goes for the local languages and the national 'stars' (no Burkinabè actor can sustain a living from working as an actor). And when the plots are relegated to a less firmly located past, the local spectators immediately recognise them as parables of, often specifically, Burkinabè events like, for instance, the assassinations of Norbert Zongo and Thomas Sankara.

In spite of their foreign funding, the paucity of their domestic audience and the often regional dimension of the issues discussed, I would, therefore, argue that, in general, the Burkinabè films are indeed 'based on productive interaction with [their] own social context'. In direct lineage from the *griot* tradition, the films comment on issues of importance to all Burkinabè, while also reflecting everyday life in the country in a way that involves banal 'aboutness'. And in a globalised media scene dominated by foreign images, the mere presentation of local issues that touch upon the spectators' own lives, set in immediately recognisable surroundings, contributes to reinforcing a certain national awareness and a sense of belonging. In this sense, the films can be said to participate – along with television, newspapers and other media and cultural artefacts – in creating what is referred to in the discourse of political philosophy as a national communicative space (Schlesinger 2000).

This communicative space is, however, not necessarily in keeping with official national policy. For the most part, it is not, for the films usually side with 'the common man'. This figure is often embodied in the immensely popular Burkinabè actor, Abdoulaye Komboudri, who again and again personifies a simple but (street-)wise and often necessarily somewhat criminal character. Known as 'Fils de l'homme' ('Son of man', in *Wendemi – L'Enfant du bon dieu*), 'L'homme du peuple' ('Man of the people', in *Laafi*) or 'Je m'en fous' ('I don't care', in *Silmandé-Tourbillon*), this character stands in stark contrast with the political and financial élite of the country. In this sense, the films can be said to constitute not only a national cinema but, indeed, a national popular cinema, despite the fact that they are rare guests on the domestic screens.

Yet, it is important to note that Burkina Faso's reputation as a pioneering film nation and the recognition that Burkinabè films have received internationally have also prompted the government officially to brand Burkina Faso as Africa's number one film nation – a national self-image designed to attract international respect and, not least, international currency from the thousands of foreigners who, mainly for this very reason, attend the FESPACO festival.

In both these respects, however opposed they may be, Burkinabè cinema is undeniably a national cinema. But with regard to the prevalent concepts of national cinema, it is, just as undeniably, a national cinema with a difference. This is not to say that the theories are necessarily wrong, but it does highlight their Euro-centricity and, to the extent that at least some of them claim to be universal, it lays bare the falsity of such a claim. In order for the concept of national cinema to be a useful tool, we need to keep it elastic, constantly to inspect, discuss and adjust it in relation to specific contexts. Burkina Faso is just one such specific context that severely challenges predominant theories of a national cinema, but outside Hollywood and Europe there are many more such 'challenges'. A national framework may not be the most obvious way of approaching these cinemas, but, perhaps for this very reason, it may also serve fruitfully to highlight aspects of these films that would not normally be identified through the usual combination of economic, cultural, aesthetic and historical approaches.

WORKS CITED

Akomfrah, John. 2006. 'On the National in African Cinema/s. A Conversation'. In Valentina Vitali and Paul Willemen (eds), *Theorising National Cinema*. London: British Film Institute. pp. 274–92.

Bachy, Victor. 1983. *La Haute-Volta et le cinéma*. Brussels: OCIC/L'Harmattan.

Diawara, Manthia. 1998. 'Toward a Regional Imaginary in Africa'. In Fredric Jameson and Masao Miyoshi (eds), *The Cultures of Globalization*. Durham, NC: Duke University Press. pp. 103–24.

Gellner, Ernest. 1983. *Nations and Nationalism*. Oxford: Blackwell.

Hien, Pierre Clavier. 2003. 'La Dénomination de l'espace dans la construction du Burkina Faso (1919–2001)'. In Richard Kuba, Carola Lentz and Claude Nurukyor Somda (eds), *Histoire du peuplement et relations interethniques au Burkina Faso*. Paris: Karthala. pp. 23–40.

Higson, Andrew. 1989. 'The Concept of National Cinema'. *Screen*, Vol. 30, No. 4. pp. 36–46.

Higson, Andrew. 2000. 'The Limiting Imagination of National Cinema'. In Mette Hjort and Scott MacKenzie (eds), *Cinema and Nation*. London: Routledge. pp. 63–74.

Hjort, Mette. 2000. 'Themes of Nation'. In Mette Hjort and Scott MacKenzie (eds), *Cinema and Nation*. London: Routledge. pp. 63–74.

Hoefert de Turégano, Teresa. 2004. *African Cinema and Europe: Close-Up on Burkina Faso*. Florence: European Press Academic Publishing.

Jørholt, Eva. 2001. 'Africa's Modern Cinematic Griots. Oral tradition and West African cinema'. In Maria Eriksson Baaz and Mai Palmberg (eds), *Same and Other. Negotiating African Identity in Cultural Production*. Uppsala: Nordiska Afrika Institutet. pp. 95–117.

Kedourie, Elie. 1970. *Nationalism in Asia and Africa*. London: Frank Cass.

Kouyaté, Dany. 2002. 'Universel comme le conte'. Interview with Olivier Barlet, *Africultures*, 3 September.

Sama, Emmanuel. 1996. 'African Films are Foreigners in their Own Countries'. In Imruh Bakari and Mbye Cham (eds), *African Experiences of Cinema*. London: British Film Institute. pp. 148–61.

Schlesinger, Philip. 2000. 'The Sociological Scope of "National Cinema"'. In Mette Hjort and Scott MacKenzie (eds), *Cinema and Nation*. London: Routledge. pp. 19–31.

Stoneman, Rod. 1994. 'African Cinema: Addressee Unknown'. *Kinema*, Spring. http://www.kinema.uwaterloo.ca/stonm941.htm.

Ukadike, Nwachukwu Frank. 2002. *Questioning African Cinema – Conversations with Filmmakers*. Minneapolis, MN: University of Minnesota Press.

UNESCO. 2001. *Survey on National Cinematography*. http://www.unesco.org/culture/industries/cinema/html_eng/prod.shtml.

UNESCO. 2006. *Trends in Audiovisual Markets. Regional Perspectives from the South*. http://unesdoc.unesco.org/images/0014/001461/146192e.pdf.

12. TUNISIA

Florence Martin

When *Khochkhach/La Fleur de l'oubli/The Flower of Oblivion*[1] was released in January 2006, the *Tunisois* flocked to cinemas in the city centre and in the outlying wealthy suburbs of Tunis. Overall, the film received excellent reviews in the local media and attracted more women viewers than men, a good omen for a work by pioneer feminist filmmaker Selma Baccar whose previous productions include *Fatma 75* (1976) and *Habiba M'Sika/La Danse du feu/ The Dance of Fire* (1995). On 25 May 2006, Baccar was one of ten Tunisian filmmakers invited to screen her film as part of the 'Tous les cinémas du monde' (All cinemas in the world) programme at the Cannes Film Festival. Yet, although it attracted promising critical attention and was shown at various international festivals, *The Flower of Oblivion* failed to be a major box-office hit in Tunisia, and a year later was still in search of a distributor abroad. According to critic Tahar Chikhaoui, each new Tunisian film re-awakens the nationally shared dream of the perfect cinematic work;[2] both the government and the public yearn for that special local film that can generate a general feeling of pride and (for the state) foreign currency. Such a film would also have to meet the audience's demanding expectations of a cinema that is at once accessible, popular, innovative and clearly the expression of a Tunisian *auteur*. However, the question of success for a film from such a small nation becomes even more complicated in the global context of cinema production and distribution. To understand Tunisian cinema is to investigate the history of its complex relationship with the state, with an audience at home and abroad, and the genesis of a national filmic discourse. While a thorough account of this cinema would need to address the range of documentaries, short films and feature films pro-duced in Tunisia, this essay will focus mostly on the latter category as repre-sentative of Tunisian cinema.

TUNISIAN CINEMA AS NATIONAL . . .

Flashback No. 1: Tunisian State-sponsored Cinema

On 20 March 1956, when, from a French protectorate, Tunisia became an inde-pendent developing country, cinema was not yet a national priority. Information was, however; newsreels were shot in Tunisia, sent to France to be developed, and then finally shown before the feature film at the various *ciné-clubs* scattered throughout the country. When Habib Bourguiba[3] took power on 27 July 1957, becoming president of the newly established Tunisian Republic, there was no Tunisian film laboratory, just as there was no Tunisian TV.[4]

Then in 1961, the 'Bizerte incidents'[5] – in which Tunisians were subject to French military aggression – were shot by a local camera crew and the film sent to a French laboratory, as was the usual process. This time, however, the French did not return the processed film, thus imposing their censorship from abroad. This prompted Bourguiba to ensure greater freedom of information by subsequently founding ERTT (Établissement de la Radio Télévision Tunisienne, Tunisian Radio and Television Institution) in 1961, to be inaugurated in 1966. He also created the SATPEC (Société Anonyme Tunisienne de Production et d'Expansion Cinématographique, Non-Profit Tunisian Production and Cinematographical Expansion Company) in 1964, which was inaugurated in 1968 after technicians were trained and the facilities built. In the 1970s, SATPEC played an even larger role as an importation and distribution company with a monopoly on foreign film until 1981 and as a state production company that co-produced films shot in Tunisia, whether by local filmmakers or foreigners.[6]

The creation of SATPEC was only the first step of many undertaken by a state aware of the potential impact of film as both a propaganda tool at home and an advertising agent abroad. Under Bourguiba's presidency, and since 1987 (even if to a somewhat lesser degree) under Ben Ali's leadership, the Tunisian government has developed various cultural policies meant to support cinema, and a department devoted entirely to the audio-visual arts still exists within the Ministère de la Culture et de la Sauvegarde du Patrimoine (Ministry of Culture and Heritage Preservation). This department has played a particularly crucial role in supporting the following institutions:

- Journées Cinématographiques de Carthage (JCC, Carthage Film Festival, for Arabic and African cinema). Founded in 1966, this

bi-annual event alternates with FESPACO (the African film festival in Ouagadougou, Burkina Faso).
- The Tunisian Cinémathèque. Originally created in 1954, the Cinémathèque was reopened in 1973, under the management of SATPEC.
- The Cinema Museum, created in 1998.

In addition, the Tunisian government has also issued a series of decrees designed to foster film production and diffusion, including a regime of tax breaks by which the materials imported to make a film are exonerated of all import taxes, particularly high in Tunisia. In addition, the national production of films in Tunisia is exempt from VAT. In the long history of decrees related to cinematographic production, No. 2001–717 (19 March 2001) structures how state aid for film production is dispensed in the form of 'support grants' (*primes d'encouragement*) intended to help finance the writing and the revision of a feature-film script; the production costs of a short or feature-length film; or the post-production costs of a short or feature-length film. Each grant represents up to 35 per cent of the total production cost of a feature film and 70 per cent of the total production cost of a short film. However, the Ministry of Culture does not dispense the generous aid (as of 2006, the sum can be up to 400,000 Tunisian dinars (DTN) – that is, around US$300,000 – for a feature film) that it gives to the two or three feature films it funds annually in a single lump sum. Rather, it disburses the funding in increments over the production process,[7] effectively ensuring state control at all stages of the process.

Also, in a nation where tourism is a major economic priority, the Ministry of Tourism has a vested interest in cinema's potential as an advertising agent in promoting the image of Tunisia abroad. Moreover, cinema intersects with tourism through another state institution created in 1998: the Museum of Cinema, located right next to the Ministry of Culture and Heritage Preservation in Tunis. This institution houses a permanent exhibition tracing the history of cinema in Tunisia from its perceived cultural roots (in, for instance, the popular, itinerant Theatre of Shadows, whose puppet characters were well known throughout the country) to the advent of the first Tunisian films. A key figure is represented here in the pioneering Tunisian filmmaker Albert Samama, also known as Chickli (1872–1934) and hailed as the first Maghrebi director, who made two short silent films, *Zohra* (1922) and *Aïn al-ghazal* [literally: the eye of the gazelle] (*La Fille de Carthage/The Girl from Carthage*, 1924), both of which starred his daughter Haydée. Didactic in its approach, the museum presents cinema as deeply ensconced in Tunisian culture. The museum also houses a viewing facility, reminiscent of an intimate *ciné-club* space with walls lined with posters advertising the JCC since 1966.

The state-controlled broadcaster, ERTT, is also regularly a co-producer of Tunisian films via its own production company, the ANPA (Agence Nationale de la Promotion Audiovisuelle/National Agency for the Promotion of Audio-visual Material). The role of the ANPA is both to co-subsidise[8] and to buy films (or series) for ERTT, which the latter can then decide whether or not to broadcast. In its function as a production company, the ANPA[9] can award 100,000 DNT (around US$75,000) to a filmmaker, who then, in return for the commission, cedes his or her Tunisian TV broadcast rights to ERTT (but retains the rights for foreign TV channels). Most importantly, this funding comes with an assurance that the film will be broadcast on Tunisian TV.[10]

Finally, an intra-governmental commission issues the licences under which films may be screened in Tunisian cinemas. The commission currently comprises a panel of 'film experts and intellectuals', one representative from the Ministry of Culture and one from the Ministry of Religion. The latter position was created at a time when Islamic fundamentalist movements were ravaging neighbouring Algeria, and it effectively enabled the Tunisian government to oversee what was said in the various mosques while giving some representation to religious affairs in what had hitherto been a secular state. However, this negotiation has led to predictable side-effects, including the censoring of particular scenes or the banning of some films deemed inappropriate to the cultural landscape of pious Islam.

The ERTT commission also has a representative of the Ministry of Religion with the power to stop a film from being broadcast. *Satin Rouge/Red Satin* (Raja Amari, 2002), for instance, was co-produced by the ANPA but denied broadcasting privileges ostensibly because of a fairly modest sex sequence between a woman and her daughter's boyfriend. Again, but this time for political reasons, *Visa* (Ibrahim Lataief, 2004), also co-produced by ANPA, was denied broadcasting a day before its projected date and after the filmmaker had been interviewed on TV to promote his film on the grounds that this short comedy poked fun at the Francophone government-controlled daily, *La Presse*. Moreover, these two levels of cultural/religious and political censorship determine another, more insidious phenomenon: that of self-censorship in which Tunisian authors (of written, cinematic and other texts) end up silencing what they want to say, knowing ahead of time that their work will be rejected, not shared in public.

Consequently the state plays a multiple, and to say the least, ambiguous role, as it promotes and controls, supports and silences. And yet, Tunisia is the most tolerant of Arab countries in the way it treats cinema, allowing filmmakers to handle topics often deemed taboo in other Muslim cultures, such as male homosexuality, sex before marriage and adultery. For example, *Visa* was banned in Saudi Arabia because its last scene – in which a Saudi embassy employee demands that a visa applicant recite the sura of the Cow – was viewed as poking fun at the Saudi government, and more generally at Arab identity.

Flashback No. 2: Close-up on the Individual

Tunisian filmic narratives have a rich local history upon which to reflect. At the dawn of independence there was, as in other liberated countries, an urgent need to create and portray a distinct, collective identity that could promote pride in the newly founded Republic of Tunisia. In 1966 Omar Khlifi directed the first bona fide Tunisian feature film, *The Dawn*,[11] the inaugural work in a trilogy about the nationalist struggle which was completed in the 1970s. As Roy Armes notes, this tragic story of three nationalists sacrificing their lives to independence in 1954 ends on a hopeful note: Habib Bourguiba's return from exile in June 1955 (Armes 2005: 21).

The use of a singular character to portray Tunisia on screen recurred in another 1966 feature film, Hamouda Ben Halima's *Khalifa al Aqra'/Khélifa le teigneux/Scabby Khlifa*. In contrast with the orientalist, colonial films that had framed the Tunisian countryside as an exotic landscape before independence (Benali 2005, Chapter IV) – best illustrated by the shot of the 'princess' Josephine Baker's head and naked shoulders emerging from a screen-wide cactus bush in *Princesse Tam-Tam* (Gréville, 1935) – *Khlifa* offers a refreshing look at the *medina*, the old Arabic city, through the eyes of its protagonist. Khlifa, a young orphan on the eve of manhood, is a messenger who earns a living by running errands. The camera follows him from one man's shop to one woman's home, one palatial dwelling to a humble abode, and all the spaces in between including the connecting terraces of the rooftops, the meandering alleys and the inner courtyards, thus revealing the complex network of relationships and the varied population inhabiting the *medina*. He is also a character in transition from childhood to adulthood; soon, he will lose his freedom of movement and be unable to enter the houses where women are. Eventually Khlifa has to occupy a fixed space; no longer free to wander from location to location Khlifa and his story can be read as embodying the *Zeitgeist* of a nation in its search for its own identity, as seen through a representation of the daily interactions of humble people.

Khlifa prefigured a trend in 1970s cinema, intent on focusing on social issues rather than yielding to the state's desire for a national grand narrative. For, at first, Tunisian filmmakers, like their Moroccan and Algerian counterparts, perhaps trapped by the state's eagerness to educate and inform through the careful (yet not necessarily artistic) construction of a national image (Chikhaoui 2004: 25), did not immediately turn to the immense reservoir of their own rich popular culture with its many ethnic roots including Italian, Arabic, Berber and French. However, unlike their counterparts south of the

Sahara who were also preoccupied with achieving new national filmic representation, Tunisian filmmakers had access to an alternative filmic tradition beside the Western one: Egyptian cinema, which in the 1950s and 1960s, beside numerous musicals, had produced Youssef Chahine's political narratives steeped in popular culture. Consequently, in the 1970s, Tunisian filmmakers began to turn from a national(ist) discourse to a (neo-)realist filming of the bitter starkness of social issues. For example, Brahim Babaï depicted rural migration and unemployment in *Wa Ghadan?/Et Demain?/What about Tomorrow?* (1971), while Naceur Ktari described emigration in *As-Sufara/Les Ambassadeurs/The Ambassadors* (1976), and Ridha Béhi cast a critical eye on tourism in a developing country in *Chams al Dhîba/Soleil des hyènes/Sun of the Hyenas* (1977), the story of a fishing village transformed into a resort that profits a handful and leaves the poor in the dust. Here, tourism is clearly painted as a form of neo-colonialism that the developed world imposes on the developing one.

The fate of Selma Baccar's *Fatma 75* (1976), the first feminist *documenteur* à la Agnès Varda[12] in Tunisia, indicates some of the contradictions inherent in the circumstances of film production in Tunisia during the period. Produced to celebrate the Year of the Woman, this film focused on the history of women in Tunisia from the Carthaginian era to 1975 through a montage of evocations including Kahena, the Berber queen who successfully led her troops against the Muslim invasion of the Maghreb in the seventh century AD, and Jelejel, Ibrahim Ibn el Aghleb's wife, who founded the first Koranic school for girls in the holy city of Kairouan. *Fatma 75* also featured interviews with key figures such as Bchira Ben Mrad, a famous leader of the Tunisian women's emancipation movement. And while the film credits thanked Habib Bourguiba for his role in promoting women's equality through the Code du Statut Personnel[13] Baccar also demonstrated that in 'progressive' 1975 Tunisia there was still room for improvement. For example, women did not have equal pay and when applying for a passport they still required their husband's authorisation. Unfortunately Bourguiba was not amused and *Fatma 75* was effectively banned. The official reason given by the State Secretary of Information was that some of its content (such as a sequence on sex education in school) was unfit to be shown to the public (Chikhaoui 1994). A Dutch-subtitled copy of *Fatma 75* was shown in the Netherlands (where it was co-produced), but the original French-subtitled version was to remain in the Ministry of Culture's archives for thirty years, until April 2006 when Baccar was invited to show the film in Marseille, France.

The 1980s was a decade in which Tunisian *auteurs* produced a number of films articulating what Tahar Chikhaoui has called 'the wounded or forgotten memory' (Chikhaoui 2004: 28) to be stitched together and/or healed by filming individual stories 're-membering' a trauma via flashbacks. In these films the sense of the nation recedes into the background, with the camera focused more prominently on the individual and his or her relationship to the community. For example, Nejia Ben Mabrouk's *As-Sama/La Trace/The Trace* (1985) depicts a poor young woman about to go and study in Tunis, who remembers her childhood and denounces the unfair treatment of little girls from birth ('When a boy is born, angels bear the banner of *baraka* – luck. If a girl is born, they lower their heads') to their wedding night ('On men no trace can be detected, so they do not forgive a trace'). As with *Fatma 75*, this film did not promote a positive image of women's condition in Tunisia and it met with a similar response from the government.

TUNISIAN FILMIC DISCOURSE

Despite the vagaries of the political authorities – Zine el Abidine Ben Ali's coup in 1987 simply replaced one dictatorial power with another and apparently recycled the same people from Bourguiba's regime – filmmakers could still obtain government funding, albeit with little freedom of expression if their work presented even a remotely negative image of the Tunisian government. For while on the surface the last two decades suggest an apparent lack of censorship, there is often, buried in the films, a kind of covert political expression. Often, the image of Tunisia that directors want to explore is not what is shown to tourists. For example, the Tunisian 'forgotten memory' was an aspect of what Taïeb Louhichi wished to address in his film *Dhil Al Ardh/L'Ombre de la terre/Shadow of the Earth* (1982). This film tells the story of a very small community of nomads living on the edge of the desert in isolation and poverty and harassed by the central government (since they fit no ready-made governmentally designed fixed place nomads are notoriously adept at avoiding the control of the state) (Ben Brik 2000: 82–4). Louhichi's film can be viewed as the urgent recording of a moribund culture and, as such, as an attempt to 're-member' it, in Toni Morrison's sense of the term. It is a matter, more specifically, of both recalling and re-attaching that memory to a larger narrative – here the narrative of the nomads – that has hitherto been given insufficient attention. *Shadow of the Earth* can also be seen as an emblematic narrative about certain social realities that have been systematically excised from the official discourse in Tunisia.

In addition to perfecting their skills in expressing the repressed via subtle detours and in out-manœuvring censorship, Tunisian filmmakers in the 1980s created a new, unique cinematic language, one at once highly referential and elliptical. Nouri Bouzid's films remain the most salient examplars of this. In *Rih Es-Sed/L'Homme de cendres/Man of Ashes* (1986) he tells the story of a young man about to get married who remembers being raped by his carpenter employer when he was a teenage apprentice. Bouzid suggests the repressed forced sex scene by filming around it, recording the muted isolation of the protagonist, and thus, as the latter is unearthing his individual trauma, the director brings to the screen the hidden practice of male homosexuality that a (Muslim) culture has trouble publicly acknowledging. In another of his films, *Safa'ih min dhahab* [literally: Golden Leaf]/*Les Sabots en or*/*The Golden Horseshoes* (screened in the 'Un certain regard' selection at the Cannes Festival in 1989), Bouzid depicts a political prisoner upon his release from jail, traumatised by the torture he has endured and now unable to fit into life outside. The man, an intellectual who is trying to re-attach himself to his various former communities – to his family, his circle of friends, to Tunis and to Sidi Bou Saïd – seems condemned to exclusion. He remains on the periphery of society as he wanders the streets at night, no longer recognising his own country which is now starting to bear signs of a budding Islamic fundamentalism,[14] and he is finally driven to suicide. Here the corporeal reality of torture invades the entire screen in a close-up on a naked, twisted, bound, male body writhing in pain. The sequence relies entirely on an appeal to a connotative semantic regime as the audience simply knows that the torture is taking place in one of the Ministry of Interior's cells.

This mode of construction became frequent in Tunisian films, with directors particularly intent on filming border areas between the inside and the outside, always hinting at a space elsewhere, off camera, away from confining spaces. The themes of enclosure and its corollary – a longing for open space – haunt the films of what Tunisian critic Sonia Chamkhi has termed 'New Tunisian Cinema', produced between 1980 and the mid-1990s and defined by a particular visual aesthetics and by certain structures (Chamkhi 2002). In each film an increasingly claustrophobic protagonist (for example, Youssef in *The Golden Horseshoes*, Ramla in Moncef Dhouib's *Ya Soltane Al Medina*/*Le Sultan de la médina*/*Sultan of the Medina* (1991), and Sabra in *The Trace*), who is incarcerated in the oppressively constricting space of family and society, desperately looks for an exit, his or her trajectory of desire leading further and further away – past the house gate, on to the connecting roofs of the *medina*, away from the village, the city and even the country – to a free space. Yet the dream destination remains out of reach, as illustrated by the close-ups on interstitial spaces such as windows, doors, connecting alleys and thresholds. Poised on a threshold, the camera itself titillates the viewer as it cuts from the walls of the home to the object of desire, including the frequent panning shots of the sky or the image of a bird in flight.

This mode of filming can be seen, in Stone McNeece's terms, as a Tunisian stylistic and as a form of 'image writing' (*écriture de l'image*), 'a tendency to exploit the ambiguity of connotation systems by putting on hold what the images and words refer to' (McNeece, cited in Serceau 2004: 69). The construction of meaning relies on shared references, patterns of communication and an imaginary world, and implies that the elements off screen are the ones that, literally, 'make sense'. It is an astute and effective way to film a taboo or the silence that surrounds it, as Moufida Tlatli's sequence in *Samt El Qusur/Les Silences du palais/Silences of the Palace* (1994) best illustrates (Martin 2004). The film is set, on the eve of independence, in a Bey palace divided along vertical class lines and focuses on the world of women servants imprisoned downstairs and at the beck and call of their male masters upstairs. The central protagonists are Alia and her mother Khedidja. Alia, unbeknownst to her mother, sees one of the *Beyat*, Sidi Béchir, push her mother on to her bed. The next shot is a wide angle view of the entrance to the palace in the background, and of the outside wrought iron gate slowly closing in the foreground. Alia's shadow is coming closer but by the time she reaches the gate, it is too late. Her hands grab two railings of the gate, she pushes her face in between and screams – the camera zooms in to her face and then proceeds to an extreme close-up on her open mouth, but no sound comes out. Devoid of extra-diegetic music, the entire sequence is arrestingly silent. The combination of the averting of the violation, followed by the imaging of an impossible flight with no human intervention visible, and the final culmination in a scream of pain literally and metaphorically 'inaudible' (Spaas 2000: 169–70), all point to a multiple construction of meaning off screen. The traumas unearthed are off screen, literally obscene, and the close-ups on the individuals linger on while a sober audience fills in the carefully orchestrated rests in the soundtrack.

In addition to such formal strategies, Tunisian cinema is also an open cinema in the sense that it has been distinguished by complex intercultural patterns that have become more visible since the mid-1990s. It has therefore continued to refine its language while relating to its multicultural base and the global audience it attempts to reach, as we shall see below. Tunisian filmmakers are often multilingual – Ferid Boughedir, for example, is equally at ease in Italian, French, Arabic and English – have experienced at least two cultures, and have a global cinematographic culture. Their films reflect some of this complexity; the multicultural is not necessarily portrayed as a traumatic, painful loss of grounded identity as it might be in other French post-colonial contexts, but as the accumulation of riches one brings home. Much like Odysseus and his many detours, the protagonist finally returns to the motherland, with either a romanticised vision of home, as Wahid in Ben Mahmoud's *Kouaïl Er-Roummen/Les Siestes grenadines/Pomegranate Siestas* (1998), or with a fresh look at old traditional gender roles, as Jamil in Saheb-Ettaba's *El Kotbia/La Librairie/The Bookshop* (2002). The latest Tunisian films put in motion Tunisian and European or Western elements in a structural 'transvergent' move (Novak 2002); this time, filmic expression takes on enlarged, multiple referential systems and plays with them. As a result, its kaleidoscopic meanings unfold differently for a French audience, an American audience or a Tunisian audience.

At the turn of the millennium films by a new wave of young directors such as Ibrahim Letaïef, Nadia El Fani, Mohamed Zran, Raja Amari and Nawfel Saheb-Ettaba aim to address a large Tunisian audience as well as an international one. Under their impulse, a few productions with popular appeal have appeared, such as Zran's romantic modern fairy-tale set in downtown Tunis, *El Emir/Le Prince/The Prince* (2004) or Nawfel Saheb-Ettaba's *The Bookshop* (2002), Ibrahim Letaïef's comic short films *Un Rire de trop / One Laugh too many* (1999) and *Visa* (2004), and his collection of ten shorts, *Dix courts dix longs/Ten Shorts, Ten Feature Films* (2006). Nadia El Fani, in her first feature film, *Bedwin Hacker* (2001–2) – the first Tunisian feature film to acknowledge female homosexuality and bisexuality – adopts some of the stylistics of the spy thriller such as high-tech communication devices and hacking that disrupts European TV channels, in order to subvert them and adopt other types of filmic discourse. Reality is not what is shown; the almighty police are everywhere, in Tunisia as well as in France. The result is a fast-moving film built along multiple cuts, reminiscent of the virtual realities common on computer screens, such as the ones under the scrutinising eyes of the hacker and the detective.

In contrast, Ibrahim Letaïef, director of *Visa* (2004), uses comedy to denounce on one level the plight of Tunisians who want to emigrate and are caught in a maze of adverse bureaucratic rules, and on another to reflect a general malaise of split identity, as Rachid faces the choice between France (Western and Mediterranean culture) and Saudi Arabia (Muslim culture), only to be rejected eventually by both. He is currently working on his first feature film, *Flouss Académie* (Moolah Academy), an entertaining detective thriller (complete with a middle-aged detective recently returned to the old country) that will use comedy to target a few other sacred cows.

Since the 1990s Tunisian cinema has diversified its thematic palette considerably, from some of the side-effects of present-day globalisation to the uncovering of a mythical past. Hence, some films focus on sexual tourism (Nouri Bouzid's *Bezness* [1991]), on the exploitation of little girls from the country who become indentured servants to urban families (Bouzid's *Araïs al-Teïn/Les Poupées d'argile/Clay Dolls* [2002, Silver Tanit[15]], or on poverty and survival in a poor neighbourhood (Mohamed Zran's *Essaïda* [1995]). At the other end of the spectrum a few directors seem to take their inspiration from the oral traditions of the past, and create films with a mythical aura. Such is the case for the series of intensely original and poetic films by Nacer Khemir, who, after *El Haimoune/Les Baliseurs du désert/The Wanderers* (1984), went on to direct *Tawk al hamama al mafkoud/Le Collier perdu de la colombe/The Dove's Lost Necklace* (1991) and *Bab 'Aziz/Le Prince qui contemplait son âme/The Prince Who Contemplated His Soul* (2005), vast frescoes shot in the desert, in keeping with the spirit of Khemir's one-man shows around the world in which he narrates tales from *The Arabian Nights*. In between these two extremes, other films tell the hitherto untold history of women at mid-distance, such as Moufida Tlatli's second feature film, *La Saison des hommes/Season of Men* (2000).

Finally, there is the beautiful documentary by Mahmoud Ben Mahmoud, *Wajd/Les Mille et une voix/A Thousand and One Voices* (2001), on the Sufi musical tradition throughout the Muslim world (starting in Tunisia and travelling to Egypt, Turkey, India and Senegal), which points to another strand of global, cultural and political preoccupations beyond Tunisian horizons. In a similar vein Ahmed Baha Eddine Attia produced a collective series of five shorts by five different Arab filmmakers[16] titled *Harb El Khalij . . . wa baad?/La Guerre du golfe . . . et après?/The Gulf War . . . What Next?* (1991); Ridha Béhi shot *Les Hirondelles ne meurent pas à Jérusalem/Sparrows Don't Die in Jerusalem* (1994) on the Israeli–Palestinian conflict.

Yet, paradoxically, given the variety of its production and its increasing visibility abroad, most Tunisian films continue to struggle to find an audience at home. After a period of renewed interest from the mid-1980s to the mid-1990s – in which each of Nouri Bouzid's three films (released in 1986, 1989 and 1992 respectively) found an audience of more than 200,000 viewers, in which Férid Boughedir's *Asfour Stah/Halfaouine* sold 500,000 tickets in 1990, and in which Tlatli's *Silences of the Palace* sold 300,000 in 1994 – the audience for Tunisian films seems to have steadily decreased in the domestic market. *Red Satin*, for example, sold only 35,000 tickets in 2002 (Barlet 2004). Various factors contribute to this new paradoxical double play of Tunisian cinema, as it sees its audience expand abroad and shrink at home.

SHOOT LOCALLY, SCREEN GLOBALLY?

Globalisation has had clearly positive as well as perverse side-effects on the funding, the distribution and, to some degree, the primary material of cinema in Tunisia. Beyond government funding, filmmakers can also apply to various European co-production venues of great impact, such as the Hubert Bals fund in the Netherlands, Fonds Sud in France, and even European TV channel film production companies like Arte or Canal +. In each case, the selection occurs at the script stage. Most Tunisian directors are also scriptwriters, producers and at times actors as well in their own films (e.g. Mohamed Smaïl in *Ghodoua Nahrek/Demain je brûle/Tomorrow, I am Leaving*, 1998). Dora Bouchoucha, who heads her own production company, Nomadis, is a full-time producer who also organises writing workshops for directors so as to help them find funds in various places. The intention of these workshops, interestingly named *Sud Écritures*, is to organise brainstorming and rewriting sessions once a year for the selected authors of submitted scripts, with the help of film professionals. The revised scripts can then be submitted to some of the European funding schemes noted above, for instance.[17]

As an unintended result, for example, there was a wave in the 1990s of scripts that seemed to coincide with pre-fabricated 'neo-orientalist' images of Tunisia replete with shots of couscous, *hammam* or Moorish baths, sea, sex and sun, all of which catered to the a priori of members of the various commissions abroad. The subsequent laminated scripts led to a repetition of similar tropes and narratives. Seemingly compulsory sequences shot in the *hammam* and on the terraces, for instance, appear in *Halfaouine* (1990), *Sultan of the Medina* (1991) and *Halk El Wad/Un Été à la Goulette/A Summer in La Goulette* (1994).

Clearly, this may not be the kind of representation that a Tunisian audience craves to see year after year, helping to explain the lack of enthusiasm for local films in Tunisia today. But there are other issues in this regard. First of all, film piracy via illegal videotapes and now DVDs (burned at home as well as in any cybercafé) has become institutionalised in Tunisia, and while there are laws prohibiting such practices, local feature films, some of them not yet even released commercially, are readily available for 2.5 DNT (about US$1.50) on the street. Rampant piracy has developed into a parallel economy that serves everybody and, although the police are omnipresent in the urban centres, they rarely raid the places that copy films, and thus break global as well as national copyright laws, unless they wish to close them down for other reasons. As a result, film buffs can watch films at home or in a café offering a large screen, which is cheaper and more comfortable than a film theatre.

There is no multiplex in Tunisia, even if the government has talked about helping to create some over the past few years, and the deplorable state of film theatres today does not help cinema. Characterised by defective sound systems, limping projection devices, antediluvian seats whose springs have given up a long time ago, and old, musty carpeting, everything about them seems to conspire to make film-viewing a less than satisfying experience with a negative result on the number of people coming to watch films. In Le Majestic in Bizerte, for instance, admissions have dropped from 178,814 in 1991 to 51,654 in 2001 (Hadda 2002). Given their shrinking patronage, theatres have also substantially decreased in number nationally from 92 in 1981 to 35 in 2004, according to the Tunisian press – a rather sad phenomenon, given the past enthusiastic crowds of cinephiles who congregated to watch films in the 1970s *cinéclubs*. Furthermore, the springing forest of satellite dishes on most roofs signals another entertainment medium; people can buy a pirated *décodeur* on the black market for a pittance and have access to, among other programmes, films broadcast by hundreds of TV channels from Europe and the Arab world. As Ella Shohat argues, this global invasion of images, all the way into the hearth, mediates the 'imagined communities' and representations:

> In a transnational world typified by the global circulation of images and sounds, goods, and peoples, media spectatorship impacts complexly on

national identity, communal belonging, and political affiliations. By facilitating a mediated engagement with distant peoples, the media 'deterritorialize' the process of imagining communities. (Shohat 1997)

This globalised media spectatorship that is experienced in the privacy of one's own home in Tunisia sets the stage for a complex imagining of often clashing identities (as *Visa* showed). In Tunisian cinema, Shohat's 'deterritorialization' actually stimulates today's borderless cinema, as *Bedwin Hacker* and other films demonstrate. On a more mundane level, easy access to global media ruins the career of a film in theatres.

Finally, the release of a film is neither preceded nor accompanied by any sort of advertising or marketing campaign. The local distribution system lacks the resources for this and has to rely on foreign publicity for its imported films – as everywhere else, American blockbusters reign supreme at the box office – and does without for its domestic ones. Under the circumstances, it takes miraculous powers for a Tunisian film to make a profit on Tunisian soil. Raja Amari's *Red Satin*, for instance, sold 35,000 admission tickets in Tunisia and 111,234 in France in 2002.

> For *Red Satin*, we had to provide posters and film copies ourselves, buy advertising spaces, head the promotion ourselves. The film stayed on the marquis for 13 weeks – a record in Tunisia – but, according to our distributors, generated no profit. Some Tunisian films are distributed in France but not in Tunisia, whether it be Ridha Béhi's last film, *The Magic Box*, or Nadia El Fani's *Bedwin Hacker*. (Bouchoucha 2003)

Bedwin Hacker addressed culturally sensitive issues such as female bisexuality and this might explain why its career was short-lived on the big screens of Tunisia (notwithstanding its circulation as a DVD or DVX). But such was not the case for Ridha Béhi's film which contained nothing culturally, religiously or politically incorrect, but seemed to have no distribution in place. This problem is, in the words of Moufida Tlatli, shared by other Tunisian directors: 'The cinemas in Tunisia mainly show American, Egyptian and Bollywood films . . . It is a paradox that globalisation threatens diversity in our cinemas, while international funding helps sustain Tunisian cinema' (Fallaux et al. 2003: 12). In the end, Tunisian cinema has come to be increasingly characterised by films that may be shot locally but viewed primarily by audiences outside the country, unless in pirated form.

Nevertheless one can be optimistic about the contemporary effervescence of Tunisian cinema. It seems healthy and, judging from its works in progress, promises to continue to produce a wide range of fascinating films. Part of its sense of unease in the global landscape might reside, ironically enough, in

Tunisia's own geo-political and geo-cultural location. As Chikhaoui points out, it is in the 'Maghreb': that is, in the 'West' (in Arabic) – West of the Middle East, of the Arabian Peninsula, but not Western all the way. It is also 'South' for Europe, and uneasily receives the label of 'Cinéma du Sud' (Cinema of the South) from the financial deciders of the North (and West!) (Chikhaoui 2004). Caught in the middle of a mediatised double pull – to simplify, a Western secular world and a Muslim religious one – Tunisian cinema has evolved some imaginative strategies to create filmic narratives that avoid various levels of censorship at home through the use of nuances. Its narrative and visual detours have in turn produced aesthetics reminiscent of ancient arabesques, an area in which it has achieved a rare level of mastery and independence.

NOTES

1. Tunisian films usually come out with two titles simultaneously: one in Arabic and one in French, although the French one is often not a translation of the Arabic one. Here, for instance, *khochkhach* means 'opium tea' in Tunisian dialect.
2. Tahar Chikhaoui, interviewed by the author on 6 February 2006, in Tunis.
3. Habib ben Ali Bourguiba (1903–2000) 'negotiated an internal autonomy' with France, (re)gaining the Tunisian territory minus the strategic naval base of Bizerte, which remained a French military base.
4. Broadcasting existed in Tunisia; Radio-Tunis had been inaugurated, under the French regime, on the eve of the Second World War, in 1938, and was 'tunisified' in 1957.
5. As the Algerian war proceeded, Franco-Tunisian relations deteriorated, the hostilities culminating in the following two related 'incidents' (a French code term for bloody confrontations). Tunisian villages along the border often provided shelter to Algerian nationalists. On 8 February 1958, French army planes took off from Algeria and bombed the Tunisian village of Sakiet-Sidi-Youssef, killing sixty-eight Tunisians and injuring a hundred more. In 1961, the French refused to evacuate the naval base of Bizerte. Tunisian troops surrounded the French base on 19 July 1961. Two days later, the French army besieged the entire town, killing 1,300 Tunisians. It took a UN resolution to reach a cease-fire on 22 July.
6. This generous offer had a few perverse side-effects. Intellectual European filmmakers, for example, used it to shoot films that were commercial fiascos, a case in point being Alain Robbe-Grillet's *L'Eden et après* (1969).
7. The Ministry gives grants out along the following strict schedule, which allows some amount of control at various points in the making of the film:

   – 10 per cent upon signing the agreement (based on the proposed script).
   – 40 per cent at the beginning of the shooting of the film (based on a revised script and *note d'intention*).
   – 40 per cent at the end of the shooting of the film (based on film rushes).
   – 10 per cent upon the delivery of two copies of the finished product (to be archived at the Ministry of Culture).

8. The term 'subsidy' is crucial here for the ANPA. The government, in its various guises, is very careful about its use of terminology to designate its aid to filmmaking for it wants to project an image of patron of the arts, not of a self-promoting body. '(Co)-producing' would immediately imply that only films that toe the party

line are subsidised by the state, and point to the (sadly very real) subtext of censorship in Tunisia.

9. Khaled Njah, director of programming at the ANPA (interviewed on 10 October 2005) also insists that, from 2005 on, each film receiving some financial aid from ANPA is first released commercially and then broadcast on TV. The fact that the ANPA is no longer titled 'co-producer' means that the filmmaker and his or her production company have no obligation to the ANPA when their film is released abroad.

10. This system does not always work smoothly. Some films end up being subsidised by ANPA but, once presented to the ERTT commission that gives the green light to film broadcasting, may be banned from TV. Usually, this is due to the subject of the film when it is at odds with the cultural environment. For instance, *Fatma* by Khaled Ghorbal (2001) was not allowed to be broadcast, ostensibly because it dealt with the still taboo topic of the virginity of brides.

11. Coincidentally, *The Dawn* came out in the same year as Gillo Pontecorvo's *Battle of Algiers*, which was on a similar theme and perhaps on a grander scale (the massive crowds in the Italo-Algerian film were the locomotives of history, while Khlifi concentrated on individual fates).

12. French filmmaker Agnès Varda coined this term for her own documentaries spliced with historical or whimsical recreations. The suffix '-*menteur*' (liar in French) points to the unreliability of the pseudo-neutral distance of the filmmaker.

13. Adopted on 13 August 1956, this new code of law guaranteed women's rights, while respecting the spirit of Islamic law. For instance, it outlawed polygamy, abolished men's renouncement of their wives (replaced by judicial divorce with equal rights for men and women), and gave women the right to vote.

14. The film is of autobiographical inspiration. Bouzid spent five years in jail for his Trotskyist political views under Bourguiba's regime (1973–9), during which he underwent interrogations and torture. The film was made under Ben Ali's regime and was not censored, since it referred to Bourguiba's era.

15. The Carthage Film Festival (Journées Cinématographiques de Carthage) awards prizes called 'tanits' (named after Tanit, the Carthage goddess): gold, silver and bronze, for the best Arab or African film presented. As in most festivals, the awards are given in various categories (such as best film, best actress, best actor, best script and so on).

16. The following directors: Borhane Alaouié from Lebanon, Néjia Ben Mabrouk and Nouri Bouzid from Tunisia, Elia Suleïman from Palestine, and Mustapha Derkaoui from Morocco.

17. Ibrahim Letaïef has also started to set up the same type of workshop for young filmmakers coming out of cinema schools in order to help them create and finance their first short films.

Works Cited

Alion, Yves (ed.). 2004. *Les Silences du palais: Un film de Moufida Tlatli. L'Avant-Scène Cinéma*, No. 536, November.

Armes, Roy. 2005. *Postcolonial Images: Studies in North African Film*. Bloomington, IN: Indiana University Press.

Bachy, Victor. 1978. *Le Cinéma de Tunisie*. Tunis: Société Tunisienne de Diffusion.

Barlet, Olivier. 2004. 'La Crise du cinéma tunisien'. *Africultures*, 14 October. http://www.africultures.com/index.asp?menu=affiche_article&no=3568.

Benali, Abdelkader. 1998. *Le Cinéma colonial au Maghreb*. Paris: Éditions du Cerf.

Ben Brik, Taoufik. 2000. *Une si douce dictature*. Paris: La Découverte.

Bouchoucha, Dora. 2003. *Actes du Colloque de Namur: 'La diffusion, promotion et distribution des films francophones: réalités et perspectives'*. http://www.cinemasfrancophones.org/upload/actes_colloque_namur_2003.doc.

Chamkhi, Sonia. 2002. *Cinéma tunisien nouveau – Parcours autres*. Tunis: Sud.

Chikhaoui, Tahar. 1994. 'Une Affaire de femmes/Stories of Women'. *Africultures*, No. 8, second quarter. http://www.africultures.com/revue_africultures/articles/ecrans_afrique/8/8_08.pdf.

Chikhaoui, Tahar. 2004. 'Maghreb: de l'épopée au regard intime'. In Jean-Michel Frodon, (ed.), *Au Sud du cinéma: Films d'Afrique, d'Asie et d'Amérique Latine*. Paris: Cahiers du Cinéma/Arte. pp. 22–39.

Fallaux, Émile, and Malu Halasa, Nupu Press (eds). 2003. *Funding the Art of World Cinema. True Variety*. Rotterdam: International Film Festival Rotterdam.

Hadda, Mohamed Hédi. 2002. In *Bab el Web*, 16 June. http://www.bab-el-web.com/archives/article.asp?ID=5214.

Khelil, Hédi. 2002. *Le Parcours et la trace: Témoignages et documents sur le cinéma tunisien*. Tunis: Médiacom.

Khlifi, Omar. 1970. *L'Histoire du cinéma en Tunisie*. Tunis: Société Tunisienne de Diffusion.

Martin, Florence. 2004. 'Silence and Scream: Moufida Tlatli's Cinematic Suite'. *Studies in French Cinema*, Vol. 4, No. 3. pp. 175–85.

Martin, Florence. 2006. '*Satin rouge* de Raja Amari: l'expression féminine sens dessus dessous'. In Guy Degas (ed.), *Expressions tunisiennes*, special issue of *Expressions Maghrébines*, Vol. 5, No. 1, Summer, pp. 53–65.

Mulvey, Laura. 1995. 'Moving Bodies: Interview with Moufida Tlatli'. *Sight and Sound*, Vol. 5, No. 3. pp. 18–20.

Novak, Marcos. 2002. 'Speciation, Transvergence, Allogenesis: Notes on the Production of the Alien'. *Architectural Design*, 72/3. http://www.mat.ucsb.edu/~marcos/transvergence.pdf.

Serceau, Michel (ed.). 2004. *Cinémas du Maghreb. Cinémaction*, No 111.

Shohat, Ella. 1997. 'Framing Post-Third-Worldist Culture: Gender and Nation in Middle Eastern/North African Film and Video', Jouvert. http://social.chass.ncsu.edu/jouvert/v1i1/shohat.htm.

Spaas, Lieve. 2000. *The Francophone Film: A Struggle for Identity*. Manchester: Manchester University Press.

NOTES ON CONTRIBUTORS

Ackbar Abbas is Professor of Comparative Literature at the University of California, Irvine. He was previously Professor of Comparative Literature at the University of Hong Kong, where he also served as Head of Department. He is the author of *Hong Kong: Culture and the Politics of Disappearance* (University of Minnesota Press 1997) and is co-editor, with John Nguyet Erni, of *Internationalizing Cultural Studies: An Anthology* (Blackwell 2004).

Jeremy Fernando is a doctoral candidate at the European Graduate School in Saas Fee in Switzerland. He is currently tutoring at the School of Humanities and Social Sciences at the Nanyang Technological University, Singapore, and is the author of 'The Spectre of the National that Haunts Singapore (Cinema), Or, You Can Only See Ghosts if You are Blind', published in the e-journal *Border lands* (2006).

Mette Hjort is Professor and Program Director of Visual Studies at Lingnan University in Hong Kong. Previous appointments include positions as Director of Cultural Studies at McGill University in Canada, Professor of Intercultural Studies at Aalborg University in Denmark, and Head of Comparative Literature at the University of Hong Kong. She is the author of *The Strategy of Letters* (Harvard University Press 1993), *Small Nation, Global Cinema* (University of Minnesota Press 2005) and *Stanley Kwan's Center Stage* (Hong Kong University Press 2006), and the editor or co-editor of numerous volumes, including *Purity and Provocation: Dogme 95* (British Film Institute 2003) and

Cinema and Nation (Routledge 2000). She has also published an interview book (together with Ib Bondebjerg) entitled *The Danish Directors* (Intellect 2001). She is series editor, with Peter Schepelern, of the Nordic Film Classics Series, published by the University of Washington Press, and is one of the general editors of the Hong Kong Film Classics Series, published by Hong Kong University Press.

Dina Iordanova holds the Chair in Film Studies at the University of St Andrews in Scotland, where she also directs the Centre for Film Studies. She has written extensively on the cinema of Eastern Europe and the Balkans, and runs projects in the area of international and transnational cinema. Her research approaches cinema on a meta-national level and focuses on the dynamics of transnationalism in cinema; she has a special interest in issues related to cinema at the periphery. Monographs include *Cinema of Flames: Balkan Film, Culture and the Media* (British Film Institute 2001), *Emir Kusturica* (BFI 2002) and *Cinema of the Other Europe* (Wallflower 2003). She is the editor of the *Companion to Russian and Eastern European Cinema* (2000) and of *Cinema of the Balkans* (Wallflower 2006). She has guest-edited a number of themed journal issues: *Framework* on images of Gypsies in international cinema (Autumn 2003), *South Asian Popular Culture* on the theme of *Indian Cinema Abroad: Historiography of Transnational Cinematic Exchanges* (Autumn 2006), *Kinokultura* on Bulgarian cinema (Autumn 2006), *Cineaste* on South East European Film (2007), *Third Text* on Romanies and Representation (2008), and *Film International* on Film Festivals (2008).

Eva Jørholt is Associate Professor of Film Studies at the University of Copenhagen. She has worked with Deleuzian film theory (for example, 'The Metaphor Made Flesh: A Philosophy of the Body Disguised as Biological Horror Film', in *Micropolitics of Media Culture*, ed. Patricia Pisters, Amsterdam University Press 2001). In recent years her main interest has been West African cinema, on which she has written several articles that have been published by the Nordic Africa Institute in Uppsala, Sweden, and in the Danish Film Institute/Cinematheque's bi-annual film magazine, *Kosmorama*, of which she is now the editor-in-chief.

Ana M. López is Senior Associate Provost and Director of the Cuban Studies Institute at Tulane University. She teaches film and cultural studies in the Department of Communication and is affiliated with the Center for Latin American Studies and the Women's Studies Program. She is the co-editor of *Mediating Two Worlds* (British Film Institute 1993), *The Ethnic Eye: Latino Media Arts* (University of Minnesota Press 1996) and *The Encyclopedia of Contemporary Latin American and Caribbean Cultures* (Routledge 2000), a two-volume primer on Latin American culture. A monograph, *Third and Imperfect: The New Latin American Cinema*, is forthcoming from the University of Minnesota Press. She has also written numerous chapters and articles for scholarly journals such as *Cinema Journal, Quarterly Review of Film and Video, Wide Angle, Revista Canadiense de Estudios Hispánicos, Nuevo Texto Crítico, Cinemais, Radical History Review* and *Jumpcut.*

Florence Martin is Professor of French and Francophone Studies at Goucher College, in Baltimore (USA), and sits on the editorial board of *Studies in French Cinema* (UK). The author of two books in French, *Bessie Smith* (Parenthèses 1996) and *De la Guyane à la diaspora africaine* (Karthala 2002), she is currently working on a book manuscript in English, *Veils and Screens: Maghrebi Women's Cinema.* Her most recent publications include articles on Tunisian directors (Raja Amari, Moufida Tlatli, Nadia El Fani) and Algerian director–writer Assia Djebar, published in France, the UK and the USA.

Martin McLoone is Professor of Media Studies (Film, Television and Photography) attached to the Centre for Media Research at the University of Ulster, Coleraine. He is the author of *Irish Film: The Emergence of a Contemporary Cinema* (BFI 2000), and has contributed to and edited *Television and Irish Society* (Irish Film Institute 1984), *Culture, Identity and Broadcasting in Ireland* (Institute of Irish Studies 1991), *Border Crossing: Film in Ireland, Britain and Europe* (Institute of Irish Studies/BFI 1994), *Broadcasting in a Divided Community: Seventy Years of the BBC in Northern Ireland* (Institute of Irish Studies 1996) and *Big Picture, Small Screen: the Relations between Film and Television* (John Libbey/University of Luton Press 1996).

Jonathan Murray teaches in the Centre for Visual and Cultural Studies at Edinburgh College of Art. He is the author of *That Thinking Feeling: A Research Guide to Scottish Cinema* (Edinburgh College of Art/Scottish Screen 2005) and co-editor of *Constructing the Wicker Man: Film and Cultural Studies Perspectives* (University of Glasgow 2005), and has published a range of scholarly articles on Scottish film culture past and present. His current research projects include monographs on the filmmaker Bill Forsyth and Scottish cinema from the 1970s to the present.

Björn Norðfjörð is an Assistant Professor at the University of Iceland and the Head of its Film Studies programme. His Icelandic publications include essays on both Icelandic and American cinema, and forthcoming publications in English include an essay on the transnational musical and a monograph on Dagur Kári's *Noi Albino.*

Duncan Petrie is Professor of Film at the University of Auckland. He has published extensively in the fields of British and Scottish cinema, being the author of *Creativity and Constraint in the British Film Industry* (Macmillan 1991), *The British Cinematographer* (British Film Institute 1996), *Screening Scotland* (British Film Institute 2000) and *Contemporary Scottish Fictions* (Edinburgh University Press 2004), and editor or co-editor of a further nine books. In addition to the work on New Zealand cinema included in this volume, he has also completed a study of New Zealand cinematography for Random House.

Tan See Kam is Associate Professor of Communication at the University of Macau, Macao Special Administrative Region, China. He has publications in *Asian Cinema, Cinemaya, Jumpcut, Screen, Social Semiotics, South East Asian Journal of Social Sciences, Media Asia, Intermedia, Antithesis* and *Journal of Homosexuality*. He also has book chapters in *Queer Asian Cinema: Shadows in the Shade* (Harrington Park Press 2000), *Between Home and World: A Reader in Hong Kong Cinema* (Oxford University Press 2004), *Chinese Films in Focus: 25 New Takes* (British Film Institute 2003) and *Outer Limits: A Reader in Communication Across Cultures* (Language Australia 2004). He has co-edited a special issue on 'Gender in Asian Cinema' for *Asian Journal of Communication* (2001), and is co-author of two anthologies: *Hong Kong Film, Hollywood, and the New Global Cinema: No Film is an Island* (Routledge 2007) and *Chinese Connections: Critical Perspectives on Film, Identity and Diaspora* (Temple University Press, forthcoming). He is presently working on a book on Tsui Hark's *Peking Opera Blues* (Hong Kong University Press).

James Udden is currently an Assistant Professor of Film Studies at Gettysburg College in Pennsylvania. He is also an expert on Asian cinema, focusing primarily on Chinese, Japanese, Korean and Iranian cinema. He has previously published works on Taiwanese and Hong Kong cinema in publications such as *Asian Cinema, Modern Chinese Language and Literature, PostScript* and *Film International*. He is currently nearing completion of a book-length manuscript on the Taiwanese director, Hou Hsiao-hsien.

INDEX